Successful
GRANDPARENTING

Successful
GRANDPARENTING

The essential guide to one of
life's most rewarding relationships

Introduction by Claire Rayner

PUBLISHED BY THE READER'S DIGEST ASSOCIATION LIMITED
LONDON • NEW YORK • SYDNEY • CAPE TOWN • MONTREAL

A Reader's Digest Book
Published by The Reader's Digest Association Limited
11 Westferry Circus
Canary Wharf
London E14 4HE

Conceived, edited and designed by
Marshall Editions
170 Piccadilly
London W1V 9DD

ISBN 0-276-42307-0

A CIP catalogue for this book is available from the British Library.

PROJECT EDITOR Anne Yelland
ART EDITOR Frances de Rees
PICTURE EDITOR Su Alexander
DTP EDITOR Mary Pickles
COPY EDITORS Jolika Feszt, Maggi McCormick
MANAGING EDITOR Lindsay McTeague
PRODUCTION EDITOR Emma Dixon
EDITORIAL DIRECTOR Sophie Collins
ART DIRECTOR Sean Keogh
PRODUCTION Nikki Ingram

CONTRIBUTORS Sue Hubberstey (Chapters 4, 7 and 8), Janice Parrock (Chapters 2, 6, 7 and 9), June Thompson (Chapter 3), Caroline Taggart (Chapter 1), Anne Yelland (Chapter 5)

The pronouns he and she, used in alternate chapters, refer to both sexes, unless a topic applies only to a boy or girl.

Printed and bound in Italy

Contents

Introduction

It was a very surreal moment. Two a.m., a night in June, the sky cloudless. The telephone rang and I reached for it, half asleep still, irritated not for the first time that I'd agreed to have the phone on my side of the bed. And then, even before I picked up the receiver, realising what the call was about and waking up very thoroughly indeed.

The moment that you actually *know* you're a grandparent for the first time, that your baby has a baby of his own, is like – well, it's almost indescribable. The strangest jolt I'd ever experienced, and quite different from the moment I became a parent.

I heard my son's voice burbling in my ear, 'It's all right. They're both fine – he's a great big chap, with the blackest hair you ever saw, and quite, quite perfect', and managed to stammer something of my relief and delight. Then I handed the phone to my husband and lay there trying to get my head together.

Of course I'd known it was going to happen, but there is a great gulf between pregnancy and reality. The change from anonymous bump to real, breathing, separate person is of monumental significance to everyone in a family.

But why? After all, isn't a grandparent the epitome of someone taking a back seat? You've had and reared your babies; your job is done. From now on you're just an onlooker, a supernumerary. Aren't you?

Well no, you're not. First of all there is the profound effect this child has on your perception of yourself. You've been bumbling along happily enough as an average sort of adult; much the same person you've been all through your shared life with your partner, but suddenly you're jacked into Elder status. It's as though when you went to bed you were a comfortable thirtysomething and when you woke up, you discovered burglars had been in the night and stolen 30 years of your life. You see yourself in the pattern of family – even dynastic – structure as never before.

So, there is that to come to terms with. And lots of other things too.

Like, how do I behave with this small new person? How do I behave with his

WHAT CHILDREN OF ALL AGES LIKE DOING
It's easy to forget how much pleasure children derive from having an adult take the time to talk to them, share their knowledge of the world and play with them. Each chapter will remind you of what children enjoy at different ages, and how you can make the most of the time you spend together. Introducing your grandchild to the wonders of the natural world (right) may be one of the most life-enriching things you do for him.

parents so that I don't irritate or upset them as I remember being upset by my children's grandparents? (And weren't we all?) How are children reared today? What sort of toys, food, clothes do they have? Or is it all the same as it always was and will my wisdom and experience be welcome and valuable? Or must I just bite my tongue all the time from now on?

Questions like this and many more besides are answered in the splendid book you have in your hands.

I can tell you that as the weeks pleated into months after our own small Simon's birth, and he became first a personality, then a person with decided ideas and opinions of his own. ('You won't need to bother with school for him,' I told my daughter-in law when he was 18 months old. 'You should just send him straight to university.' And she agreed.) I learned more and more about the very special relationship that exists between grandparent and grandchild.

HOW CHILDREN DEVELOP
*Every child is different and some acquire physical,
mental and social skills earlier than others.
However, average ages for different skills – and
ideas for games and pastimes to complement
them (left) – are given throughout the book.*

SHARED SKILLS
*Passing on their expertise in a craft,
skill or pastime is something many
grandparents find they have the time,
inclination and patience to undertake.
If you are a keen gardener, you may
find at least one devoted student
among your grandchildren (right).*

I learned to accept that I was now one
of four in relation to this child and not
just one of a couple (the other
grandparents are quite as important as
you are). I learned to take on board
totally different ideas about the necessary
routine for a baby's life, and discovered
that new ideas were just as good as the
old ones, and sometimes better. I
relearned the skills of buying toys and
clothes, of enjoying family meals that
included a vociferous person in a high
chair. I also rediscovered the delight of
finding half-chewed apples or soggy
biscuits in my stationery drawer, and
having a suddenly weary toddler fall
asleep in my lap. Lovely, all of it.

Of course, not all the coming years will
be lovely as, I hope, other grandchildren
arrive to surround our table on special
occasions. There will be pains and
problems, fears and failures, worries of
all sorts. But I'll have this book on hand

to help me sort them out. If I need to
know the newest jargon in the baby and
child-care world (and it's one where
fashion rules as much as any other), if I
need to get my head clear on matters
ranging from infancy to adolescence, here
are the pages that will aid me.

I hope I won't have to deal with the
unpleasant things, like separation or
divorce, like illness or handicap, like
religious intolerance or child abuse or
anything painful, but of course I can't
count on having my hopes fulfilled. Having
a text that discusses such matters honestly
and clearly will be of huge benefit to me
and, by osmosis, to my much-loved
children and children-in-law. Having a
sensible, tactful, reliable Elder or two in
your private tribe can make a massive
difference to family happiness, and
therefore to grandchildren's happiness
and success in life. This has, after all, to
be what we all want for our family.

SPECIAL DAYS
Suggestions for places to visit with your grandchild, and ideas to enable you to make the most of the precious time you spend in each other's company (right), feature in every chapter.

TOYS AND GAMES
An indication of what appeals at each stage of your grandchild's life makes buying gifts, and stocking your toy cupboard for long and short visits, easy.

LOVING FRIENDSHIP
As your grandchild grows into adulthood, a relationship built on love and trust may mature into one of loyalty, respect and companionship.

Whether you've bought this book for yourself, or it's been presented to you by one of your children as a way of letting you know what's to come, you're in good hands. There is much helpful advice and many stimulating ideas here, from planning money matters to creating a 'heritage chest' for your grandchildren (an enchanting idea) and I know you'll enjoy it.

Welcome to the world of the grandparent. It's an amazing and exciting, if sometimes challenging, one. Enjoy it.

Claire Rayner

Your Newborn Grandchild

Becoming a grandparent for the first time is a unique experience. In much the same way as no one could quite prepare you for how you felt when you held your first child in your arms, so reactions to becoming a grandparent vary. But the perception that it will make you feel 'old before your time' is simply not true: it is more likely to mark the beginning of a rejuvenating and deeply rewarding period of your life.

You may feel an intensity of love that you may not have experienced since your own children were babies. You may also feel more needed than you have since your children left home, giving help and advice to the new parents as they make the transition from couple to family. And you will take great enjoyment in watching your

grandchild develop from a tiny and helpless creature into a unique human being in whom you see echoes of yourself and your children. Like many other grandparents, you will have a privileged place in his life for many years to come.

Your role as a grandparent

What sort of grandparent do you want to be?

The grandparent you want to be, or are able to be, depends on a number of factors – where you live, your relationship with the new parents, your and their financial circumstances and how healthy you are. If you live close to your child and his or her partner, you may see your new grandchild almost every day; if you live farther away or perhaps do not have a close relationship with your child or his or her partner, your contact may be sporadic.

Grandparenting is immensely rewarding – you do not have the day-to-day duties of childrearing, so you are able to be relaxed with your grandchildren in a way that parents cannot always be. Grandparents, who never seem 'too busy' and who may be more approachable than parents on some subjects, can also play an important role in a child's life. The prospect of a new baby is an opportunity to repair any rifts that might exist in the family. Sharing a grandchild may bring you closer to the other set of grandparents, too.

You will blend better into the new family if you discuss important issues with the parents-to-be before the birth. They will be thinking about how they are going to cope generally, about breast- or bottle-feeding, about whether or not the mother is going to go back to work after the baby is born and about childcare arrangements. Their attitudes may be different from yours.

Try to talk through anything that bothers you now, so that it does not become a problem later. Particularly if this is their first baby, they are probably feeling apprehensive about the responsibility they are about to take on. Don't undermine their confidence if their way is different from yours. If you are generally supportive and accommodating, they will not feel inhibited about asking your advice when they are in real doubt about what to do.

Discuss cultural or religious differences ahead of the birth if at all possible. Your son or daughter is not necessarily rejecting your beliefs in following his or her partner's wishes, but rather acknowledging how important those wishes are to them both. If such matters are discussed in principle before they become problems in practice, it will be easier for everyone to understand and accept any decisions made.

Childcare arrangements

If the mother is planning to go back to work, the parents may ask you to look after the baby on a regular basis. This is, of course, a great compliment – they are not going to entrust their child to anyone in whom they do not have absolute faith. But think carefully about what it would entail.

You would almost certainly have to spend a lot of time in the baby's home, as babies are happiest in familiar surroundings. Do your other commitments allow you to do this? Have you got the energy and the patience to cope? Will your enthusiasm last beyond the first few weeks, or will you get bored? What will happen if the new parents have a second child, or if another of your own children has a baby and wants similar help from you?

If you are happy with the prospect, this should be a period of great joy and fulfilment. If the idea does not appeal to you, it is better to say so now so that the parents can make other arrangements early on, rather than feel you have let them down later. (Realistically, you should be thinking about committing yourself for at least a year – the average period of employment for a nanny.)

Respecting rules

If you are not going to be closely involved on a daily basis, you will still want to visit your grandchild and have him come to visit you. Although nobody can be entirely consistent about parenting or grandparenting, the new parents will have ground rules that you should follow. If they ask you not to bring a toy or put a coin in your grandchild's moneybox each time you visit, don't. Respecting the parents' wishes from the start will make it easier to do so later when different views about sweets and television-watching come to the fore.

One unbreakable rule is that you should never smoke or allow anyone else to smoke near a baby or small child. Smoking dramatically increases the risk of cot death

Grandchildren bring families closer together, cementing bonds that for many reasons may have loosened over the years. This is a time for increased communication, mutual support and understanding and, in the best of circumstances, enormous happiness for all concerned.

and can cause asthma and other lasting problems. If you or your partner smoke and your house is always smoky, you may find the new parents reluctant to bring their baby to visit you: if you can't give it up, try to ensure that at least one comfortable room in the house is a permanently smoke-free zone.

Single parents

If your daughter is about to become a single mother, you may find this difficult to accept. Calm discussion is the best approach. A baby needs to be loved and cherished whether he was planned or not. If your daughter is in her 30s and felt 'time running out' when there was no long-term man in her life, she may have deliberately chosen to become pregnant, or found herself pregnant after a relationship ended and decided to bring up the baby alone.

Ask her to talk to you about this and try to understand that she is serious about motherhood and the baby, however unconventional you may feel her approach is. She is embarking on a potentially lonely road and will welcome your support if you can give it without passing judgement (see also p. 33).

In at the start

Helping to bring your grandchild into the world

Almost all mothers-to-be have someone in the delivery room to give them practical support during labour and birth. This helper is, of course, usually the baby's father, but there are many circumstances in which this may not be an option. If a man is particularly squeamish, the couple may decide it is better for him not to be there; inflexible work schedules and unpredictable babies may mean the father is away; and a woman intending to raise her child alone may not want or need a male presence. It is possible, in any of these situations, that your daughter might ask you for help. (Equally she may choose her sister or a friend, so don't be offended.)

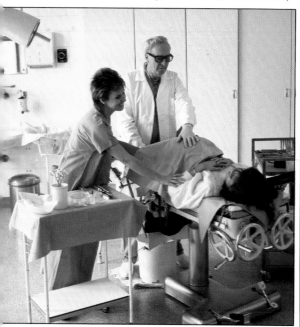

A mother-to-be usually has the oppportunity to visit a delivery room in advance of the birth; if you are to be her birth partner, go along too. It is important that you know what the various pieces of equipment are used for, as well as the mother-to-be's wishes regarding such subjects as continuous foetal monitoring and the use of a drip to speed labour.

If you are to be a 'birth partner', attend antenatal classes with your daughter so that you can brush up on what is expected. As a birth partner, you must comfort the mother-to-be, helping her to relax during the early stages of labour, but also encouraging her to breathe as she has been taught to do and advising her when she needs to push. If the labour is long, she may lose concentration and you will have to remind her what she should be doing.

The first decision your daughter may have to make is where to have her baby. You can help here – especially if she is working and you are not – by phoning or visiting suitable hospitals, chatting to the staff and finding out if their philosophies dovetail with what your daughter wants. If she thinks she would like a home birth, she may face opposition from health-care professionals. It is, however, her right to have her baby at home if she wishes. Be as supportive as possible if she has difficulty in getting her way over this, but make sure she listens to the professionals too – if complications are likely, she would be safer in hospital.

Your daughter may formulate a birth plan, which will detail her wishes and hopes for the birth. Birth plans generally include information such as whether she wishes to be given painkillers, how strongly she feels about avoiding an episiotomy or Caesarean and if she wants her baby put to her breast immediately after the birth. In a 'natural' birth, the mother avoids drugs in order to feel in touch with what her body is telling her to do. Some women accept Entonox – a mixture of gas and air, breathed in through a respirator – but no injected painkillers.

You should be part of these discussions early on: when the time comes, you are going to be the intermediary between her and the medical staff caring for her. You must be prepared to honour her wishes (think in advance about how you will cope with seeing someone you love in pain), but you should be clear on whether there is a margin for an on-the-spot change of mind if it all gets more painful than she imagined. She may not be able to make the decision when the time comes, and you may have to do it for her. Obviously, if there are serious complications with the birth; take advice from the medical staff, but if everything is straightforward they should respect the mother-to-be's wishes.

There may also be discussion about the position in which she wants to give birth. The term 'active' birth means that the

A HERITAGE CHEST

If his parents do not do so, there are all sorts of mementos of your grandchild that you might like to preserve. You don't need a special container – a cardboard box will do – but if you can afford something more worthy of the name 'heritage chest' so much the better.

Among the things you might like to collect are:
• His hospital identification tags
• His first lock of hair
• His first bootees or other 'first size' clothes
• His first tooth
• A newspaper for the day he was born
• A set of the coins that were in circulation in the year he was born (available in presentation packs).

You can continue to add to this over the years, preserving discarded toys, early attempts at writing and drawing, school reports and photographs. Most of us become more nostalgic as we grow older and there will come a day when he is grateful that you kept all this 'junk', a unique record of his childhood.

mother may stand, sit, squat, even walk around and generally take an active part in the process of giving birth. All these positions have their merits – squatting or kneeling is best for positioning the pelvic organs for the birth; standing up may be better for the baby's oxygen supply; being propped up on a bed may be more restful during a long labour and it makes it easier for doctors and midwives to help – the important things are that the mother-to-be should be comfortable and her baby safe.

Water births are increasingly popular and, although not all hospitals have facilities for them, you can buy or hire baths for home or hospital births. Some women remain in the bath throughout the birth; others use it simply to ease labour. As a birth partner, you should get into the tank with her, since supporting from outside in a long labour will put too much strain on your back. The water – the temperature is controlled by a thermostat – is reputed to relax the mother and bring stronger contractions and quicker dilatation of the cervix. Some people also believe that emerging into warm water makes birth less traumatic for the baby.

After the birth, you may find that the baby is whisked away for tests or because he needs oxygen or special care. But unless something is seriously wrong, he should be able to return to his mother. The new mother will be too tired to argue about anything at this stage, so it is up to you to make sure she is happy with what is going on. This is an important time for mother and baby and they should not be apart unless there is good reason.

Understanding the jargon
Keeping up to date with birth and childcare practices

In 1946, the first edition of Dr Benjamin Spock's *Baby and Child Care* caused a furore for its controversial suggestion that parents should respond to their babies' needs when they are expressed, rather than keep them on a rigid timetable. This seems extraordinary today, when so many well-qualified writers producing book after book of sensible and caring advice for new parents and parents-to-be echo this advice.

Prominent among today's established names are Penelope Leach, Sheila Kitzinger, Miriam Stoppard, Hugh Jolly and Alison Mackonochie, and many new parents benefit from the advice of these experts. They differ in their emphasis – Stoppard is perhaps the most practical for mothers-to-be intending to return to work, while Leach stresses bonding to the point of considering mother-and-baby as a single unit – but they all encourage a new mother to follow her instincts, find her own rhythm and do what seems best for her and her baby.

At the same time, a more flexible attitude to labour and birth has evolved: mothers-to-be are encouraged to have more say in how they deal with pregnancy and birth, and to consider their hopes and wishes for the birth. Your daughter or daughter-in-law is likely to read books and attend classes and enter her pregnancy and labour with these philosophies uppermost in her mind. If you want to keep up with her, read these books too so that you understand her thinking on various issues (if you are to be her birth partner, see pp. 14–15).

Antenatal care

Since you had your children, antenatal care and childbirth practice may have changed. Antenatal testing is now usual. The most common tests are listed below.

• An initial blood test, which determines blood group, rhesus factor, iron levels and immunity to certain diseases, notably rubella (German measles). Many couples check these factors before they conceive.

• An ultrasound scan, which may be given at any time between 16 and 20 weeks, confirms that the baby is growing normally and may identify such problems as spina bifida or heart defects. Later in pregnancy, ultrasound may be used to check the position and condition of the placenta, alerting medical staff to the chance of a Caesarean section being necessary.

Approaches in antenatal classes vary, with some following the philosophy of a particular childbirth educator. Here, couples learn exercises to help prepare the body for labour and birth. If you have been chosen to be the birth partner, you should attend these classes too.

Feeding a baby when he is hungry – rather than leaving him to scream until a feed is due – makes the whole experience calm and as rewarding for you as it is for your grandchild.

• Blood tests for genetic disorders. Some of these are most common among people of particular ethnic groups, so testing is usually offered only to those considered at risk. They include: sickle cell disease (for people of Caribbean and African origin); cystic fibrosis (which is most common among white people of northern European origin); thalassaemia (for those of Mediterranean or Asian descent); and Tay–Sachs disease (prevalent among Jews of Eastern European origin).
• Tests for chromosomal disorders, the most common of which is Down's syndrome. This is more prevalent in older mothers, so tests are usually offered only to women over the age of 35. They include chorionic villus sampling (CVS) and amniocentesis.
• Tests for neural tube defects, such as spina bifida. The most common test is the alpha-fetoprotein (AFP).

You may or may not know whether your family has opted for a particular test or be told the outcome. Having a test, getting the result and acting on it, can be emotionally draining. In these situations, take your lead from your son or daughter – if they want you to know they will tell you – and offer all the support you can.

Sometimes called parentcraft or childbirth classes, antenatal classes are intended to prepare the mother-to-be for labour and birth, and include advice on such subjects as exercise in pregnancy, massage, relaxation, pain relief in labour and breastfeeding. All stress the importance of mothers-to-be feeling in control of their labour, and of the role of the whole family in childbirth.

Immunisation

The major vaccinations for babies occur in three stages in the first two to six months of life, and consist of a triple shot against diphtheria, tetanus and whooping cough, with separate immunisation against polio, taken orally. (UK schedules also include the HIB – haemophilus influenzae type B – vaccine, which protects against a number of illnesses, notably meningitis.) MMR (measles, mumps and rubella) is given at 12–15 months.

Support groups

You may have felt isolated when you had your baby; or you may have been living with or near your family, or been sufficiently friendly with neighbours to have company and advice from women who had children of their own. Today, many new mothers do not have this informal network, and more organised support groups have grown up. There are lists of useful addresses at the end of almost every childcare book and in your local library.

If your daughter or daughter-in-law has problems, there is somebody at the end of a telephone who can give advice on breast-feeding problems, crying or colicky babies, and who can support and help her if she feels isolated, has had a multiple birth, is a single parent, or has a baby with special needs. Many associations also have local groups, where parents of babies of similar ages (or with similar problems) can meet and give mutual support.

Basic baby facts

What you may have forgotten about tiny babies' wants and needs

It is all too easy to forget how small and vulnerable new babies are, especially if the last tiny baby you held was your own. For many parents, too, the first weeks and months with a baby pass in a blur.

Babies' looks and skills

Some babies are born bald, others have a full head of dark hair, which will probably fall out and be replaced by something much lighter. If he does not have much hair, the pulse on the top of his head will be clearly visible. This is under the fontanelle, one of several soft places on the head where the bones of the skull have not yet fused together. This is normal: they close during the first couple of years of his life. His head may have been pushed slightly out of shape if he had a difficult birth, but this will correct itself after a few months. Most newborns have deep blue eyes which often change colour as they grow older.

His body may be covered with a fine 'fur' which drops out during the first few months.

His skin will be highly sensitive. Avoid using toiletries for at least the first six weeks, and after that use only specially formulated baby products. Clean his nappy area gently with moistened cottonwool and dry all the folds of the skin to prevent irritation.

The genitals of newborn babies of either sex may seem disproportionately large and swollen. This will subside after a few days.

Newborns are helpless. They can suck, cry and eliminate waste, but you have to do pretty much everything else for them. And their needs are basic. If your grandchild is crying he is probably hungry, too hot or too cold, uncomfortable (and in need of a clean nappy), bored and wanting attention or – possibly – sick or getting sick.

Your grandchild can focus on objects up to about 25 cm (10 inches) away and can mimic gestures and lip movement. Poke your tongue out at him several times and he will do the same back to you. He will also have a strong gripping reflex – even the tiniest baby can grasp and hold on to

Newborns' neck muscles are weak so you must always support the baby's head with a hand or arm when you are holding or carrying him. By the time he is two or three months old, he will have more head control, but you should still support his head until he is about six months old and holding his head upright all the time.

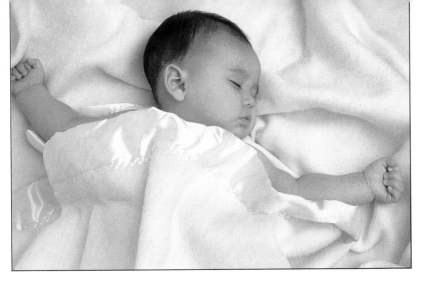

Overheating can be dangerous and is thought to be one of the contributory factors in cot death. If the room where the baby is sleeping is well-heated, don't overload him with bedclothes. Two or three layers of light covers are better than one heavy one.

your finger. He will lose this ability after about three months and have to re-learn how to hold things.

Most babies sleep when they are not being handled or fed (unless they are colicky, when they can cry a lot). But by three months your grandchild will be alert, fascinated by jewellery, anything bright and his own fingers. He will smile for the first time when he is six to eight weeks old.

Newborn babies cannot regulate their body temperature by sweating or shivering, so it is vital to make sure they are neither too hot nor too cold. Use blankets rather than a duvet so that you can remove or add layers if necessary; undress the baby only in a warm room; a lot of heat is lost through the head, so make sure he is wearing a hat in cold weather. Remember, too, that he is not getting the exercise of walking up the hill or pushing the pram, so he may not be as warm as you are. Cuddling is a good way to transfer some of your body heat to him.

How to handle a newborn

Newborns are fragile, but there is no need to be afraid of this vulnerability. Pick him up gently but with confidence, and always support his head. When you put him down to sleep lie him on his back (which has been shown to reduce the risk of cot death) and check he is comfortable: he cannot move himself out of an awkward position.

Tiny babies respond to a soothing tone of voice so if you talk reassuringly to a crying baby you may calm him. He will be startled by a loud noise, but will not normally be disturbed by noises or conversation, so once he is asleep there is no need to whisper or tiptoe around him. He may find a continuous background 'hum' soothing – if he can't sleep try turning the radio on low, or get someone to vacuum in another room.

Babies hate having things pulled over their head and some dislike being dressed and undressed. Buy clothes with wide necklines or front fastenings and change the baby's clothes no more than is necessary.

Babies' health

It is normal for a baby to lose up to 10 per cent of his birth weight in the first few days, but he should be back to birth weight by the time he is 10 days old. In the first three months of his life, a baby grows 5–7.5 cm (2–3 inches) and gains just over 2 kg (4 lb).

Babies' immune systems are not fully developed, so your grandchild has little resistance to infection. Make sure everything he touches is clean. Sterilise bottles carefully and wash your hands before feeding him. All babies regurgitate some milk after almost every feed. Put a clean towel over your shoulder before burping him. He will also have no control over his bowels or bladder and may need to have his nappy changed as much as 10 times a day. But be alert: vomiting and/or diarrhoea can quickly lead to dehydration. Contact the doctor if the baby has watery, green or smelly stools, pus or blood in his stools or if his temperature exceeds 38°C (100°F).

Gifts for the baby

Choosing clothes and equipment for a baby

It is an understandable reaction, when you hear that you are going to become a grandparent, to rush out and buy a gift – either for the baby or for the nursery. But it's wise to resist the urge until later in the pregnancy, when you have had the chance to talk through choices with the parents-to-be. Always consult the parents before you buy anything substantial or expensive for a baby. He needs only one pram, one cot and one car seat, so make sure that no one else is planning to buy the same thing and that the parents are happy with your choice.

If you can, take the prospective parents shopping with you, be honest about your price range and buy what they want. Nothing will alienate them more quickly than if you spend a lot of money on something they do not want, and are then hurt if they don't use it. Make sure it's practical, too – don't buy a large chest of drawers for a small bedroom, or a heavy pram if it will have to be carried up and down stairs.

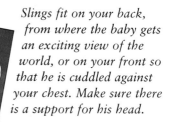

Slings fit on your back, from where the baby gets an exciting view of the world, or on your front so that he is cuddled against your chest. Make sure there is a support for his head.

bag. High prams with large wheels give a smoother 'ride', although babies do not seem too bothered about this as long as they have a comfortable mattress; smaller prams are lighter to push and easier to manoeuvre. A baby must be able to lie flat – pushchairs or strollers come later.

The law requires all babies and young children to be firmly strapped in when travelling by car. You can buy straps to hold a carrycot in place on the back seat (these can be used later to secure a toddler's seat). A rear-facing car seat is generally considered safer but do not use one if the passenger side of your car is fitted with an airbag. Babies and young children can be seriously injured or killed by the force with which these 'eject'.

Small babies can be carried against an adult's chest or back in a sling, which leaves the adult's hands free but still gives the baby reassuring warmth and closeness.

Transport

Some prams are structured so that the top lifts off the wheels and becomes a carrycot, and the chassis folds up for easy storage. Some have a wire basket underneath which is useful for shopping or for carrying a changing

A pram for city streets needs to be lightweight and easy to manoeuvre. It should also protect the baby from extreme conditions, from cold winds to blazing sun. A single chassis that can hold first a carrycot then a pushchair or stroller is more practical than a carriage pram, although the latter will last longer and can be passed down the family.

You can use these for short trips outdoors – if you walk with one for too long, you and the baby can become hot and uncomfortable – and indoors, when your warmth and proximity may help soothe a baby who is fractious.

Somewhere to sleep

Moses baskets or cradles are soft and warm for a newborn baby, as well as convenient for his parents. He will be asleep for a lot of the time, so it makes sense to be able to transport him in his bed. A cradle can sit on the floor or on a solid table so that the parents can keep an eye on the baby and he can have company while they get on with other things. One with a hood gives extra protection from the weather if you take him outside in it. If there are pets in the house – cats in particular can be jealous of new arrivals – buy a light, loose-meshed net to lie over the cradle (with the hood down) to keep inquisitive paws out.

Your grandchild will soon

A Moses basket (right) is small enough for a new baby to feel secure: many seem 'lost' in a full-size cot. Baskets are also easy to carry from room to room. Most babies need a cot from around six months. If you are buying second-hand, check the distance between the slats – safety standards specify no wider than 5–8.5 cm (2–3⅓ inches). Use sheets and blankets, with an eiderdown for winter, rather than a duvet.

From his earliest days a baby can focus on a mobile hung just out of reach above his face. If it is asymmetrical, keep him interested by changing it around every few days. When buying a mobile, hold it above your head and look up at it to get the view the baby will see: some look wonderful from the side but are uninteresting from below!

grow out of his cradle and need a full-size cot. Make sure the slats are sufficiently close together to avoid any danger of his head getting stuck (ideally, no more than 5 cm/2 inches apart) and that the sides drop down so that it is easy to lift the baby out. He will sleep in a cot for about two years, so it needs to be sturdy enough to last the course.

Bedding is important: a close-fitting foam mattress with airholes, protected by a waterproof sheet, cotton sheets and a cotton cellular blanket. Make sure these are machine-washable. Don't buy a duvet for a newborn baby – he needs layered bedding so that it is easy to remove or add a layer if he gets too hot or cold. Avoid pillows and cot bumpers in a newborn's bed, since they can reduce the baby's ability to lose heat if he becomes too hot (a possible factor in cot death). Sleeping bags may be convenient if the baby kicks off his bedclothes in the night, but make sure they allow plenty of room for him to move his feet and are loose around the neck and wrists.

Gifts for the baby

Other equipment

Around the house, you can put a baby who is beginning to take an interest in his surroundings in an infant seat, which allows him to be slightly propped up, see what is going on and have company while adults are getting on with their work. Some of these seats are of moulded plastic and adjustable – the younger the baby, the nearer to horizontal he should lie; others are of canvas, which gives him the additional fun of some gentle bouncing.

Many parents choose vinyl or wood flooring for the nursery because it is easier to keep clean, in which case a non-slip rug might be a cosy addition. A baby listener, with a speaker for the baby's room and a receiver that enables his breathing to be heard in other parts of the house, can be reassuring for new parents and alerts them as soon as he is awake.

Storage space in the nursery is essential to keep all the baby's equipment. If this is not built-in, a chest of drawers or stacking wire storage baskets may be appropriate. Soft towels, a changing mat, a bath and another non-slip mat to go next to it are also practical gifts. Changing tables are not useful for very long, so check whether this is one of the parents' priorities.

Other basics include bottles, a bottle warmer and sterilising equipment if the baby is to be bottle-fed; a nappy bag; and wipe-clean holdalls for all the other bits and pieces that accompany a small baby whenever he goes anywhere. Nappy bags or nursery organiser bags can hang over the end of the cot to hold toiletries and other essentials. If you are adept with a sewing machine you can make one of these yourself. A baby gate will become essential the moment the baby is mobile if his house (or yours) has stairs.

A car seat is a must; many designed for newborns have carrying handles that make it easy to move the baby from car to shops or home even when he is asleep.

Choose clothes that have wide 'envelope' necks and easy access to a nappy (below) to make dressing and changing easier.

Clothes

Opt for layered clothing, so that it is easy to take something off if the baby gets too hot. Choose natural fibres for garments that will be next to his skin, but since he will dribble all over even his smartest clothes, they need to be machine-washable and colour-fast.

Babies grow out of clothes quickly, so don't buy too much of any one size. In particular, don't buy a lot of first-size clothing – supposed to fit babies up to three months – until he is born and you know that he is not a 5-kg (11-pound) record breaker who will be into second sizes in a week. If in doubt about the size, buy big: loose-fitting clothes are comfortable and he will soon grow into them. Vests, T-shirts and jumpers should have wide necks so that they can be easily pulled over the head. Check whether the parents have any colour preference. Most don't choose pink for girls and blue for boys any more.

If you plan to knit or sew clothes for the newborn, be realistic about how long this will take and bear in mind his likely size and the time of year when the garments will be

CUTTING COSTS

A baby does not need everything around him to be new. If you are on a tight budget, you may be able to find a nearly-new cot or pram advertised for sale in the local paper. As long as it conforms to the approved safety standards, and is clean, stable and painted with non-toxic paint, it should be acceptable. Make sure, however, that a buggy or stroller locks into the upright position and won't inadvertently collapse, and that all the wheel locks work properly. There should also be a good harness fitted to retain the child securely.

If you have time rather than money to spare, you may be able to contribute to the nursery in a more practical way, by painting the walls, making new curtains or refurbishing an old toy box (preferably one without a lid or with hinges that hold the lid securely upright) or small chest of drawers.

An unbreakable mirror, securely attached inside the cot at the level of the child's head, will help develop his fascination for faces. A colourful line of plastic or soft teddies strung above his pram or cot will give him something else to look at, and if they rattle so much the better – the sound will intrigue him. Do not leave toys inside the cot or strung within reach of a child who could use them to pull himself up.

By about three months he will be able to hold a rattle if you put it into his hand – choose a variety of shapes and ones that make different sounds. Chewable rattles come into their own from about four months, when the gums become sensitive and teething begins. All these should be

An activity mat will give hours of fun. Choose one that is bright and includes some sounds, as well as several tactile experiences – soft, fluffy, bumpy and so on.

ready. Do not make anything too lacy – tiny fingernails are easily caught in the holes.

Don't forget head, hands and feet. Babies need hats (against sun and cold), mittens and bootees or socks. They don't need shoes until they start to walk.

Toys

Babies do not really appreciate toys until they are about six months old, but they do respond to anything that stimulates the senses. A cuddly toy for a newborn should be small, squeezable and soft to the touch; toys that squeak have added interest. All toys are sucked regularly so make sure they are washable and colour-fast. Toys with small detachable parts are usually labelled 'unsuitable for children under 36 months', so look out for this warning (see p. 57).

lightweight, so that he won't hurt himself if he hits himself on the head with them.

A cassette player and a tape of nursery rhymes or lullabies is a good gift, since babies love to be sung to. Or buy a musical box operated by pulling a string or pressing a button. He will be able to work it himself by the time he is about six months old, but can enjoy listening to it from the beginning.

Practical gifts

If you visit regularly and don't want to arrive empty-handed, why not spend some time in the chemist's and arrive with a bag of disposable nappies, wipes, creams, cotton wool and other consumables? It may not be glamorous, but the parents may be more grateful than if you buy another cuddly toy.

Financial gestures
Making your grandchild's future financially secure

Bringing up children is an expensive business; if you can afford to, you may want to help provide for your grandchildren's future. Don't worry if you cannot spare a great deal – there are many savings schemes which allow for small, regular investments as well as for lump sums. Some people – understandably – also find helping in this way more satisfying then adding to a grandchild's seemingly bottomless toy box.

For up-to-date, impartial information on investment it is best to go to an independent financial adviser; next best are the banks, building societies and insurance companies themselves, although they will advise only on their own products. Word-of-mouth recommendation is the most satisfactory way to choose a financial adviser (your accountant or lawyer may be able to recommend someone), but if you cannot find one that way, the Independent Financial Advisers Association (address in the telephone directory) will give you the name of a member in your area.

Financial advisers, whether independent or attached to a company, earn their living on commission from the companies whose policies or investments they sell, not by charging fees to their clients. They are not allowed to accept cheques payable to themselves. Steer well clear of anyone who does not adhere to this regulation.

If you are thinking in terms of investment, some of the options are discussed below.

Bank or building society account

You can open these in a child's name, in which case no one can touch the money until the child is a specified age (normally about seven years old), or in your own name on behalf of the child, in which case you become a signatory to the account and sign it over to the child when he reaches a certain age.

These accounts attract varying amounts of interest depending on the minimum sum you keep in them and the amount of notice you are required to give before making a withdrawal. You may also be able to find a special children's savings bond: this tends to attract a higher rate of interest although there may be a minimum investment.

COLLECTABLES

It is not only financial investments that increase in value with the passage of time. Any number of more tangible gifts may also be seen as assets. Paintings or prints, furniture, books, dolls and dolls' houses, china or porcelain, wine or port may all be worth appreciably more by the time your grandchild grows up, as well as being agreeable possessions in themselves. But if you are not well informed on the subject, be sure to ask the advice of an expert before investing in any of these commodities.

A leather-bound book of Victorian poetry may 'feel' like a precious antique, but if it turns out to be one volume from a six-volume set it is unlikely to interest a connoisseur. You may prefer to buy a first edition of a 'current' novelist you admire in the hope that his or her work becomes better known. If you want to buy a bottle of port that can be enjoyed on your grandchild's 18th birthday, consult a reputable wine merchant to ensure that you buy a vintage that will still be drinkable then.

Banks and building societies normally pay interest net of basic rate income tax, but a parent or guardian can apply to have this waived when the account is in the name of a child under 16. A child is not allowed to earn more than £100 a year tax-free interest on money given to him or her by a parent, but these rules do not apply to gifts from grandparents.

National Savings' Children's Bond

These can be bought over the counter at the post office and offer no-risk investment and tax-free interest. The minimum investment is £100, the maximum £10,000. Premium bonds, which pay no interest but may win a jackpot of a million pounds, are part of the same system.

Be honest about your circumstances, what you can afford and how long you are willing to have money tied up. A reputable financial adviser should have a range of schemes to meet your precise needs.

Unit trusts

These may be risky in the short term, but are reliable over a period of 10 to 20 years. There are special children's funds which can be opened with a minimum of £50, or with regular payments of at least £20 a month or £50 a year.

Second-hand endowment policies

These are ideal if you have a lump sum to invest and are looking for a return in six or seven years – for school fees, perhaps.

Covenants

These were once a popular way of passing on money to grandchildren, but a change in the law in the late 1980s took away the tax benefits unless the recipient was a charity. As a result, they are now less attractive than the other options mentioned above.

Thinking ahead

A good rule of thumb is that the longer you intend to leave the money invested, the more risks you can afford to take. If you want a quick return, go for safety. But whatever you decide, however much you feel you can afford to put aside, bear in mind the possibility of future grandchildren and calculate whether you can do the same for them. It is much better to be less generous now and give everyone a fair share in the long term than to make promises you find you cannot keep or to offend the parents of your second and subsequent grandchildren by appearing to favour the first. If no other grandchildren come along or your financial circumstances change, you can always make further provisions at a later date.

Gifts for new mums

Congratulating the new mother of your precious grandchild

Once the excitement of bringing home the baby amid congratulatory flowers and champagne is over, it is easy for new mothers to suffer an identity crisis. Strangers talk to the baby and ignore the mother completely or view her only as an extension of him, asking how old he is and what his name is. Friends who do not normally give the parents presents arrive laden with cuddly toys or clothes for the baby. The mothers who view their baby as an extension of themselves will revel in this. Others will not.

It is important, therefore, to remember that a mother is still a woman in her own right. She is also in a new and possibly frightening situation, and she needs pampering. Send her a glorious bouquet three weeks after the birth, when most of the initial deluge of flowers have died.

Arrange a massage or a half-day at a health club if she is willing to leave the baby for a length of time. (If you offer to look after him, you have the added bonus of having your grandchild to yourself for a while.) Or treat her to a series of yoga classes to help her get back in shape – and offer to go with her to keep her company. Some hair loss is common during and immediately after pregnancy, so being treated to a visit to the hairdresser is another good morale booster.

The essential oils used in aromatherapy, which she can put in the bath or use for massage, feel and smell wonderfully luxurious. They interact with the systems of the body in various ways, stimulating, calming or healing, depending on the oil. Among the most common, bergamot and lavender will relax her after a stressful day – and lavender also helps to heal stretched or stitched tissues after the birth; rose, jasmine and ylang ylang are also relaxing; and rosemary is a great tonic for general fatigue.

Pregnancy makes some women feel unattractive and almost all have to adapt their wardrobe to their increased size. Buy her something feminine such as perfume, silk underwear or a lacy nightdress – these are not things she is likely to buy for

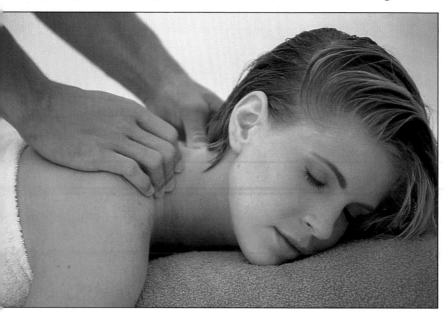

A bottle of her favourite perfume is an instant antidote to baby wipes and lotions, and can be applied liberally when a mother is feeling low. A massage (left) will soothe away tension and the minor aches of the first few weeks after the birth, allowing her to focus on her own body rather than her baby's.

A warm bath filled with luxury oils or essences (right) will revive tired limbs – or help a new mum relax sufficently to get a few hours of much-needed sleep. Silk underwear (below) will remind her that she is still a woman, as well as a mother.

out when necessary. If she is breast-feeding avoid anything too spicy, which might upset the baby's digestion, but don't worry too much about fattening foods, as breast-feeding will help her to lose much of the weight she has gained during pregnancy.

However she chooses to feed her baby, a new mother is going to spend a lot of the next few months doing it. A comfortable chair that gives adequate support to her back – her feet should touch the floor – is essential. If she has one already, you could buy a large, cheerful cushion for it – she can either put this at the base of her spine for added support, or use it to lie the baby on to bring him up to a comfortable level for feeding. Make sure it is washable.

A new parent wants to record her baby's every gesture. Photograph albums fill up quickly and it doesn't matter if she is given several. If she is a keen photographer some accessory for her camera, or even a new camera, may be a welcome present, but consult her or her partner first – don't spend a lot of money until you are sure you are buying the right thing. Record books of the 'baby's first smile, baby's first tooth' variety can be fun, and many of these have room for other photographs too.

A few CDs or tapes of music you know she likes, or some not-too-demanding books that she can read for the odd few minutes, might encourage her to find some time for herself. Childcare experts believe that even half an hour a day relaxing and looking after her own needs (and not feeling guilty about it) will help keep the new mother on an even keel – which is as beneficial for the baby as it is for her.

herself at this time,
but they may help her feel better about herself. Or take her shopping (the baby can come too) and buy her a new dress or a sumptuous sweater. If you have a piece of jewellery that belonged to your own mother, this might be the time to pass it on, but if you have other daughters or daughters-in-law and are likely to have more grandchildren, consider whether you are going to be able to make similar gestures every time.

Practical gifts

Although they frequently don't have the time or energy to cook much, new mothers (particularly those who breast-feed) need to eat well. Make some of her favourite meals that can go in the freezer and be brought

It is also important for new parents to be able to spend time together as a couple. Offer to babysit occasionally so that they can go out together, secure in the knowledge that their baby is being well looked after.

Then and now:

Breast or bottle?

Arguments in favour of breast- and bottle-feeding wax and wane in popularity. The best way to feed a baby is the way his mother feels most comfortable with; whatever her decision, supporting her is in everyone's interests.

THEN

In the 1990s the experts are unanimous: 'breast is best'. After a generation when bottle-feeding was the norm, breast-feeding is returning to popularity in many parts of the world, coinciding with the emphasis researchers and writers place on bonding between mother and baby, and also perhaps with the massive upsurge of interest in natural foods and medicines.

Bottle-feeding last became fashionable in the 1960s when, in the days of Women's Liberation, an increasing number of women were returning to work soon after giving birth. Breast-feeding came to be seen as something primitive or faintly distasteful. In a manner strangely reminiscent of Victorian times, many newborn babies were carried off not to wet nurses but to be bottle-fed, so that the new mother could either rest or get on with her life.

One respected baby expert writing in the mid-1970s put this question into the mouth of one of his imaginary readers: 'Why bother to understand the complexities of breast-feeding when bottle-feeding is a perfectly good alternative and when breast-feeding seems to be so exhausting, restricting and difficult?' Although he goes on to give a sympathetic and balanced account of the benefits of breast-feeding, it is a question which would hardly occur to mothers and childcare writers today.

Why breast-feed?

The arguments in favour of breast-feeding are compelling. Breast milk is easier to digest than formula milk, so breast-fed babies are less likely to suffer from constipation or wind. They also produce less waste, because a higher percentage of the milk is absorbed into the system. It is difficult to overfeed a breast-fed baby, so the risk of obesity is lessened. Breast-feeding also stimulates the production of the hormone oxytocin, which helps the womb to return to its previous size and shape, enabling the new mother to regain her figure more quickly.

Breast milk contains some of the mother's immunities that help a baby to fight off infection. It is also thought that it can be useful in the prevention of allergies, and recent research in the United States suggests that it can also protect against otitis media, a common childhood infection of the middle ear. It is more

NOW

Bottle-feeding (far left) has tended to be associated with feeding on schedule; today (left) mothers are more concerned to feed when their baby clearly needs milk or comfort. This approach also reduces the likelihood that a mother will have insufficient milk – one of the major reasons for giving up breast-feeding.

convenient, with no bottles or sterilising units to worry about. The milk is also always available and at the right temperature for the baby – and even becomes thinner in consistency when the weather is hot.

Learning to express milk is reasonably straightforward. It means that a baby can be fed breast milk when his mother is out at work, or in the middle of the night so that she can get a few hours' unbroken sleep and her partner does not feel left out of this intensely personal relationship.

Bottle-feeding
It is argued that bottle-feeding gives the new mother more freedom. She will not have the uncomfortably heavy breasts associated with breast-feeding since, if they are not stimulated by the baby's suckling, her breasts' unused milk supply will soon dry up. (But it is a fact that once the supply-and-demand of breast-feeding has settled down, her breasts will not overproduce and discomfort will be less of a problem.) She will not have to express milk if she has too much or if she is going to be unable to feed the baby herself for a while. Nor must she face the emotional

distress of 'failing' at breast-feeding, which many new mothers find difficult at first if they do not get the support they need. She will not suffer from sore nipples or potentially embarrassing leakages, or have to deal with the disapproval of strangers if she feeds her baby in a public place. There also need be no concerns about feeding the baby when the mother is ill.

The father of a bottle-fed baby can be involved from the start, which reduces the risk of his feeling jealous of the intimate relationship between mother and baby; it also means that he can do some night feeds.

But formula cannot duplicate colostrum, the thin watery fluid containing antibodies to help build up the baby's resistance to disease, which is secreted by the breasts in the first few days after childbirth. It is widely believed that a new mother should breast-feed for the first few days in order to give the baby this benefit, whatever her plans for feeding thereafter.

Personal choices
If your daughter or your son's partner opts for bottle when you believe in breast, or vice versa, do not be alarmed. How to feed her baby is a choice that every woman has to make for herself, unless she is advised not to breast-feed because of a problem of her own such as heart or kidney disease. Breast-feeding gives a baby all the nutrients he needs; but continued research and development has meant that formulas today are almost as good. As long as the mother (or whoever is giving the bottle) is relaxed and both parties are comfortable, feeding by whichever method should be an intimate and satisfying experience for all concerned.

I don't love the baby

Coming to terms with negative feelings about the new arrival

There is an in-built assumption in our society that everyone loves babies. But, in fact, many people do not, and there is no reason why they should: babies can do little, cry a lot, are sick over your clothes with monotonous regularity and can wear the nerves of the most committed carer to shreds in a very short time. Naturally your child loves his or her new baby and assumes that you will do the same, but circumstances and your own personality may make this difficult, initially at least.

If you live too far away for regular contact, you cannot be expected to bond with him as you would if you saw him every day, nor can he be expected to react to you with pleased familiarity. Take heart from the positive side of this situation: you only see his good points – blissfully asleep in a photograph or smiling into the video camera.

People unused to dealing with babies – and many of today's new grandfathers in particular had little to do with bringing up their own children – are often uncertain around them. If your grandchild senses this, he is more likely to cry when you hold him and reinforce your awkwardness. If you are uncertain, don't insist on having your 'turn' to cuddle him. In fact, many babies show by crying how much they dislike the kind of 'pass the baby' that tends to go on with newborns, and the new parents – especially if they lack confidence themselves – may prefer to become used to handling him before they allow others to have a go. Certainly most new parents will prefer your reticence to your insistence on gathering the baby up in an 'I know best' manner.

Try not to worry. There is no law that says you have to love your grandchild from the moment he is born. Lots of people find tiny babies uninteresting – you may be one of those who responds better when he starts to respond to you. You may find it reassuring to know that many new mothers don't immediately 'fall in love' with their baby, but say that the bond grows over the first weeks and months of his life. And it will between you and your grandchild.

If your grandchild is premature you may see him for the first time in an incubator, linked up to monitors and tubes. The fact that you cannot hold or cuddle a baby at this stage makes getting to know him more difficult, but providing there are no additional complications, he should be out of special care in a matter of days or, at worst, weeks. Then you can belatedly get on with the important business of being close to him.

Some babies are born with conditions that need almost immediate surgery. In

While most adults are overwhelmed by feelings of protectiveness towards premature babies, many find it hard to feel love for these tiny creatures. This, and his parents' undoubted concern for his wellbeing to the exclusion of all else, may make for a less than auspicious start to your relationship with your grandchild.

An irritable grandchild who cries a lot, even when he appears to be clean and fed, will not necessarily bring joy to the heart of every grandparent. Don't worry if initially you feel only relief as you leave his home: with time, you will come to love and appreciate him.

these circumstances, you are unlikely to be able to relate to your grandchild for the first months, or even perhaps most of the first year of his life. Everyone's attention is concentrated on simply keeping him alive. Most babies who go through this traumatic start go on to live perfectly healthy lives; many of them become very tough, having learned to fight from such an early age.

And, of course, some babies are born with problems for which there is no cure. If your grandchild has special needs, you may have to draw on all your inner strength to accept his unique place in your family (see pp. 60–61).

CASE HISTORY

My first grandson was born abroad and was over a year old when I saw him for the first time. I was excited at the idea of having a grandchild, and liked looking at the photographs my daughter sent regularly, but in fact his birth had no day-to-day effect on my life.

By the time my second grandson was born, my daughter and her family were back in this country, but too far away for regular visits and I was still not really involved in their lives. I wasn't disappointed, exactly, but my husband and I had a business, so it was difficult for us to go away anywhere. I accepted that I simply didn't see enough of the boys to get to know them and feel close to them.

I have never been the type to peer into prams and coo at other people's babies. I even found my own children more interesting only as they grew older and we were able to have real conversations. I tried not to worry too much that I was not closer to my grandchildren and was sure that in time a relationship would grow. A couple of years ago my husband and I decided to sell our business and retire.

Our first treat was to go for an extended visit to my daughter's. We took the boys to school some mornings, helped with homework, spent hours chatting, read to them at bedtime and took them – both separately and then together – out for a burger. I think that visit marked the start of our real relationship with them.

The children are seven and nine now, very bright, with great senses of humour. We see them fairly often and I feel I appreciate them as people whereas I couldn't respond to them as babies.

Sharing the baby

Giving all the family time to spend with the baby

However much you love him, it is important to remember that your grandchild is not your baby. Particularly if he is his parents' first child, they need to spend all the time they can with him in the first weeks, learning to deal with his needs, adapting to the changes in their family, their relationship with each other and their sleep patterns.

New mothers are often amazed at how much time caring for the baby takes, and how difficult it is to accomplish anything else. You will give valuable support, and may be more appreciated, if you offer to do the ironing or cook the dinner rather than look after the baby.

It is also important to remember that there are other friends and relatives who feel they have a 'claim' on your grandchild: the other grandparents, in particular, but also uncles, aunts and close friends all want to get to know him. Too many visitors, or one who stays too long, can wear out both parents at a time when they need all their spare energy. If you live close enough to

New fathers are sometimes reticent about handling their babies, as if somehow their partners 'know' how to do it better. By encouraging your son to care for his child from the start, you are helping him to lay the foundations of a close, loving relationship.

visit regularly, limit yourself to an hour at a time, unless you are invited to stay on – in which case make yourself useful.

If you are staying with the new parents, you will be there to help and should not expect them to entertain you. Do not be offended if they leave you alone all evening because they are looking after the baby or if they collapse hours before you are ready to go to bed. If there is nothing else for you

It is only natural to want to get the whole family together to celebrate the new arrival, but consider carefully whether this will put undue strain on the parents. Keep any gathering short and informal and be prepared for the parents to leave once everyone has seen and cooed over the baby.

to do, indulge yourself with reading, sewing or watching television and be ready to talk or lend a hand when required. You may be rewarded later in the evening by a cosy hour's chat with your son or son-in-law after mother and baby are asleep.

Try not to be possessive or to feel neglected if you hear that someone else has been invited around when you were not. This is especially important if you are the parents of the new father. A new mother is likely be more eager to have the support of her own mother and/or sisters or girlfriends of her own age who have children and can share recent experiences.

It is easy for the paternal grandmother to feel left out, but important that she should not give way to hurt or jealousy. Enough powerful, unfamiliar emotions are at work at this time without adding to them. If you are cheerful, helpful and understanding now, your visits will be all the more welcome later when things have settled down.

New fathers often feel neglected because their partner has to give so much time and energy to the baby. His parents can play a useful role here, reminding him that the baby is helpless and does indeed need all the attention the new mother is giving him, but that this does not mean that anyone loves or appreciates the new father less. Encourage him to learn how to care for the baby, too – cuddling him, changing his nappy, washing him and preparing him for bed.

A single parent will appreciate all the help you can offer, but don't limit yourself to babysitting: it may be more useful to get the numbers of support groups she could contact, or to help her fill out forms for the benefits to which she is entitled.

SINGLE-PARENT FAMILIES

If your daughter is a single parent, you may be called upon to provide the emotional and practical support that would otherwise come from the father. This might encompass anything from doing the shopping or accompanying her to postnatal checkups to simply 'being there' – in person or on the phone – if she needs you. If you find it difficult to accept her situation, try to discuss it calmly. The future wellbeing of mother and baby are what matters, and if you alienate your daughter by expressing disapproval you may miss out on one of life's most rewarding relationships.

Many childcare experts give the grandfather a special role in a single-parent family. He can introduce the baby to the idea that there are people who look and dress differently from his mother and have deeper voices but who are still friendly and trustworthy. Other experts point to the danger of a single mother desperately trying to provide for her baby's every need in order to compensate for the lack of a father. This may cause the child to have unreasonable expectations of other people later in life. Grandparents can ease the burden here, by providing loving and reliable support for mother and child.

A single mother may experience more financial hardship than one who is part of a couple, simply because she is trying to do two jobs in one and is likely either to have to give up work or to pay for childcare. If you can look after the baby on a regular basis while she is at work, this will help her enormously. But don't feel guilty if you can't do so: you might also be in full-time employment yourself, have other commitments or simply feel that your parenting days are over. In addition to all the emotional support you can give, help her to find out about the financial support to which she is legally entitled and the most effective ways to obtain maintenance from the child's father, if she is unable to do this unofficially.

Common dilemma: Am I interfering?

Knowing when and how to offer support and help

The line between giving sound advice and interfering is a fine one. Your common sense and the nature of your relationship with the new parents are your best guides. Attitudes to many aspects of childrearing, and to working mothers, have changed enormously since you were a new parent; while no one is saying that your way was wrong, it was not necessarily the only right way either.

If you are in your 50s or 60s, it is likely that you were given firm instructions about how to deal with your newborn baby: feed him every four hours, no more, no less; don't pick him up every time he cries or you will spoil him for life. Today's thinking is much less rigid, with many experts believing that it is wrong to leave a newborn baby to cry. Watching as your daughter or daughter-in-law cuddles her crying baby may bring back unhappy memories of 'not being allowed' to do the same for yours, but you must not allow this to form the basis of a criticism. Talking to her about your feelings may deepen the understanding between you, but it will not do so if you show resentment at her having a more rewarding time than you did.

Whether she chooses to breast- or bottle-feed is up to her, and whatever decision she makes deserves your whole-hearted support – regardless of your views on the subject. Pointing out the advantages of formula if she is convinced that she wants to breast-feed but is having trouble, for example, is less helpful than suggesting she ask a post-natal nurse or lactation counsellor for professional advice. Similarly, if she has tried breast-feeding and given up, don't add to her possible feelings of guilt at having 'failed', but praise the fact that her baby is now clearly more settled and obviously thriving.

Your son's priorities will of necessity change once he is a father: if he normally comes round at the weekend to tidy your garden, he may find he hasn't time now, for example. Ask someone else to help out for a while, so that you are not adding to his already overstretched schedule.

The new mother is probably reading books or leaflets that were not available in your day. Ask if you can read them too. They may give you a clearer idea of the thinking behind modern approaches to childrearing.

Domestic arrangements

You may be surprised by the extent to which the new father is involved with the baby. Many men feel left out of the intimate mother–baby relationship and need to find ways of bonding with their child. Getting up early, changing the baby's nappy and spending half an hour alone with him before the mother wakes up may be a special time for a father, not a sign that his partner is lazy or taking him for granted.

The same applies to household chores. Most women find it hard to keep on top of the housework when they are coping with the demands of a new baby, however immaculate their house usually used to be. You may not like to see your son having to prepare his own meals or do his own laundry, but many couples share domestic jobs anyway, and he may regard this as normal. The worst thing you can do at this time is sow seeds of discontent between the new parents. They are having to adjust to a new situation, neither of them is getting as much sleep as they are used to, and criticising the new mother to her partner – even if he is your son – is not going to help.

It is also none of your business whether the new mother chooses to go back to work. She may have to do so for purely financial reasons and may feel guilty about 'abandoning' her baby. If you were a full-time mother, your daughter may feel she is unable to live up to your standards, or that she has to compete with you to prove that she, too, is a good mother. Don't let any disapproval of yours reinforce these unnecessary and negative feelings.

If you don't live close to the new parents, or don't see them regularly, you will find that you see them even less and that they telephone less frequently. Try not to be hurt. Ask if there is a particular time of day that is convenient for you to phone, but don't take offence if you ring and find the baby screaming and the parents too harassed to talk. Don't make demands of the new parents: they are busy with their new child, and that must be their first priority.

Postnatal illness

You may be the first person to recognise any emotional problems the new mother is having. Most people think of postnatal depression as occurring in the first few weeks, but this is not necessarily the case.

Offering to take the baby out for a couple of hours gives new parents the opportunity to catch up on some sleep or have an uninterrupted meal together. But don't force your presence too often: the new parents need time together with their baby, simply learning to be a family.

A new mother can feel tearful, unable to cope, alienated from the baby, terrified that something is going to happen to him at any time during the first year after the birth. She may manage to look after the baby's needs but be totally incapable of running her house or the rest of her life.

She needs help, but should be discouraged from the 'easy' option of taking tranquillisers or antidepressants. The effects of drugs can be passed to the baby through breast milk, and some are addictive. A better approach is to offer to take on some of the daily chores that are getting on top of her. Look after the baby for an hour so that she can get some fresh air or have a nap; encourage her to talk about her feelings. Depression is often at its worst first thing in the morning, so if you can be there to make breakfast or deal with the older children, she may be better able to cope later in the day. If the depression lasts more than about 10 days, encourage her to seek help from her doctor (who can monitor the effect of any tranquillisers he or she prescribes), or a counsellor or psychotherapist.

From a distance
Establishing a relationship when you don't live close

If your grandchild lives too far away for you to visit regularly, it is inevitable that you will miss out on some of the pleasures of grandparenting. But there are many ways in which you can compensate for the distance between you, right from the start.

The telephone is the nearest to first-hand contact you are going to be able to have on a regular basis, but you will have to accept that, initially at least, the new parents are going to be tired and busy and it may not always be convenient to chat. Be understanding about this – things will calm down in a few months, the baby may settle into a routine and you can establish what is likely to be a convenient time of day for you to ring. Even quite young babies are fascinated by the telephone and your grandchild may be able to gurgle to you from an early age.

If you think or know that they would ring more often if they could afford it, offer – tactfully – to pay (or contribute to) their phone bill. Explain that they will be doing

you a favour, keeping you in touch with them and your grandchild. And if you can't afford to phone often, be meticulous about birthdays and other special occasions. Get several members of the family together so that everyone can have a quick chat – you will feel you have been in touch more closely than you can be by letter.

You are likely to find that even regular correspondents write fewer letters when there is a new baby in the house. Remind yourself how busy they are with the new baby and don't take offence. Keep writing to them. There is nothing to stop you writing to your grandchild long before he is able to read. If he has been receiving letters from granny and granddad for as long as he can remember, it may become a natural thing for him to start writing to you as soon as he is old enough.

Photographs and videos will also help you stay in touch. Encourage the new parents to send photos

Your grandchild may laugh, cry, gurgle and chatter to you from as early as a few months old. Ask his parents how he spends his day so that you can visualise what he may be doing at odd moments when he is in your thoughts.

CASE HISTORY

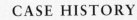

*A*fter my marriage broke up, I was transferred to an office in my home town, 300 kilometres from my ex-wife and teenage daughters. I managed to keep up a good relationship with both my daughters, who came for long visits during school and college holidays. But when they started work, they had a limited amount of free time and I was still working myself, so although we kept in touch by phone we saw a good deal less of each other.

Then Jenny got married and had a little boy. I took a long weekend to go down and meet James when he was three weeks old. He was delightful and I was so proud of him – it was good to have a grandchild, and a boy in the family at last! But I knew I wouldn't be able to visit on a regular basis and they were often too busy or too tired to chat on the phone. I was also aware that my ex-wife saw a lot of them, and I was jealous. I felt I was missing out on something special.

After six weeks of sulking I decided to buy them a video camera and asked them to film James whenever they had a spare moment. I wasn't expecting them to have much time at first, but in fact when the baby was just over three months old they were able to send me an hour-long film that I can watch whenever I like. It ends with a close-up of James smiling at the camera and it always makes me want to smile back.

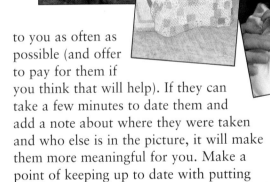

to you as often as possible (and offer to pay for them if you think that will help). If they can take a few minutes to date them and add a note about where they were taken and who else is in the picture, it will make them more meaningful for you. Make a point of keeping up to date with putting the photos in albums or display folders and captioning them so that they are a readily accessible source of enjoyment, rather than a higgledy-piggledy collection of pictures.

If the new parents don't have a camcorder, consider hiring one for them for a week or two so that you can have moving pictures of your new grandchild. (You could also arrange to do this on special occasions, such as his first Christmas.) Make sure your video systems are compatible: those in Australia, New Zealand and the UK are not usually compatible with those used in North

America and parts of mainland Europe. Find a reliable company that will convert one system to the other for you (look in the Yellow Pages under 'Video Services').

You will discover you rapidly become an expert in postable presents. This is easy with babies, whose clothes and toys tend to be small, light and unbreakable anyway. And if you and your grandchild live in different countries, always ask his parents if there is anything in particular they would like from 'home' before sending presents: even in these days of globalisation, there may be a favourite item from a particular shop that is unavailable on the other side of the world.

CHAPTER TWO

Older Babies
3 to 15 months

The period between 3 and 15 months is one of tremendous change in your grandchild's life. In the space of a year she will develop from a helpless baby into a self-motivated little person. Her progression into an individual with character and looks all her own may appear to come about overnight. So much happens, in fact, that you may feel that it all goes by too fast: you are likely to be surprised by how quickly she walks, plays and generally wants to communicate with you.

Even if you don't live close by, and there are other children clamouring for your time and attention when you visit, make a special effort to notice as much of what she achieves as possible. Take mental pictures of her early steps, sounds and words and enjoy getting to know her. Chat to her whenever you are involved in the everyday activities she experiences, such as nappy changing and feeding, and tell her about yourself, your family and her place in it so that she comes to know your voice.

Basic baby skills

What you can expect your grandchild to do at this stage

This is one of the most exciting and rewarding periods of babyhood, when a child is past being a completely helpless bundle and really begins to communicate and develop as an individual.

You will probably find that your grandchild has learned something new each time you visit. Enjoy everything she does but don't compare her development with that of your own children. It is galling for a parent to be told that other people's children have walked quicker or spoken earlier, because it implies that their child is slow or inferior in some way. And memory is highly selective: we all have a habit of improving on the facts when it comes to our own children.

You may be able to spend time enjoying the baby's new skills without feeling guilty about what else you should be doing, a luxury her parents may not have. Join her as she explores the textures on her activity mat, stacks her bricks and posts her shapes. And share her delight in repetitive games

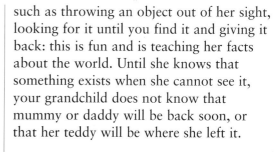

such as throwing an object out of her sight, looking for it until you find it and giving it back: this is fun and is teaching her facts about the world. Until she knows that something exists when she cannot see it, your grandchild does not know that mummy or daddy will be back soon, or that her teddy will be where she left it.

Talking to your grandchild

When you speak to a baby of this age you introduce her to the way in which language and communication work. Don't be self-conscious about it or perturbed that, initially at least, you may not get much response. Almost before you know it, you will be having 'real' conversations.

Before she can sit up, a baby watches your face when you hold her close and if you purse your lips and make a face she will imitate your action. When your grandchild starts 'cooing' to you, follow your instincts and 'coo' back so that she knows that her efforts to communicate have received a response.

Make a time when the house is quiet, so your grandchild has your undivided attention. Talk about anything you like but leave pauses for her to join in, even if it's just to raise her hand or chuckle.

Don't sit your grandchild in front of the TV or a video while you do something else. Although this will hold her interest because of the fast-moving images, she will soon learn that there is no point in trying to communicate with it. Taken to extremes, this will inhibit her ability to focus on one quiet speaker.

If, when you are out for a walk, you point to the birds and tell your grandchild what they are, he will soon point the birds out to you and make what for him is an appropriate sound to identify them.

How your grandchild develops

This chart gives an indication of what your grandchild may be able to do at different ages. But all babies are different. Use this as a broad guide only: some babies will reach these stages sooner, others later.

PHYSICAL	MANIPULATIVE	SOCIAL	LANGUAGE
FOUR MONTHS She can sit without her head wobbling as long as she is supported. Between four and five months, she may roll over from her front on to her back.	She is beginning to develop hand–eye coordination and will examine her own hands, feet and other small objects, as well as her reflection in a mirror. She can reach for objects and may put them in her mouth to 'gum'.	If you are a frequent visitor, she will be able to recognise your voice. She attracts attention by wriggling about and enjoys new faces, toys and places.	She 'talks' to objects and people and can pronounce the sounds 'h', 'b', 'p', 'f' and 'n'. She laughs in response to the sound of your jolly speech or laughter.
NINE MONTHS She rolls, crawls and shuffles around to get to toys she wants or to you. She tries to pull herself up and uses furniture and your legs as props to help in exploring her surroundings.	She enjoys examining objects, and turns them around to look at from all angles. She will start to pick up things using her thumb and forefinger.	She may become 'clingy' and wary of strangers. She shouts to attract attention. She is happy to play by herself for 10–15 minutes. She loves interactive games such as dropping and throwing objects away. She is delighted when you applaud her actions.	She knows your name and can understand, but does not always respond to, 'No' and 'Please give me'. She babbles in a mixture of her own language and bits of ours.
FOURTEEN MONTHS She can sit down from a standing position and totter around quite fast, often falling down and getting up again in quick succession. She is becoming aware of the danger of walking down stairs and falling off things and needs close supervision. She can see and follow fast-moving objects.	She loves pushing items into holes and hiding things from you. She understands the concept of 'hide and seek' games and will concentrate on shape sorters for up to 20 minutes.	She can express feelings of fear, annoyance and jealousy through shouting and crying. She has a favourite comforter. She points a lot to show things to you.	She has a vocabulary of around three words or relevant signs or sounds at 12 months, and more than 20 by 18 months. 'Puss' may refer to all animals. She understands short sentences like 'Please give me the teddy', and uses single word sentences to make her own needs known, such as 'Ball' for 'I want my ball'.

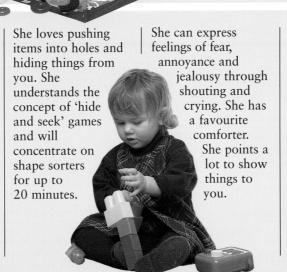

Toys for older babies

Choosing play materials to help your grandchild's development

Today most people are aware that play and learning are synonymous. Manufacturers have also caught on to this idea and almost everything is now described as an 'aid to learning'. Don't let this tempt you to buy more sophisticated or expensive toys than you think suitable. In her first year or so, your grandchild will be delighted and stimulated by the most basic of toys as long as she also has company. This does not mean you should do everything for her but be on hand, taking an interest in her endeavours so that she can play with increased confidence.

TYPE OF TOY	PLAY VALUE

BRICKS

Good-quality coloured wooden bricks, held in a box or trolley, last longer and are sturdier than plastic. Wooden bricks can be used in a multitude of ways and will be enjoyed by your grandchild well into her school years. Under six months, soft cloth blocks are a good choice.

Bricks can be used to identify and name colours. From about a year, stacking aids hand–eye coordination, the ability to concentrate and understanding of spatial concepts. Building and knocking down promotes feelings of control and is fun. The trolley provides storage and is a push-along aid to walking.

ACTIVITY MAT

This can be rolled up and transported to different places to offset baby boredom. It must be washable and made from high-quality materials, with no sharp edges.

The mirror, flaps and shaker toys incorporated encourage the baby to discover and explore using pincer grip and fine hand movements. Different textures encourage tactile development. Bright colour contrasts stimulate visual interest.

SHAPE SORTER

Large wooden or plastic pieces endure even when sucked and are easy for the baby to grasp and manipulate.

Playing with shapes helps the baby to learn about space and the relationships between objects. It is not important at first which shape is forced into which hole; making them disappear and retrieving them holds the interest. Placing the correct shape into each hole comes later, as do identifying and naming shapes.

CONSTRUCTION SETS

Concentrate on one kind and make sure it can be added to with more sophisticated components as the baby gets older. A foundation board allows the baby to fix pieces firmly, avoiding much frustration.

Large pieces encourage the development of the building skills she will acquire throughout her childhood. Additionally, fitting pieces, such as people, cars and trains, aid imaginative play.

SOFT TOYS

Large numbers of soft toys are unnecessary but one or two are invaluable. Make sure soft toys are washable and, if you can, buy two the same to minimise distress if one is lost.

A soft toy is a comfort object first and foremost; as she gets older, some will be useful as props – for guests at a tea party, an audience for a story and patients to be nursed.

The treasure basket

Find a clean basket with no sharp edges that is big enough for the child to dip into without her being able to see everything inside – but not too big. Inside, place a collection of safe objects for your grandchild to touch and explore. Include wooden or plastic spoons; plastic bricks; squares of fabric of different textures – cotton, corduroy, felt; wooden curtain rings; various plastic containers; a set of measuring cups; an unbreakable mirror.

Most inexpensive wooden and plastic household items will be suitable, but always check to ensure that there are no detachable small parts. Adding new items to the basket every so often will provide a child with endless interest and delight.

TYPE OF TOY	PLAY VALUE
BOOKS Choose laminated board, plastic or vinyl which can be easily wiped clean.	It is never too early to sit with a baby and encourage her to turn the pages. Point out shapes and colours and she will do the same. Let her take one or two softer ones into her cot with her at night so that they become 'friends'.
BATH TOYS A set of buckets with holes and strainers make bathtime a pleasure.	Water is a fascinating medium with a texture unlike anything else a child plays with. She can explore filling and emptying, pouring and straining. Demonstrate them to excite her curiosity, then allow her to experiment while you watch.
ACTIVITY CENTRE This can be fixed almost anywhere. Vary its position for maximum interest.	Dials, pull cords and squeezy buttons teach the baby that she can elicit a reaction and a sound. Mirrors (perhaps large eyes on a teddy) encourage the baby to focus and concentrate.
BOUNCING CRADLE TOYS These have taken over from the old-style row of beads or teddies that were fixed across large prams. They clip on to the front of the baby rocker or bouncing cradle and are cheap enough to buy more than one set for variety.	The baby can finger them and move them along, and will soon learn that if she reaches out to hit them she will make them turn over. Later she may start to babble to them.
PAPER AND CRAYONS Choose thick, non-toxic wax crayons and large sheets of paper.	At around 15 months, babies thoroughly enjoy your simple efforts to draw basic shapes they recognise and will begin to place their marks on paper and to start to recognise different colours and textures.

Then and now:

Daycare

As it becomes more common for both parents to work outside the home, and for single parents to combine parenting and a career, your grandchild's early life is likely to include at least one professional carer who is not a member of her immediate family.

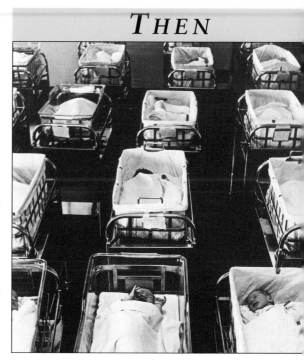

THEN

If you and your partner both had full-time jobs when your children were babies, you were in a minority – most mothers stayed at home with their children. Even 20 years ago, many of those who worked had two choices of carer: a family member or – for those who had the means – someone to live in and look after the children. Professional daycare provision was rare and different in ideology from what we now know that babies need. Babies who had professional daycare led regimented lives with set feeding times, enforced naps, daily 'airings' in all weathers, and even prescribed times for 'potty training' at a very early age.

Working parents today are likely to be able to choose between a number of options: nursery provision, a live-in or daily nanny or au pair, a childminder, a workplace crèche or a family member. And professional childcare is more child centred. A baby may be encouraged to sleep at a given time, say after a meal; she will also be placed in her cot when she shows signs of needing a rest, but kept awake, stimulated and played with if she

shows no desire to sleep. Nor are babies forced into toilet training. Nursery staff generally listen to parents' wishes, in addition to taking cues from the baby.

In the past, babies were often left to amuse themselves for long periods. Now we know that babies need stimulation. Toys and play equipment which help the baby's development are an important part of any nursery, and professional nannies and carers receive instruction on this aspect of care during their training. Nurseries are likely to emulate a home environment with cosy furniture, pictures and colourful mobiles instead of the sterile, hospital-like appearance of yesterday's nurseries.

Some workplaces now provide crèches for the children of employees. These are run along similar lines to nurseries and the parent may be encouraged to pop in and visit for a short while during the day.

Home-based care

Care in a home environment – whether it is your grandchild's home or that of a childminder – has many advantages. A

NOW

Although babies often received loving care in large nurseries, the stimulation of one-to-one contact was missing (far left). Care in the home, whether by a childminder, nanny or au pair, is often more fun for children and more rewarding for their carers (left).

nanny or childminder can have the sort of one-to-one relationship that your grandchild's parents may have with her. And toys and activities are on a smaller, domestic scale than in a nursery or crèche.

Regardless of how close by you live, it is important to accept that the carer is being paid to look after your grandchild and is a professional. While it is acceptable to visit your grandchild occasionally during the day if you have liaised with the carer in advance, do not pop around whenever you feel like it or take your grandchild away from the house on your own. In doing so, you will put the carer in a difficult position, as well as undermining the parents' arrangement.

If you witness things involving your grandchild and her carer of which you do not approve, you must decide whether it is important enough to inform her parents. Although, for example, you may feel that a carer's manner or choice of vocabulary when speaking to your grandchild is unsuitable, this may be something that does not concern the parents. But in the unlikely event of the carer acting negligently and putting your grandchild in danger, obviously you need to inform the parents immediately.

Doing it yourself

Once, the first person a working mother turned to for help with childcare was her own mother, but families are often not sufficiently close geographically for this to be an option today. In cultures in which grandparents automatically assume the day-to-day care of their grandchildren, there is often also an extended family of aunts, uncles and others.

If you are asked to be wholly responsible for your grandchild, weigh up the pros and cons before committing yourself.
• Do you feel physically able to cope?
• Are you ready to give up your time to what most people admit is an exhausting way to spend your days?
• Will you be able to make your ideas on childrearing blend amicably with those of your grandchild's parents?
• Can you discuss what you will be paid for your services objectively?

REASSURANCES FOR YOU

The number of children a childminder can care for at any one time is restricted by law. Childminders' homes are inspected regularly to make sure that they comply with safety standards. Approval from local council or government authorities is usually necessary. Nannies should have references, which your grandchild's parents will have checked.

For successful registration and operation, daycare centres, including those in the workplace, need to satisfy a number of criteria in areas such as staff-to-children ratios and building and safety regulations.

Basic baby care

What you may have forgotten about caring for babies

Fashions in childcare come and go: depending on your age, you may find your grandchild is being changed and fed in much the same way as you looked after your own children's needs, or you may find her care very different. In case it is all new to you or you have forgotten some things in the intervening years, these pointers will help you to look after your grandchild.

Nappy changing

Volunteering to change the baby's nappy may be the best received of all your offers of practical help and it is a good way to get used to handling your grandchild.

Put her on a flat surface that is the right height for your back. Keep your eyes and one hand on her all the time (you don't want her to perfect her ability to roll over when you are changing her). If you use a barrier cream on her bottom, be careful not to get it on the tapes of a disposable – they won't stick if you do. Many professionals advise against using baby powder, as the fine particles may exacerbate breathing problems in some babies.

Baby foods

Most parents start to think about introducing solid food into their baby's diet when she is about three months old. Your own children may still have been totally milk-fed at this stage. A baby's digestive system is better equipped to deal with milk than anything else, so if you find the parents need reassurance in deciding to delay solids, back them up. There is no hard evidence to suggest that introducing solid foods makes a baby sleep through the night, and certainly babies need milk above all else until they are at least six months old.

If your grandchild is bottle-fed, you can enjoy feeding her to give her parents a rest. Seat yourself comfortably and give her your undivided attention, communicating by using lots of eye contact. Bottle-feeding can be a very cosy and satisfying time for you and the baby. Stories abound of putting rusks – or a little extra formula – into babies' bottles as a way to fill them up so that they sleep through the night. Don't do this. Nor is it safe to reheat a bottle in the microwave: this causes hot spots in the milk which can scald a baby's mouth.

Once weaning has begun in earnest you can give lots of help in what can often be a frustrating business. If you are able to take a turn at feeding the baby it will give her

Nappy changing is not a chore to be rushed through. You can make it into a pleasurable experience for both of you. Spend this time chatting to your grandchild, making eye contact with her. Most babies like being without a nappy for a while, simply kicking their legs and enjoying the freedom of movement.

WHICH NAPPY?

• **Disposables** are convenient, and since you buy them as needed, they do not involve a large initial financial outlay, although they can prove costly in the long run. But they do have ecological drawbacks: it takes years for a disposable nappy to begin breaking down in a landfill site, and a lot of trees are felled to provide the wood pulp needed to manufacture the nappies in the first place.

• **Fitted reusables** are made from cloth, but shaped like disposables, and fasten with Velcro at the sides. They are used in conjunction with liners and, unlike true terries, there is no folding or pinning involved. They are expensive but long-lived and can be passed down the family.

• **Terry nappies** have to be washed and dried and are expensive to buy initially, but even taking these factors into account they are more ecologically friendly and economical than either of the other options in the long run.

The easiest fold is probably the kite: place the clean nappy on a flat surface in a diamond shape with points at north, south, east and west. Bring west and east into the centre so that lines south-west and south-east sit side by side. Bring the north point down to the middle of the kite, then fold up the double layer at south until the nappy is the right size for the baby. You could offer to sit and fold several of these so that there is always one to hand.

In addition to contributing to the initial cost of the nappies you may wish to help, either by laundering some of them yourself to save the parents work, or by paying for a nappy laundering service to reduce the strain.

parents a chance to see that there is nothing personal in her habit of turning her head aside when the spoon is heading her way or in throwing the food on the floor.

If her parents give you jars of baby food to feed your grandchild when you are looking after her, follow the instructions printed on the side; but if they don't object, purée (when she is very young) or mash (as she gets older) some vegetables or fruit you are going to eat with your own meal. As long as you leave out salt and sugar and use fresh, quality ingredients you will be doing what is best for your grandchild. Once she reaches 9 or 10 months of age, and assuming her parents are not vegetarians, add some finely chopped meat or fish to the vegetables and include some 'finger' foods that she can pick up and eat herself. The advertising that surrounds prepared baby foods has taken away confidence in our ability to make fresh,

healthy food for babies ourselves. If her parents tend to rely on prepared foods, you may be able to persuade them that in this case the old ways are the best.

Under six months
The most suitable foods for babies under six months are: baby rice (specially manufactured and gluten free) mixed with cooled, boiled water, formula or expressed breast milk; puréed or mashed fruit; and puréed or mashed vegetables.

Until she is at least six months old (many doctors recommend at least a year), do not give your grandchild eggs; wheat products, such as bread and cereals; cheese, yoghurt, fromage frais, cow's milk; citrus fruit; onions, peppers, chillis; high-fat and fried foods.

Your adopted or fostered grandchild
Welcoming a child who is not a blood relative into your family

Fostering and adoption do not happen overnight. If you become a grandparent in this way, you will have a period – rather like a pregnancy – when arrangements are being finalised, during which you can become accustomed to the idea of the new addition to the family.

The legal and social circumstances surrounding fostering and adoption have changed considerably in recent years, so your child and his or her partner will usually be aware of the baby's circumstances and birth history. Social workers encourage adoptive parents to make a diary, with photographs where possible, to explain the child's origins to her as soon as she is old enough. Contact with her natural parents will also usually be encouraged. All this differs completely from the secrecy that used to surround adoption. However uncomfortable you may feel, this has been shown to be the best thing for adopted children in the long run.

A wholehearted welcome

If your grandchild has not yet been adopted, you may be involved in what can seem a long and tense build-up to the final legal arrangements. Be on hand, if you can, to support the waiting parents and empathise with what they are going through.

When your grandchild arrives, you will start getting to know her in some ways that are similar to when you meet your 'natural' grandchildren for the first time and in others very different. First of all, you must accept wholeheartedly that this baby is a wanted and loved member of your family, just as if the new parents had conceived her. On the one hand this is easy because she is an innocent child; on the other, it is difficult since she comes with a background and family that are not your own. Accepting her origins without judgment or fear is the key to being able to love her without reservation.

In the days and weeks after her arrival there will be great excitement on the part of the parents and any siblings. Enjoy everyone's happiness and take your time to become familiar with the new child. It may be very apparent that the baby bears no resemblance to your family, as other new arrivals have, but don't let this concern you. For inexplicable reasons, adopted children often develop the looks of their adoptive family.

If your new grandchild is being fostered rather than adopted, there is no need to feel insecure about her place in your family. Long-term fostering usually happens because of the natural parents' refusal or

Acknowledge racial characteristics which differ from your own as you would the fact that your grandchild's hair is red and yours blonde. Such traits will make no difference to her parents and other members of the immediate family.

grandchildren that they hold a superior position in your affections: you will hinder their acceptance of their new sibling.

Practical arrangements

Most people treat the arrival of an adopted grandchild as they would a birth. Baby gifts, presents for the new parents and a celebration party all contribute to the integration of this much-wanted child into your family.

Many couples adopt because they are unable to have children of their own. The arrival of an adopted baby may signal the end of a period of unhappiness and is an occasion for celebration.

unavailability to agree to adoption. Social workers tell foster parents if the child is likely to return to her natural parents, so don't worry that she will be taken away; simply start loving and caring for her.

You must be scrupulously fair in your dealings with all your grandchildren. Work on any negative feelings about the new baby before they start to cause problems. If you are worried, consult an outsider rather than the parents. Your family doctor will listen to your concerns and can put you in touch with a counsellor if you wish.

It may help you to look outside yourself and see how your other grandchildren, if you have them, are coping. However excited they seem at the prospect of such a romantic addition to the family, when the reality hits home they may experience a mixture of emotions which the parents are too busy to appreciate fully. Younger children may see the newcomer as a usurper to their parents' love in much the same way as a newborn child would be, only more so, because the parents made a more active choice over this arrival. Give extra time and attention to your existing grandchildren, while leaving space to get to know the new child. Never imply to other

CASE STUDY

My daughter Clare is an only child and once she reached her 30s I did drop hints about being a granny. But she didn't want to settle down. I was astounded when she came back from a trip abroad with a photo of a baby she was going to adopt. She had visited a friend who was a doctor at an orphanage, seen this boy and knew instantly that he had to be hers.

I thought it was a ludicrous idea and assumed she'd come to her senses. We knew nothing about this child; the country was unstable and his parents were missing or dead. And my daughter would be a single mother. When I realised Clare meant to go through with it, I was terrified for her.

When Clare brought Mikael home, I knew I should be pleased, but I couldn't accept that she was bringing a stranger into our family. He was about two but looked younger; he was small and thin but had the eyes of an old man. His stare made me uneasy, but I could see that he needed looking after and began to understand part of what had moved Clare so much.

That was two years ago. Mikael didn't say a word for six months, but gradually started to talk and to fill out and grow. He's a nice boy, although I still find it hard to accept that this is my grandchild. But I know my daughter is happy, and I'm very proud of what she has done.

Naming ceremonies

Christenings and other special ways to welcome a child to the world

A christening or other naming ceremony is an important rite for many families. But such celebrations can be the cause of disagreements in some families.

Practical arrangements

If you have a family heirloom christening robe you would like your grandchild to wear, feel free to show it to the parents but do not put pressure on them to accept it. The other grandparents may also have a gown they would like worn and, despite the importance this issue often assumes, the gown your grandchild wears at her christening will be quickly forgotten as she reaches other milestones in her life.

If there is no family gown, you might contribute to the event by making one or having one made. Many families embroider the name of each child who wears the gown into the hem to make it a unique heirloom. Alternative keepsakes are a shawl, a tapestry block or sampler embroidered with your grandchild's name and date of birth, or a porcelain plate including these details.

It is up to the parents whom they choose as godparents, who is invited to the event and to any party. But you could offer to make or buy a christening cake or, if your house is larger than theirs, offer it as the venue. Or, simply ask the parents what you can do to help them enjoy the event.

Many parents, especially with a first baby, feel they should organise everything to do with this first milestone in their child's life themselves. If you find that you have to take a back seat, look for something imaginative to satisfy your need to be a part of the proceedings without stepping on anyone's toes. Taking informal photographs during the day and making albums for you, the parents and other grandparents to keep will be greatly appreciated. You could also make a video of the event although, since this is more

A Christian priest sprinkles the baby's forehead with water, symbolising Christ's baptism in the River Jordan. The ceremony allows other members of the parents' church to welcome the newborn into their community.

The imposing setting of a Greek Orthodox christening emphasises that this is an important rite of passage for both baby and parents.

DIFFERENT CUSTOMS

In many cultures the ceremony to mark a child's entrance into the world takes place very shortly after birth.

Circumcision
In Jewish families this takes place on or before a boy's eighth day. The operation is conducted by a mohel in the presence of the parents, family and a rabbi. Prayers are said by the rabbi and the child is given a Hebrew name in addition to the name he will be known by. The ceremony is usually followed by a family party. Nowadays both boys and girls are named and blessed in the synagogue.

Humanist ceremony
A naming ceremony without religious content can be arranged through humanist societies. Two or more adults promise to act as guardians to the child. Appropriate poetry may be read, either by a representative from a humanist society or by the parents, to welcome the child into the world. The ceremony is often concluded with planting a tree for the child in the family garden.

Hindu ceremonies
At birth a sacred formula is whispered into the child's ear and she is given gold dipped in honey to suck. The naming ceremony takes place on the 12th day. The child's name is not disclosed in advance in case evil spirits carry her away before she has received the ritual protection, signified by the tying on of scarlet threads. A piece of gold is given for luck.

Sikh ceremonies
Soon after birth the baby is named in the presence of the Adi Granth (sacred book). The book is opened at random and the first letter on the left-hand page is taken as the child's initial. Water and sugar are placed on the child's lips. Prayers are offered to commit her to God's grace and express the hope that she will live as a true Sikh. The ceremony ends with a special meal prepared by the community.

Islam
New life is seen as a gift from God, in recognition of which the baby's family gives food, money and clothes to the poor. Allah's name and the *adham* (prayer) are whispered into the ear of the newborn and on the seventh day she is named and her head is shaved to remove the uncleanliness of the birth and encourage the hair to grow thicker. A feast, to which relatives and friends are invited, is held at the naming ceremony.

intrusive than still photograhy, you should check that the parents want you to do this.

Christenings often bring to the fore any debate concerning family names. You may not have been aware of the parents' wish to use or exclude traditional family names. Remember that there are two families and that passing on everyone's 'traditional' name might not be an option. You may, of course, find the choice of name odd, or even hilarious. Vogues for names come and go, so it is unlikely that parents will pick names that would have been your choice. But your grandchild's personality is much more important than what she is called.

Silver is a traditional material for christening gifts, with photograph frames and tooth fairy containers popular. But china mugs and money boxes are also perennial presents.

Non-religious parents
If you have strong religious beliefs and the parents do not, you may find it hard to accept that your grandchild will not be christened. You may find it helps to talk to your priest or pastor about your feelings: he may be able to offer you some consolation. It may help to bear in mind that your grandchild will be able to choose for herself, when she is old enough, whether or not she wishes to be baptised.

Toddlers
15 months to 3 years

It is easy to forget how quickly children grow. In what seems no time at all, your 'baby' grandchild has learned to walk and begun to talk to you in recognisable words or signs. He has become a (sometimes wilful) little person with a mind of his own. Life for a toddler is one big adventure, which he will be delighted to share.

You may be surprised at the speed with which your grandchild masters new skills at this stage. In the toddler years he will go from tottering on unsure feet to climbing stairs with confidence; from calling every man he sees 'Dada' to being able to name clearly most of his friends and family. He will advance from throwing – in frustration – a brick that won't fit a shape sorter to sitting and completing a jigsaw puzzle. His artistic efforts will progress from crayon scribbles to pictures with named elements such as the sun and Mummy.

Toddlers love life and if you can provide a few props and an interested presence, these years will be full of fun for you both.

What toddlers like doing

Games, toys and activities to satisfy the most energetic grandchild

Whether you see your grandchild regularly or only occasionally, you want the time you spend with him to be enjoyable and special. Obviously, what you do together depends to some extent on your circumstances and how active you are. Fortunately young children enjoy simple indoor and outdoor activities, so entertaining them does not need to be costly or sophisticated. And because children learn by imitating the actions and behaviour of other people, as well as through play and exploring the world around them, the time you spend doing things with your grandchild can also help his physical, mental and social skills.

Make sure that the activities you plan are suitable for your grandchild's age and stage of development (see pp. 58–59). Allow for the fact that toddlers seem to have boundless energy and can be demanding and tiring. Bear in mind, too, that although they may have a short attention span when

doing some things and grow bored easily, they also have an amazing capacity for repetitive action with other games. Plan a variety of things to do which will suit both your paces, and include active and passive pastimes during the day.

Outdoors

One of the simplest and most enjoyable outdoor activities you can share with your grandchild is to go for a walk. Once he has found his feet, he may not want to sit in his buggy or stroller, but take it with you just in case (you may have to carry him if you don't). And, depending on where you are going, consider using a harness and reins for road safety. If you need to be somewhere by a certain time, allow for the fact that toddlers love to dawdle when walking.

Point out items of interest such as a bird, cat or dog, or goods in shop windows. Look out, too, for things which you can take home and use later, such as an interestingly shaped stone, pebble or shell, feathers, leaves or pine cones.

If your grandchild is used to travelling by car, he will find it a treat to go for a ride on a bus or train. And take him to a 'child friendly' restaurant and let him choose his own drink or something to eat.

Toddlers also love gardening. Donate some ground for him to dig with his own miniature tools and perhaps sow with seeds, or ask him to help you rake up leaves. You could fix him a swing, make a little house to play in, or provide a sandpit or paddling pool (for safety, see pp. 66–69).

Weather wise

Toddlers usually need to work off some energy outdoors, so unless the weather is really bad, don't let it prevent you from donning suitable clothes and going out,

Farms are fun, especially when there are baby animals to see and hold. But toddlers find many activities exciting: going to the park to feed the ducks, running around or playing on the slide or swings; a trip to the beach; or even a visit to the shops to pick up a newspaper or some groceries.

This is the stage at which your grandchild may have unbridled energy and a boundless capacity for 'fun'. If you can find an outdoor activity you all enjoy, you will have hours of pleasure together.

even if only for a short time. On rainy days, children love wearing wellingtons and splashing through puddles. Point out the different-shaped clouds or reflections in puddles, and look out for a rainbow. In the snow, take your grandchild for a ride on a sled, build a snowman together, look for icicles, or let him help you to clear a path.

Indoors
Playing with household items will give your grandchild hours of fun, and you can take part in many activities together around the home. Talk to him and involve him in what you are doing. If he is old enough to understand, make up simple stories with him as the hero or tell stories about your childhood. He will also love to hear you sing funny ditties or nonsense rhymes.

• Helping you
From the age of about 18 months, your grandchild will love to copy what you are doing. 'Helping' around the house – dusting, tidying up, drying dishes – or cleaning the

car will be fun for him, and you can also help him learn. When dusting, identify the types of furniture; when drying up tell him the names and colours of the pieces of crockery, say whether a plate is large or small, count the number of spoons.

• Water play
Let your grandchild help you wash small pieces of crockery or cutlery, or his own tea set. Be careful not to give him sharp knives or anything precious that he might break. Give him a bowl of water with some plastic containers such as washing-up liquid bottles, food containers or cups to play with.

Add some glycerine to detergent and water to make soap bubbles to blow. Make a simple blower by twisting the end of a thin piece of wire or a pipe cleaner into a ring.

• Make believe
If you provide a few basic props such as cardboard boxes, curtains, blankets and cushions, and a corner of your room, your grandchild will be able to use his own imagination to entertain himself – and you. He will also enjoy activities such as inviting you to tea, 'cooking' using a saucepan and wooden spoons, or playing 'shop' with a few tins, empty packets and plastic bottles.

• Creative play
Dried pasta can be threaded and used as jewellery; pieces of newspaper or wallpaper can be used for drawing or finger painting; pictures can be cut out of magazines with blunt scissors; a saucepan or box can be beaten with a spoon to make a drum, and containers with tight-fitting tops can be filled with dried peas or lentils for shaking.

• Other activities
Toddlers carry their enthusiasm for some activities through to their preschool years and beyond. Dressing up, baking and all sorts of drawing and writing are obvious examples of skills which, once learned, are perfected over the years (see pp. 76–79).

What toddlers like doing

Books for toddlers

It is never too early to encourage a child's interest in reading. Most children love looking at books from an early age. If your grandchild is coming to visit, remind his parents to bring some of his favourite books. Make a point of sitting down with him at least once a day and looking at books, if only for a few minutes. Point out objects or read him a story. You may also like to keep a small selection of books in your house especially for your grandchild to look at.

Books are also ideal presents. Suitable books for toddlers include ones which have moving parts or make a noise; ones with lots of pictures to encourage chatting; and perennial favourites such as simple fairytales and nursery rhymes which you can teach your grandchild to sing.

Choosing toys

Your grandchild learns many skills through playing, so if you like buying him toys, it makes sense to give him ones that will help his developing skills. Playing with different types of toys can help him distinguish between shapes, sizes, colours and weight; stimulate his imagination and creativity; and help to develop spatial awareness, manual dexterity and other skills.

To be beneficial, a toy needs to be appropriate for your grandchild's age, personality and stage of development. Avoid buying expensive porcelain dolls or complicated train sets, for example, until your grandchild is old enough to appreciate them. Choose toys that have plenty of play potential, lots of features, bright colours and are fun. And, of course, don't assume that only girls enjoy playing with tea sets and pushing dolls and toys around in buggies, or that only boys like construction sets.

Toy safety

Some children stop putting everything into their mouths at about a year, but many still mouth and suck a lot of toys well past this age. For this reason, safety measures when buying toys are vital.

A walk along the seashore is an opportunity for splashing and water play, as well as for hunting for shells and seaweed. It is never too soon to teach a toddler the names of different shells, or to listen to the calls of some of the seabirds. He won't remember them all but you are sowing the seeds of what may develop into a lifelong interest in the natural world around him.

Check with parents before buying your grandchild a large piece of outdoor play equipment, since many gardens simply are not big enough. Make the most of what is on offer in local parks and playgrounds.

• Buy toys from reputable manufacturers or those which carry an appropriate safety standards symbol. Take extra care if buying second-hand (especially from garage sales), or if shopping at markets, since goods sold here may not conform to safety standards.
• Take safety messages such as 'Not suitable for children under three years' seriously. Children under three have generally not developed a 'gagging' reflex, so they cannot cough up small bits that they swallow or inhale.
• Make sure that the toy has no sharp edges or detachable small parts. Any piece that can be removed during normal play and that fits into a 35mm film canister is small enough to choke a young child.

Sharp edges on plastic toys can scratch and detachable pieces are all too easy for a child to swallow. Both are common. Many toys – such as dolls – are not dangerous in themselves, but their accessories, such as shoes, jewellery and combs, can be.

TEMPER TANTRUMS

The majority of children of between one and four years old have occasional tantrums; 20 per cent of two year olds have one or more every day. Often these short outbursts are quickly over, but in some children they develop into full-blown episodes.

At their most extreme, children lie on the ground, scream and kick, or throw things. If your grandchild has tantrums when he is with his parents, do not undermine their authority by interfering or criticising. If he has them with his parents, he is likely to have them with you, although less frequently.

When he has a tantrum with you, try to work out why and as far as possible avoid these trigger situations. Tantrums are more common when a child is tired, hungry or overexcited; the most usual causes are not being allowed to do something he wants to do, being made to do something he doesn't want to, or simply frustration at his limited capabilities.

How you deal with a tantrum depends on the age and temperament of your grandchild. If his parents have a method that works, follow this. Whatever you do, stay calm and avoid bribes, smacking or threats.

Diversion tactics may prevent a threatened tantrum, or halt one. Choices ('Do you want to go to the park or do some painting?') are better than open-ended questions ('What shall we do now?'). If this does not work, try ignoring the child, put him in a different room until the tantrum is over, or leave the room so that he does not have an audience.

If you are out, decide whether to stay put until the tantrum blows over or remove him from the scene. If you can't pick him up and take him to the car, for example, hug him, which works well with some children.

Once the tantrum is over, tell him that you still love him even if you do not approve of his behaviour, then let the matter rest.

What toddlers like doing

How your grandchild develops

You will no doubt take pride in watching your grandchild acquire certain skills, but try not to compare his development with that of other children. All children develop at their own rate, and there is a wide range of average. The majority, however, will have acquired certain skills by the time they reach a certain age. Here is a guide to the stages of a child's development at particular ages, with suggestions of suitable toys to buy and activities to do. Remember, most toys and activities will cover more than one age range.

PHYSICAL

15–18 MONTHS
Walks around furniture or alone with hesitation
Explores and is 'into everything'
Can throw a ball and push a large toy
May place one brick on top of another
Starts to climb on chairs and scramble up stairs
Drinks from cup without spilling and takes spoon to mouth to feed himself

MENTAL AND SOCIAL

Jabbers and says a few words
May start temper tantrums
Carries objects around
Knows some body parts such as nose or eyes
Understands simple requests such as 'Please shut the door'
Puts simple shapes into posting box or puzzles

18 MONTHS–2 YEARS
Walks steadily
May have started running
Climbs on chairs
Squats to pick up a toy without falling over
Walks up stairs with helping hand

Starts to join words
Looks at books and points
Copies adult activities
Favourite word is 'no'
Tries to join in nursery rhymes
Scribbles vigorously
Can be quite aggressive and likes his own way
Unscrews lids and turns door handles
Takes off shoes and socks

2–3 YEARS
Runs everywhere
Kicks ball firmly
Jumps
Climbs easy nursery apparatus

Joins in nursery rhymes
Vocabulary expands; he can make sentences
Copies circles and lines
Knows some colours
Can count to five
Usually dry during day
Helps with dressing himself

3 YEARS
Climbs with increasing agility
Rides tricycle using pedals and steers round corners
Hops and stands on tiptoe
Kicks ball forcibly
Dances
Catches ball with two hands

Many who, what, why questions, but grammar may be incorrect
Builds tower of nine bricks
Knows several nursery rhymes
Counts up to ten
Cuts with blunt scissors
Draws person with head
Gives name, age and sex
Eats with fork and spoon
May have imaginary playmate

These are the ages when the world around them becomes a fascinating place for children. A walk often beomes a nature trail as you pick up leaves, examine plants and see how many birds you can spot.

SUITABLE TOYS INCLUDE

Baby books; stacking toys; simple insert toys such as posting boxes to aid manipulation; toys that make noises such as drums; wooden building bricks; push-and-pull toys to aid balance; chatter telephones to help speech; colouring materials; large soft balls; handbag or box full of safe interesting objects to rummage through.

Tea sets for pretend play; interlocking blocks and bricks for building; more advanced picture books with simple stories; miniature household objects such as brush and dustpan; musical toys with nursery rhymes; crayons and paper; play dough or modelling clay; simple dolls; simple puzzles; balls; wheeled toys; stacking toys.

Finger paints; play house; push-and-ride toys; first jigsaws and large puzzles; simple climbing toys; construction toys; sandpit; bucket and spade; soft dolls and teddies.

Dressing-up clothes; blunt scissors and magazines for cutting up; simple 'snap' cards; colouring books; toy tools, tricycle or pedal car; picture books; glove puppets; toy farms; powder paints and chunky paint brushes; chunky chalks and chalkboard; chef set; fix-it kit; doctor's set; easy musical instruments; shopping basket; accessories such as handbags and artificial flowers (with no detachable small parts).

ACTIVITIES CAN INCLUDE

Throwing a soft ball for him to pick up; simple movement games such as 'Ring-a-Rosy'; crawl and chase; simple hide and seek; holding his arms and dancing to music; sandpit; water play; building towers and knocking them down; looking at books; drawing with crayons; banging saucepans or boxes with a wooden spoon.

Kicking or rolling balls; simple chasing; household 'cleaning' such as sweeping and dusting; simple puzzles; make-believe play such as making tea with miniature tea sets; talking on a pretend phone; singing nursery rhymes; reading simple stories to him; songs with simple actions; splashing through puddles; feeding the ducks.

Musical games; going to park to play on under-fives' equipment; or to beach with bucket and spade; filling and pulling a small cart or trailer; simple ball games; doing puzzles; pretend play; dressing up; painting; telling stories; printing with potato pieces; hiding a few toys or edible treats for him to track down.

Helping with baking; gardening; dressing up; going for rides on tricycle; playing simple card or board games; cutting out pictures; making dough models; playing ball; colouring pictures; pasta or paper shapes to glue on; vegetables cut up for block painting; pretend play; trips to the library; zoo or nature activities.

Your special-needs grandchild

When extra love, caring and support are required

If your grandchild has special needs – a term that covers minor physical defects, learning problems, allergic reactions, chronic illness or permanent disability – your role is to give extra love and support to your family and to the growing child.

In the case of severe disability, you may need to call upon all your inner resources to be able to support your grandchild's parents and siblings. If the disability is not life-threatening but something to be accepted, you must be positive in your comments and attitude in order to give your best to the child.

Find out as much as you can about the disability so that you can assess how best to help your grandchild and his family. His parents may be wrapped up in the medical aspects of his condition, initially at least. Get in touch with an appropriate support group or a sympathetic doctor with a view to contacting the parents and families of other children who share your grandchild's special needs. Today we tend to expect that all children will be born 'perfect' and it is hard to accept that this is not the case. It may help to remember that one in five children has special needs at some point in childhood.

When you are first told of your grandchild's condition you may feel frightened for his future. This is natural, but all you really need to bear in mind as he reaches the age at which other children are walking and talking is that normal development may be slower, and the milestones you remember in your own children's childhood could happen later. This does not mean that you should not have high hopes for him, however: the key lies in maintaining a positive outlook.

Other people's reactions

You may find it difficult to cope with some people's reactions to your grandchild. While it is charitable to be tolerant of others' ignorance, don't waste energy educating casual acquaintances unless you feel it is a point of principle that they should not be allowed to offer condolences or make crass, ill-informed comments. In such situations you are likely to make new friends and find support from surprising sources. The important thing is not to let the strength that may be needed within the family be sapped by people outside it.

Your role in the family

Assess whether your grandchild's parents need extra practical support – around the house, for example – or someone to listen to their concerns and fears, or whether you can be of more use making sure any financial help or other benefits to which the family is entitled are forthcoming.

Many toys need little or only slight adaptation to suit children with developmental delay. The families of children with the same condition as your grandchild may be able to tell you what they found useful. Check, too, whether there are any toy libraries in your area; these are often a good source of specialist toys.

The temptation to step in and 'help' a child with special needs can be overwhelming, but like all toddlers your grandchild wants and needs to learn to do things for himself. Give him the opportunity to be as independent as possible from toddlerhood onward.

It is important to remember that a special-needs child is only one member of the family. Don't overlook the needs of the other children: they may be overwhelmed by their sibling's demands. Perhaps you can give them the extra time and attention that their parents cannot provide. If, however, the special-needs child is their first-born, his parents may opt for counselling if they wish to have a second child. When a sibling arrives, your role will be the same as that of any grandparent – to let the first-born know he is special to you.

Even when they have accepted that life is different from what they expected and adjusted and organised things accordingly, the parents of children with special needs often cannot find time for themselves. When you feel confident that you can care for your grandchild, offer the parents a short break. Undoubtedly they will need some persuading in the circumstances, but you will be contributing to their inner resources considerably if you can manage to release them from the burden of care for a time.

Above all, your grandchild needs to be treated as any other child – loved, kissed, hugged, played with and (perhaps most difficult) taught reasonable limits.

THE DEATH OF A CHILD

A child's death is devastating. Parents, grandparents, siblings, relatives, friends, the doctors and nurses who cared for him – everyone who knows you and your grandchild will be affected by what is often seen as an unnatural course of events. However much we grieve when elderly people die, we also know, and ultimately accept, that this is a part of the life cycle; but when a child dies there is an unbearable sense of waste and injustice.

If your grandchild has severe disabilities, his parents may have been warned – and told you – that he may not live long, but this will not ease your grief and loss when the time comes. Do not try to offer consolation to your grandchild's parents along the lines that their child was suffering and could not have led the life of other children, unless that is clearly what they believe. And do not feel obliged to be comforted by this knowledge yourself. You have the right to grieve over the loss of a child, whatever his state of health: your grandchild deserves this from you.

Research suggests that families who are close and loving recover from this kind of loss more quickly than others; this is obviously a time for binding together and sharing the pain. However outraged you feel at what has happened, don't let your anger dominate your contact with the parents. Be led by their feelings and save your own extremes of grief for a close friend or appropriate support group. If you are the parents' sole emotional support, you may feel the need to contact a grief counsellor as an outlet for some of your own sorrow.

You will also need to keep a watchful eye on any siblings, who may find the whole business frightening and bewildering. Children feel grief deeply but express it differently from adults, perhaps through behavioural difficulties, regression to baby habits or fears concerning their own mortality. Because of the powerful feelings they are witnessing, it may also seem to them that everyone loved the dead child more than they love the children who are living. Their parents may be too distressed to notice their other children's difficulties fully; it may be left to you to provide the reassurance that is needed.

What toddlers wear

Choosing clothes for your toddler grandchild

Like many grandparents, you may enjoy buying clothes for your grandchild, especially if your children were girls and your grandchild is a boy, or vice versa.

Perhaps money and the range of clothes available were more limited when your children were young. Today you are more likely to be overwhelmed by choice and find it difficult to select something appropriate, particularly if you do not live close and have only a vague idea of what he usually wears or how extensive his wardrobe is. Picking the right size may also be difficult, as some clothes manufacturers use the child's height as a measurement, and others use the age. Always check with your grandchild's parents what he measures now and what kind of clothes he needs before you buy.

Practical clothing

Most of the time your grandchild probably wears practical clothes such as sweaters, T-shirts, dungarees or trousers, which can cope with the rough and tumble of an active child's life and be laundered easily. Much as you may long to dress your granddaughter in frilly dresses or your grandson in trousers, tie and waistcoat, such clothes are likely to be appreciated for special occasions only: most parents consider the hand washing, careful ironing or dry cleaning they need take too much time for everyday wear. Such clothes are usually also expensive. If you are intent on buying 'special' clothes, it is worth remembering that smart summer clothes often wash and dry more easily than those for winter.

Hats and caps are useful both summer and winter, and fashionable for both boys and girls these days. Your grandchild may be delighted to receive a trendy baseball cap (which he can wear back to front).

If you enjoy knitting, either by hand or machine, you may find that providing your grandchildren with sweaters is much appreciated, especially if you can depict animals or favourite characters on them. (Bur remember that some characters become outmoded even faster than your grandchild grows.) Unless you are knitting for a special occasion, use machine-washable wool – there is plenty of choice of colour and texture.

Even at an early age, many children have a definite dress sense, or strong likes and dislikes, and may refuse to wear certain clothes. So don't be hurt if your grandchild sometimes declines to wear what you have bought or made for her. If you don't make a fuss, the chances are that the next time you see her, she will be sporting in delight what she once wholeheartedly rejected.

Even the most sociable toddlers are rarely invited to enough parties to make a wardrobe full of special party clothes worthwhile. Check what your granddaughter has before buying another pretty dress.

Shoes

It is vital for young feet to have shoes that fit well, so it is best not to buy these unless your grandchild is with you for a fitting. Children grow out of shoes quickly but even shoes in good condition should not be passed on because each child moulds the shoes to suit his feet. Although you may prefer your grandchild to have leather shoes, many children today wear sneakers or trainers which are cheaper and perfectly adequate for growing feet.

If his parents are willing, you may like to take your grandchild shopping for shoes. Choose a time when the shops are not busy. Be guided by his parents' wishes: if they have requested trainers, don't be seduced by party shoes. If you can't find what you want at the first shop, try another but if you are still unsuccessful check your grandchild's reaction. Having been promised shoes some children are reluctant to go home without them; others are easily bored by shopping and resent going from shop to shop, and repeatedly trying on different items.

TIPS ON BUYING CLOTHES

If you find the choice in children's clothes overwhelming, these guidelines may help.

• Consider safety and practicality. Avoid clothes with drawstring hoods which could strangle a child. Try to buy clothes with a flameproof or fire-resistant label. If he is not potty-trained, check ease of opening. If he is, remember that elastic waistbands are easier to manage than zips, buttons and poppers.

• Don't buy something that just fits, even if it is a bargain, as children grow very quickly. Buy casual clothes such as T-shirts and sweaters in slightly larger sizes so that your grandchild gets more wear from them.

• If you have promised to buy an outfit for a special occasion, take extra care that you have the right size to avoid disappointment.

• If the parents are on a tight budget, buy clothes that can double up, such as colourful cotton vests that can also be worn as T-shirts.

• As a treat, buy your grandchild 'fashion' clothing such as items depicting film characters, but make sure they are the right size for immediate use and be prepared for them to be discarded early. Clothes featuring characters from a favourite book are also popular.

• Once they are potty-trained, most children consider gifts of underwear a sign that they are 'grown up'.

• Colours that you may consider unsuitable for a child – such as black – may be popular with (and suit) your grandchild.

• It is easier for parents to change clothes that do not fit if you buy them from nationwide stores.

• Buy basic clothes such as nightwear, socks, sweaters and T-shirts during the sales even if they are a size too big for your grandchild – you can easily keep them until he is older.

• As a general rule, buy clothes that are tough, practical and easily laundered.

Then and now:

Potty training

Dispensing with piles of nappies to be washed and dried was once a priority, and young children were encouraged to use a potty from the time they could sit upright. Today, attitudes are more relaxed.

THEN

Potty training often became something of a battle of wills as children were encouraged to sit there until they 'performed' (above); today many children treat the potty as another toy, to be carried from room to room for use when they remember or feel the need (above right).

When your children were growing up, getting them potty trained as early as possible may have been part of the routine. Before a child was a year old, parents would often sit him on a potty regularly. Even just a few years ago, children were expected to be potty trained by the age of 18 months to two years.

Today, however, it is accepted that 'catching' a bowel motion or urine by putting a child on the potty from an early age was not toilet training but simply observation on the part of the parent. For the child himself it was an involuntary reflex action, and often when he grew older he refused to 'perform' to order, which resulted in tension or frustration between parents and child.

Even if you feel that your grandchild has reached the stage when he should be dry – during the day at least – don't comment on it or compare him with other children. If you are involved in potty training, go along with what his parents have said or want to do. It is important that all his carers do the same thing, so that he does not get confused with different messages. Similarly, you must know the words he uses when he wants to use the potty.

Tips for successful potty training

Keeping a relaxed attitude is essential if you are involved in potty training your grandchild. If you are upset by a puddle on your new carpet or upholstery, don't show it. Getting cross may frighten him or make him more nervous about potty training – and maintaining a good relationship with your grandchild is more important. Clean up in a matter-of-fact way, and suggest that next time he should tell you if he wants to use the potty.

If your grandchild is coming to stay, remind his parents to bring his potty, or take him shopping to choose one for use

NOW

especially in your house. Buy one with a rigid base to stop it from toppling, and for boys make sure it has a splash guard. When your grandchild is not using it, keep the potty within easy reach in a warm room. If possible, place it on a firm washable floor surface or use some waterproof material to cover the carpet. If your grandchild moves it, make sure you always know where he has left it: there are few things more frustrating than not being able to find the potty when he has remembered he needs to use it.

Encourage your grandchild to sit on the potty after every meal and at various times of the day for a short period, but don't make a fuss if he doesn't want to. Praise him when he uses the potty successfully.

Trainer pants are easier for a child to pull up and down and are more 'grown up' than nappies – or consider trainer nappies which can be pulled up and down

like pants. As your grandchild starts to get trained you may wish to buy special knickers or underpants as a present.

All children eventually gain control over their bladder and bowels, and your grandchild is unlikely to need nappies when he goes to preschool. Indeed, some nurseries and preschool groups will not accept children until they are potty trained.

POINTS TO REMEMBER

• To become potty trained a child must be able to make the connection between the physical signs from his bladder or bowels and the passing of urine or faeces.

• Early advancement in skills such as walking or talking does not necessarily mean that your grandchild is old enough to be potty trained.

• The earliest time to start potty training is around 18 months, but for most children two years is more realistic. Some children may not be ready until nearer their third birthday. Girls are frequently ready a little earlier than boys.

• There is no fixed method of potty training: what works for one child may not work for another.

• Some children learn more quickly than others, so don't compare one grandchild with another, or with a friend's grandchild.

• Your grandchild may be unable to urinate on an unfamiliar potty or toilet.

• Young children cannot put off passing urine until it is convenient.

• Accidents may happen even after the child is trained.

• Even if a child is potty trained during the day, night-time control can take months longer. Bedwetting can occur in otherwise normal children for several years.

• If you go out with your grandchild, don't forget to take spare underwear and clothes in case he has an accident.

When a toddler comes to visit

Making your home safe for your grandchild

Accidents in or around the home are the most common cause of death or injury among children between the ages of one and five. It is not simply that small children are 'accident-prone'. Toddlers are active and curious, and the average home today has numerous potentially hazardous gadgets and appliances. Although nobody can make a house completely accident-proof, you will be able to relax and enjoy your toddler grandchild's visit more if you spend a few moments making your house as safe as possible. What's more, you will find that as you get older, many of these safety procedures will also make your home safer for you.

If your grandchild is an infrequent visitor, you may find it more economical to rent or borrow larger items, such as a fireguard, rather than buy them. Certain safety measures – removing scatter rugs when he comes or putting breakables out of reach, for example – cost nothing. Some items, such as safety gates and a car seat, can 'travel' with your grandchild.

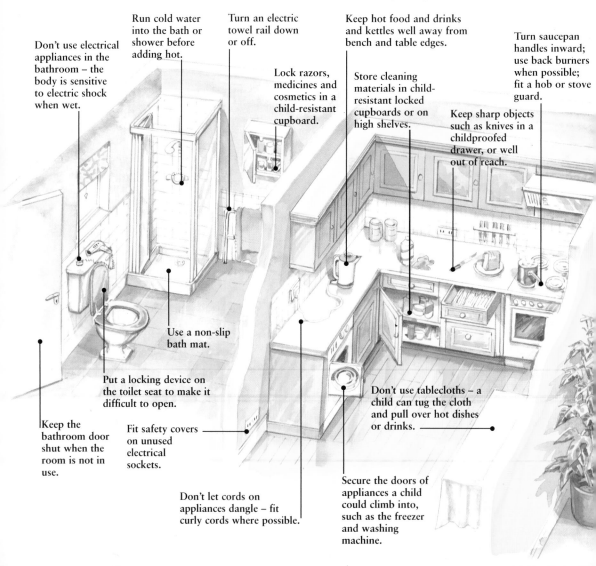

Don't use electrical appliances in the bathroom – the body is sensitive to electric shock when wet.

Run cold water into the bath or shower before adding hot.

Turn an electric towel rail down or off.

Lock razors, medicines and cosmetics in a child-resistant cupboard.

Keep hot food and drinks and kettles well away from bench and table edges.

Store cleaning materials in child-resistant locked cupboards or on high shelves.

Turn saucepan handles inward; use back burners when possible; fit a hob or stove guard.

Keep sharp objects such as knives in a childproofed drawer, or well out of reach.

Use a non-slip bath mat.

Put a locking device on the toilet seat to make it difficult to open.

Keep the bathroom door shut when the room is not in use.

Fit safety covers on unused electrical sockets.

Don't use tablecloths – a child can tug the cloth and pull over hot dishes or drinks.

Don't let cords on appliances dangle – fit curly cords where possible.

Secure the doors of appliances a child could climb into, such as the freezer and washing machine.

There are two ways in which to approach home safety: doing a room-by-room hazard check, and being aware of the most common causes of accidents in and around the home among the under-fives. These are: burns and scalds; drowning; poisoning; falls; and choking, suffocation and strangulation.

Burns and scalds

Because young children have thinner skin than adults, they are more susceptible to burns and scalds at lower temperatures.
• As soon as he is old enough to understand, teach your grandchild not to touch without your permission anything in the kitchen that might be hot. This includes such items as the oven, hotplates, taps, saucepans, kettle and teapot.

• Turn the thermostat on your hot-water system down to 50°C (120°F) to help prevent scalding.
• Always run cold water into the bath or shower first, then add hot. Shield the hot tap with a face cloth or towel.
• Keep matches and lighters out of sight and reach.
• Keep hot food and drinks out of reach; never carry a hot drink and your grandchild at the same time.
• Install – and regularly check – smoke detectors.
• Fit a fixed guard around all fires – whether they are gas, electric or open – and wood-burning stoves.
• Position movable heaters where they cannot be knocked over.

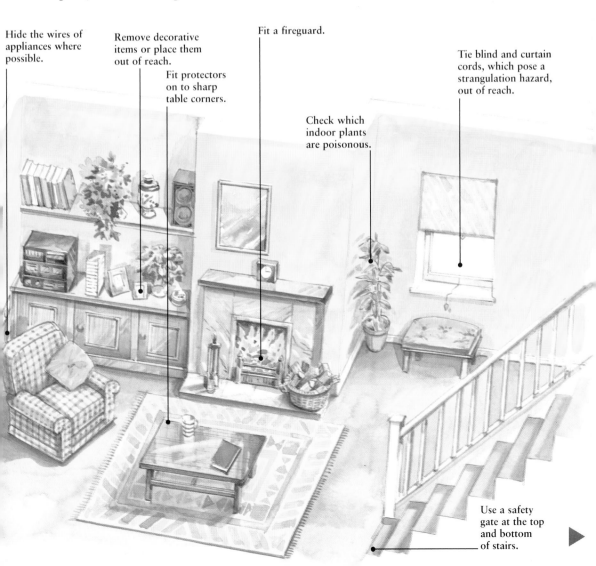

Hide the wires of appliances where possible.

Remove decorative items or place them out of reach.

Fit protectors on to sharp table corners.

Fit a fireguard.

Check which indoor plants are poisonous.

Tie blind and curtain cords, which pose a strangulation hazard, out of reach.

Use a safety gate at the top and bottom of stairs.

When a toddler comes to visit

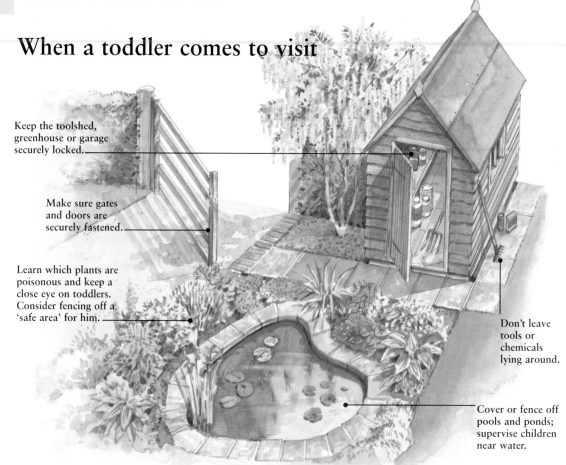

Keep the toolshed, greenhouse or garage securely locked.

Make sure gates and doors are securely fastened.

Learn which plants are poisonous and keep a close eye on toddlers. Consider fencing off a 'safe area' for him.

Don't leave tools or chemicals lying around.

Cover or fence off pools and ponds; supervise children near water.

Drowning

Young children are fascinated by water, but can drown quickly in a few centimetres.
• Don't leave buckets of water around.
• Never leave a child in the bath unattended, even for a few seconds.
• If you have a swimming pool, install a fence with a self-closing gate that latches firmly. But still be vigilant.
• Always supervise a child near water, even in a shallow paddling pool.
• Cover garden pools or fishponds with wire mesh or strong board, or fence them off.
• Make sure you know how to resuscitate a child who may have water in his lungs.

Poisoning

• Don't leave medicines in pockets or handbags. Paracetamol, in particular, is a common cause of medicinal poisoning.
• Never refer to medicines as sweets.
• Buy medicines and other potentially

harmful products in child-resistant containers, but remember that these are not 100 per cent 'childproof'.
• Put poisonous indoor plants on high shelves; teach your grandchild not to eat or pick anything from the garden without showing you first.
• Keep all potentially harmful products – medicines, pesticides, household cleaners – locked away and out of reach.

Falls

• Don't leave anything lying around in the garden that a child could trip over.
• Remove scatter rugs from polished floors.
• Put up safety gates to stop a toddler from going up or down stairs.
• Be extra vigilant if you have banisters with vertical bars that a child could squeeze through, or horizontal bars that he could climb over.
• Keep doors to balconies securely locked.

• Install window locks on all accessible windows, but make sure these can easily be opened by an adult in an emergency.
• Keep dark areas such as landings well lit.

Choking, suffocation, strangulation
• Insist that a child stay still while eating. Running around with food in his mouth invites choking.
• Do not give under-fives boiled sweets or whole nuts.
• Don't leave small objects, such as coins or button batteries, lying around.
• Only buy toys suitable for your grandchild's age. Most toy-related choking accidents occur with toys not recommended for under-threes because of small parts.
• Deflated or burst balloons are a hazard for a small child who may suck one into his mouth and choke or suffocate.
• Keep polythene and plastic bags hidden.
• Make sure there are no loose or dangling wires or cords which a child could wrap around his neck.

In the car
The law states that all children must be carried in an approved restraint appropriate to their weight, size and age. In some Australian states there are also restrictions about where a child can sit in the car, but children are generally safer in the back seat. If your grandchild is staying with you, ask his parents to leave you his car seat.

When to call a doctor
While your first-aid kit will deal with minor emergencies, always remember that accidents are not the only potential problem when your grandchild is with you. It is easy to forget how quickly a small child can become unwell or how a minor illness may suddenly get worse.

A fever or high temperature is common when a child is not well. To help bring this down, undress him and keep him cool. Sponge him with tepid water and give him plenty of fluids. A child with a fever or mild pain can also be given an appropriate dose of paracetamol for his age. Never give aspirin to a baby or child unless prescribed by the doctor.

Call the doctor if the child:
• Has a temperature above 38.6°C (101°F).
• Is drowsy, losing consciousness or cannot be woken.
• Has a convulsion (fit) or seems limp.
• Appears to have severe abdominal pain.
• Has difficulty breathing or turns blue.
• Has prolonged diarrhoea or vomiting.
• Has an unusual rash.
• Appears grey or ashen.
• Has a severe head injury, or if a head injury is followed by vomiting or loss of consciousness.
• Has swallowed a poisonous substance.
• Has a condition such as asthma or epilepsy when seems to have worsened or does not respond to the usual treatment.
If you are in any doubt, call the doctor.

SAFETY CHECKLIST

• Are chemicals and medicines out of sight and out of reach?

• Is the hot-water thermostat turned down?

• Are all gates and toolsheds locked?

• Are guards fitted to all fires?

• Is there any access to open water?

• Are there any trailing tablecloths, flexes, wires or curtain cords?

• Are safety locks fitted to windows?

• Is safety glass or film fitted on glass doors and tables? Are there safety gates on the stairs?

• Are there any garden tools or other sharp objects lying around?

• Are there any small objects lying around?

• Is the first-aid kit fully stocked?

Feeding a toddler
Coping with fussy children with minuscule appetites

Your grandchild's eating habits can be one of the biggest sources of friction between you and his parents. You may think that his parents are too strict about not allowing him treats (particularly sweets) or too lax in allowing him to be picky. His parents may feel that you are setting him on the road to tooth decay and poor habits by giving him sugary foods or that you are unrealistically strict about his behaviour at mealtimes.

You may find that you disapprove of the kind of food that your grandchild prefers, or worry that he seems to have an impossibly small appetite or a limited diet of two or three favourite foods. You may also find it difficult not to get upset if your grandchild wastes food, especially if you have lavished time and attention on preparing a meal, or if you remember days when food was less plentiful than it is now.

If it is any consolation, his parents may also be concerned about your grandchild's eating habits, convinced that he doesn't eat enough and might be hungry. They may also have to sit and watch as he eats with relish at your house something he won't touch at home. If this happens, make the dish a treat that he gets only at Granny's house.

Don't allow your grandchild's eating habits to be a source of vexation within your family. Come to an amicable agreement with his parents about what foods are or are not allowed and what constitutes acceptable behaviour. Don't let your grandchild hear you discussing any feeding problems or let him know that you are worried about them – he will revel in being the centre of attention.

Common feeding problems
Young children have small stomachs which cannot cope with large quantities of food, so most toddlers prefer to eat small meals with snacks in between. Make sure that such snacks are healthy and give sugary treats only occasionally. Too many high-fibre foods can also fill children up without providing enough calories; high-fibre low-fat diets are inappropriate for the under-fives who need plenty of calories for energy. Some children who suffer from a poor appetite and low weight gain may be filling up on sugary drinks, which provide empty calories.

Once he is happy in a high chair and can feed himself a spoonful every so often, introduce your grandchild to the idea that meals are social occasions for all the family. He will feel very grown up if you give him the same food as you are having, and you may even find that he cheerfully eats foods that he used to throw on the floor.

THE GOLDEN RULES

- Don't fuss over, bribe or force a child to eat.
- Don't show concern if he does not eat.
- Don't get upset if he rejects your lovingly cooked meal in favour of a packet meal or fast food.
- Expect a toddler to make a mess, and cover the floor with newspaper. Don't demand perfect table manners.
- Don't use sweets, cakes or biscuits as a bribe or a reward for good behaviour.
- Give small portions, and let your grandchild ask for more if he wants it.
- If he is old enough, involve your grandchild in selecting and preparing food.
- Don't undermine parents' rules about when – or if – sweets are allowed.
- Don't give foods that may cause choking: whole nuts, chunks of meat or popcorn.
- Don't let him fill up on squash or juice. And don't give him tea to drink with a meal – this can prevent the absorption of iron.

It may also help you to know that almost every family has a tale of a child who went through a phase of eating only cornflakes or baked beans or strawberry yoghurt for days at a time. Fads of this kind are usually harmless and are best left to run their course. If you are worried, you may be able to find subtle ways of introducing a wider variety of food – blending fruit into a milk shake or adding it to good quality ice cream or jelly, for example, or grating some cheese on the baked beans or hamburger.

Some children are more adventurous about food they have helped to prepare. Let your grandchild stir a jelly or cake mix, spread peanut butter or honey on his sandwich, sprinkle cheese on his pizza and select the fruit and vegetables in the supermarket.

Rest assured that if your grandchild eats something every day, or over several days, from each of the groups of food listed here he is likely to be getting a balanced diet. And if he is growing normally and has plenty of energy, he is getting enough food.

- Proteins such as meat, poultry, fish, eggs, beans, lentils and other pulses, tofu
- Starchy foods such as bread, pasta, rice, corn, millet, oatmeal, yams, potatoes, breakfast cereals
- Fruit and vegetables, both fresh and frozen; check the salt and sugar content of tinned fruit and vegetables and choose fruit tinned in juice rather than syrup
- Dairy products, such as milk, cheese, yoghurt and butter

Healthy snacks

- Milk shakes with no added sugar
- Sandwiches filled with smooth peanut butter (make sure your grandchild is not allergic to nuts), cream cheese, fruit spread or yeast or vegetable extract
- Slices of apple, banana, peach, strawberries or seedless grapes
- Frozen yoghurt
- Pitta bread, bagels, muffins, chapattis
- Small pieces of raw vegetables or soft dried fruits
- Breakfast cereals with no added sugar
- Cubes or sticks of cheese
- Pieces of home-made pizza

The vegetarian toddler

There are two concerns with a vegetarian diet for children. First, vegetarian foods generally have a high fibre content. To make sure that your grandchild gets enough energy, give him small, frequent meals and plenty of nutritious snacks. Also, children who do not eat meat may not get enough iron (breakfast cereals and pulses are good sources of iron). To help iron absorption, give foods or drinks containing vitamin C when you serve iron-rich foods.

From a distance
Keeping in touch with your toddler grandchild

If your grandchild lives near enough for you to see him regularly, keeping in touch is fairly easy. But today it is rare to find a child who has four grandparents within easy reach. And, although modern transport is often fast and efficient, few people have the time or money to simply drop everything whenever they wish to see their grandchildren.

When your grandchild is young, you will have to rely on his parents to keep up the contact. But if they lead busy lives, or your relationship with them is not especially good, communication may be difficult. If you feel that you are losing touch with your grandchild, mention it to his parents and discuss ways in which this can be improved.

Try to do this without acrimony or getting upset, as they may have no idea how

Almost all children love using the telephone from a very early age. If you can think of ways to make your calls extra special for your grandchild, so much the better. You could, for example, sing him a nursery rhyme or get your dog to bark a greeting. On special occasions, consider reading him a short story.

you feel, or they may have problems of which you are unaware. But you may have to accept that you are the one who has to make the most effort to keep in touch, especially when your grandchild is young.

Fortunately, new means of communication make keeping in touch from a distance easier than it was a generation ago. Keeping in touch will also become easier as your grandchild grows older and is able to write, telephone or visit by himself (see pp.108-109).

Telephoning
Talking on the telephone is one of the easiest and quickest ways to maintain contact with your grandchild. As soon as he is old enough, set aside a regular time each week or month when you make a telephone call to your grandchild only, rather than including him in the family call.

Check with the parents what day and time are best so that your calls are not at an inconvenient hour and do not clash with bedtime. If you usually ring at a regular time, and know that you cannot make this one day, tell your grandchild or his parents in advance to avoid disappointing him.

Don't be surprised, however, if your grandchild does not seem to respond to you when you talk. You cannot see each other but he may well be nodding his head as he listens, or simply not have enough words in his vocabulary to answer you fully. He is also likely to hold things up to the telephone for you to see – and it may take all your ingenuity to work out what he is holding!

Video and tape recording
If you don't own a camcorder, consider hiring one from time to time (see pp. 36–37). Include a special message for your grandchild on a video you are sending

to your family, or make one especially for him.

Even young children often have good memories and certainly by two and a half or three your grandchild may remember a visit to your house. Show yourself doing something he particularly liked while he was with you – such as baking a cake or visiting the park and feeding the ducks, or show him how 'his' flowers are progressing in the garden.

If he has never seen your home, make him a video tour of your house and garden, showing him the room where he will sleep if he comes to visit. And continue to ask his parents to reciprocate by sending you an occasional video of him too.

Make audio cassettes regularly, and be sure to send a special message for his birthday or for a festive occasion such as Christmas. Tell him what you have been doing, or what you will do when he comes to stay with you or you visit him. If you are confident, record yourself singing some songs for him. Ask if he can sing or talk into a tape for you to listen to as well.

Making pictures

If his parents have been sending photographs since he was a baby, ask them to continue to do so now. Except for holidays, busy parents tend to take fewer pictures as their children grow, but encourage them to send a duplicate set of prints each time they complete a roll of film. Send him photographs of yourself and of your house and pets if you have them. Make a special photograph album of all family members, including your parents, to share with him as he gets older.

If you and his parents have access to a fax machine, send drawings and short letters and stories regularly. Ask his parents to send you a copy of something he has done

When you live far away, little gifts can make you seem more real to your grandchild. Holiday souvenirs are an obvious choice, but you can also send simple, everyday items such as a small drawing book and some thick crayons or a hair slide.

at playschool or nursery each week. (This has the advantage that your grandchild keeps the original: some children can be very proprietorial about their 'work'.)

Send postcards addressed especially to your grandchild. Don't restrict yourself to holiday locations (although these will make a fascinating record for him when he is a little older), but include pictures of the area where you live.

STORIES

All children love stories and from toddlerhood up respond to simple tales recounted with expression. Stories settle fractious children for a nap or a sleep and can relieve the monotony of a car journey for a short time. You can buy cassettes of well-loved children's stories, often with an accompanying book. But it is more personal – and more special for your grandchild – to record one or two favourites from a book of fairytales or other stories yourself. Keep the stories short for the very young; you can begin to increase their complexity or record chapters at a time when your grandchild is older. Send these tapes regularly.

If you are good at storytelling (see pp. 94–95), you could also record your own inventions, perhaps making them personal to your grandchild or to any special objects he likes to play with at your house.

Preschoolers
3 to 5 years

*In her preschool years your grandchild
begins to learn many of the skills of
socialisation and independence she
will need for the rest of her life. These
are fascinating years and experiencing
the novelty of the world through her
eyes can give you immense pleasure.
Gradually she will start to move
away from her immediate family of
parents and siblings in preparation*

*for nursery or school. You can help in this
transitional period by gently introducing her to
new surroundings and experiences.*

  *Because she is interested in everything around
her, the time you spend together can be
tremendously rewarding. Her thirst for
knowledge will lead her to ask endless questions
and to be willing to learn anything you can teach
her. This time can be as precious to you as your
own child's preschool years. But now you
probably have more time, more patience and
perhaps a more relaxed approach
to childrearing. You also have the
chance to do all those things
you wish you had
done with your
own child but
somehow never
got around to!*

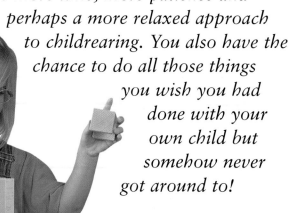

What preschoolers like doing

A host of games and activities fills a young child's day

Children of three and four are constantly busy. They play – as they did when they were younger – but now their play is more considered and organised. Through play of all kinds, young children begin to develop the skills they will need in the real world; the rehearsal for life has begun in earnest.

When your grandchild is with you, provide her with the materials she needs to fuel her creative, imaginative and physical abilities, then stand back and watch her take off. Her ingenuity, resourcefulness and determination will surprise you.

Creative play

All young children love to draw and paint and the ability to create recognisable pictures gradually develops as they get older. By the age of four your grandchild will be able to draw people with bodies, heads and the right number of limbs, for example. Art materials of all kinds are essential. She needs pencils,

crayons, felt-tip pens (buy washable ones in case she decides to draw on the wall), washable paints, large brushes and plenty of paper, preferably in different colours. When she draws a picture for you always praise it. If you don't recognise what it is, don't ask 'What's that?' but suggest she tells you about it.

Making collages is also popular. Save catalogues with lots of pictures for her to paste on to sheets of paper. She may do some snipping with blunt-nosed, child-sized scissors but it's unlikely she will be able to follow a straight line. If she gets frustrated, encourage her to tear out the picture carefully instead.

She will feel very proud when she visits you if the pictures she has created for you are displayed on your pinboard or a cupboard door, or stuck with a magnet to the fridge door. An even better idea is to keep a record of her artistic development by punching holes in drawings and paintings and storing them in a loose-leaf folder. You will enjoy looking at these together and she will be encouraged to make more special pictures for you.

You may recall from when you were bringing up your own child how things you had previously regarded as rubbish suddenly became valuable playthings. Save cereal and egg boxes, cotton reels and shoe boxes, scraps of

Even babies often discard a new toy in favour of the box it came in, but by the time your grandchild is three a box has much more play potential. Don't throw away the boxes in which new household appliances are delivered – in no time at all she will have converted them into a house, car, shop, spaceship, boat, castle or countless other things.

wool and plastic drinking straws so that your grandchild has a wealth of things to sort, cut, glue and paint. It is fascinating to see what a young child can create out of the most unlikely material.

Imaginative play

Three and four year olds are beginning to sort out the differences between the world of the imagination and the real world. One way in which they do this is through role play – taking on a different persona in order to find out how it feels to be mother, father, nursery teacher, doctor, nurse or any of the other people they meet in their daily life. For many children, the most satisfying part of 'let's pretend' is that temporarily they have control over the actions of the adults they have become. You will be amazed at the way they mimic the speech and mannerisms of the adults in their lives.

A large selection of dressing-up clothes is a wonderful way to keep a child of this age occupied for hours. Your grandchild will probably be used to ready-made or bought outfits from playgroup or nursery school, but it's just as much fun for her to dress up in your old petticoat, nightdress, waistcoat or hat. If you are handy with a needle or sewing machine, you can make costumes more or less on demand, but don't worry if your skills do not lie in this direction. With a bead necklace and an adult-sized handbag or briefcase or a tie and felt hat or baseball cap for props a little girl can instantly become 'Mummy' or 'Daddy'. She will copy her parent's mannerisms and tone of voice and be very, very serious. It can be amusing to see your adult child through the eyes of the next generation but be sure to laugh with, rather than at, your grandchild.

Dressing up at this age is also about fantasy play – pretending to be the characters your grandchild knows through nursery rhymes, television programmes and books. Curtains, especially those in heavy fabrics such as velvet, make wonderful cloaks for a pretend king or queen (old

Face painting gives you a chance to practise creating a 'picture' in a new medium, but it can also be a valuable prop in fantasy play, helping you in your efforts to be cats in the garden, tigers in the jungle or clowns at the circus.

bath towels are a good substitute). An old lace curtain can transform your granddaughter into a princess (or a bride). Add belts, necklaces, earrings, combs, discarded spectacles – preferably with the lenses removed – and a tiara or crown. Scarves and any other strips of material, the flimsier and shinier the better, are also useful additions to the dressing-up box.

Dressing up is as enjoyable for boys as it is for girls. All children enjoy the tactile experience of satin and velvet, so much of the old clothing and furnishings you put aside for your granddaughter's pleasure can be utilised with great effect by your grandson, too.

With play of this sort you are also laying the foundations for later drama sessions, when children can act out favourite fairy stories and nursery rhymes. Don't force this but be ready to follow your grandchild's lead when the time comes.

Finally, dressing up is even more fun if you can provide a full-length mirror so that fashionable creations can be examined in all their glory. And if you have a mirror with folding 'wings', so much the better.

What preschoolers like doing

The right setting

Satisfactory role play requires an appropriate setting – 'mummies and daddies' is invariably played in a 'home corner', for example, but that can be simply a rug or cushions in the corner of the room. Ready-made play furniture can be too realistic, thereby restricting its use and curtailing your grandchild's chance for imaginative play. Playhouses are attractive and have their place but your grandchild will manage just as well with a sheet or bedspread stretched over two dining chairs. This also makes a great den or tent.

Playing shops is a great favourite, largely because shopping is one of your grandchild's everyday experiences. A board balanced on two chairs makes an excellent counter. You also need to provide items to sell, a bag and some money – small coins, odd bits of

Play structures do not need to be particularly high in order for children to practise their physical skills. The most important factor is that a piece of equipment offers plenty of opportunity to develop different skills, such as climbing, swinging and balancing.

foreign currency left over from a holiday, or make your own from cardboard circles covered in foil.

The easiest shop to re-create is a supermarket with tins and packets from your store cupboard, but it is possible to 'sell' almost anything. You will probably be expected to play both customer and shopkeeper in turns to prolong the game.

There is great learning potential in playing restaurants or offices. For a restaurant you need a table and chairs – preferably child-sized – some play food and a pad on which to scribble down orders. Plan the menus and set the table, then take your place and give your grandchild your order. Again, be prepared to reverse roles.

An office can be brought to life with old diaries, cheque stubs, forms and brochures. A toy telephone is a must, and a toy computer – or, even better, access to a real one – will develop valuable skills.

Being helpful

Preschoolers are naturally helpful and happy to do household chores. Remove any small or precious ornaments, then give your grandchild a duster and let her get to work. She will happily help you to hang out the washing and sort the dry laundry. She may well enjoy setting the table, which will also help her counting skills. When you go to the supermarket, let her select goods and put them in the trolley. This might slow your progress but small responsibilities such as these help to build self-esteem.

Outdoor play

If you have a garden you may want to buy equipment to help your grandchildren expend some of their energy when they come to see you. When considering a large purchase, look for an activity centre that features a climbing frame, slide, bars to swing on and a tunnel to crawl through.

You may feel alarmed as you watch your

Playing shops is not simply great role play, it also helps your grandchild to develop early maths skills through counting out coins, giving change and handing you – and any other customers – the right number of items.

grandchild scale the equipment, but children only gain confidence by being allowed to test their abilities. Praise her enthusiasm, rather than worrying about potential hazards. But if she is reluctant to climb and slide, don't force her. Children do vary enormously in the ages at which they acquire physical skills.

You may prefer a piece of equipment that can be packed away when your grandchild is not with you. If so, look for one that can be easily slotted together, but remember that constant erecting and dismantling may mean that bolts and screws work loose, so check over the equipment before it is used.

If you are a competent carpenter and have a suitable tree in your garden, a treehouse is a good idea for older preschoolers. A low platform may be more suitable than one high in the branches in case your grandchild is reluctant to climb down (or wants you to climb up with her). Add a safety rail and some kind of cover – such as a tarpaulin – and your grandchild will have hours of fun tucked away inside, whatever the weather outside.

Summer garden play is incomplete without a paddling pool or sandpit. An inflatable paddling pool is easy to store when it is not in use; if you provide a sandpit in your garden, keep it covered between play sessions so that it isn't used by cats or birds.

If you don't have the space or resources to provide a paddling pool or sandpit, there will probably be a public park near where you live to which you can take your grandchild when she comes to visit.

Keep hoops and a skipping rope or two with which to devise an obstacle course. A large cardboard box makes an ideal prop – when open-ended on its side it makes a tunnel to crawl through or hide in. See p. 68 for reminders on safety in the garden.

Chatting

Above all, preschoolers love talking, and as a grandparent you may have more time to listen and more patience to answer her endless questions than anyone else. Make allowances for a lively imagination if she describes some unlikely behaviour at home, but see pp. 96-97 for what to do if you suspect that something is amiss.

HANDY TIPS

• Store felt-tip pens in sealed jars to stop them from drying out.

• Use a kitchen cutlery tray to store art supplies and keep them separated.

• Dressing-up clothes are more appealing if they are not creased and crumpled – keep things like princesses' dresses hanging in a cupboard or folded flat in a drawer.

• Your grandchild will need an overall to protect her clothes from paint and glue. An old shirt worn back to front is a good alternative to a shop-bought coverall.

• Plastic stackable crates are the ideal way to store playthings in the garage, shed or loft when they are not needed.

Toys for preschoolers

Choosing gifts that complement your grandchild's developing skills

Preschool children can make excellent use of homemade items (see pp. 76-79), so there is no need to buy lots of toys and games for when your grandchild comes to play – or to stay – at your house. There will be times, however, when you want to buy something special – perhaps if she is coming for an extended visit, or if more than one is coming and you want to have enough variety to keep them all interested. And, of course, you may want to buy toys for birthday and Christmas presents.

Check the recommended age on the box of all toys, especially those for younger preschoolers, but if you find something that is technically 'too old' which you think your grandchild will love, be guided by your instincts. Some children develop skills in certain areas much more quickly than others. If you are planning to buy expensive items, ask her parents if it is appropriate and what she has already. Near or – worse – exact duplications are a sure recipe for tears, particularly on a special occasion such as a birthday.

The chart opposite gives ideas for toys suitable for three to five year olds, and indicates their developmental value. Keep an open mind when choosing gifts – some boys enjoy pushing toys and animals around in dolls' prams, and girls are as adept with construction kits as their brothers.

TYPE OF TOY

Creative

These toys and materials enable children to express themselves; many such materials also encourage manipulative skills.

Manipulative

These toys enable children to practise moving their hands; many also encourage spatial awareness.

Imaginative

These are props that enable children to 'be' someone else for a time.

Outdoor

This is a self-evident category, but don't forget that some indoor equipment can be taken outside – use bath toys in the paddling pool, for example, and kitchen measures and pourers in the sandpit.

Technological

This category covers everything from toys that encourage simple pre-maths and pre-spelling skills to interactive computer games.

Importance

Children can explore different media and work out the differences between them. They also help their observational skills. By the time children reach three or four years of age, they start to draw what they see around them. Observation is a key skill in learning to read.

Without the ability to manipulate small objects, everyday life would be almost impossible. Manipulative skills are vital for everything from holding a pencil to doing up a button.

Pretending to be somebody different is the first step in learning how others feel. Until she can do this, a child has no concept of why hurting someone else is so bad, nor can she relate to characters in stories, such as sharing Goldilocks' surprise when the bears find her.

Outdoors, children can use boundless energy and make more mess and noise than most of us can cope with indoors. A lot of outdoor equipment also encourages physical skills – running, climbing, balancing.

Learning how new technology works is an important part of primary education; familiarity with a keyboard and mouse is useful; computer games help children to learn pre-reading skills, counting and problem-solving.

Toy suggestions

Crayons, felt-tip pens, paintbox and brushes, chalks, easel, colouring books, blocks of different coloured paper or rolls of paper for the easel; modelling clay; face paints; musical instruments – tambourines, drums, castanets, xylophones.

Construction sets of all kinds (many offer opportunity for expansion as children get older); beads and strings for threading; sewing cards; jigsaw puzzles with large pieces; miniature tool kit.

Tea sets; miniature domestic equipment such as ironing board and iron, dustpan and brush; baby doll, cots and beds, dolls' house and furniture; cash register, play groceries; dressing-up costumes, especially doctor's and nurse's uniforms plus play first-aid kit, hats and helmets (firefighter, police officer and so on); play camera, binoculars, telephone.

Miniature gardening tools, wheelbarrow; skipping ropes, hoops, balls of all shapes and sizes; bug boxes; sandpit; paddling pool and water play equipment – plastic containers, scoops and water wheels; swing, activity centre; tricycle, scooter, roller skates (for older preschoolers).

There is a wealth of early years' programs on the market – some excellent, others indifferent. If you are not up-to-date on new technology, check magazines or ask in computer stores for suitable programs and learn alongside your grandchild.

Then and now:

Early years education

The value of preschool education in developing children's social and intellectual skills is unquestioned, although to you a three year old may still seem too young to spend time in a learning environment.

THEN

Preschool groups were once a preparation for school, with all children engaged in the same 'learning' activities (above); today, more emphasis is placed on play and self-motivation (above right).

If you believe that a young child's place is in the home with her mother or another carer until she is legally required to go to school, you may feel a few pangs on hearing that your three or four year old grandchild is to start attending a playgroup or nursery school. Particularly if your own children stayed at home happily with you, with lots of activities to occupy them and seemingly endless visits from friends, you may feel that a more structured environment is unnecessary for your grandchild. It may help you to know, therefore, that preschool education has been thoroughly evaluated over the past few decades and it is now widely accepted that every child benefits from attending a playgroup or nursery for at least part of her day.

In the past, early years educationalists tended to concentrate on children from what were considered to be disadvantaged homes, largely those from poor families in urban areas. Such children, it was believed, did not get stimulation at home, so the nurseries took over parts of the parental role. The result was that nursery education was primarily on offer to the poor, for whom it was provided free or at low cost, and to the children of wealthy parents who could afford private nursery fees. The children of the majority of families missed out.

The playgroup movement was started in the 1960s to give more children the advantages of a preschool experience in the absence of government investment. A study by Professor Kathy Silva at the London Institute of Education observed that children tend to play in a more complex way when they are playing with others compared with when they are playing alone.

It is no longer believed that nurseries can usurp the parents' role. People working with preschool children accept that parents must always be a child's 'first educators' and that their role is to complement this

NOW

home relationship. Far from attempting to supplant parents, nursery teachers and other staff aim to work in partnership with them so that they are well informed about and involved in their child's progress at all times.

The preschool experience

Nurseries and kindergartens give children the opportunity to develop self-reliance and to learn to cooperate with others. They offer equipment, toys and games that may not be available at home and plenty of space to play – an important factor for those who live in cramped conditions. Some preschool experience also makes the transition from home to school easier. The prime objective is not to teach reading, writing and early maths – although a child who wants to get on with these skills will not be held back – but to provide the groundwork so that these skills become easier to learn once a child starts school.

If your grandchild attends a daycare centre, she may also be receiving some preschool education, perhaps spending part of the day engaged in a variety of structured activities. But she should still have time for free play and naps as if she were at home.

INFLUENCES ON EARLY EDUCATION

Friedrich Froebel
Many of the ideas of Froebel, the German educational philosospher who established the first kindergarten in 1836, are still in use today. He believed that play was a serious, significant activity for small children and developed educational materials such as geometrical shapes to encourage children to learn through play. In 1826 he wrote that 'the focus of play at this age is the core of the whole future'.

Maria Montessori
The first Montessori nursery, the Casa dei Bambini (children's house), opened in 1907 for children living in the industrial areas of Rome. Montessori believed she could compensate for the experiences children missed by not living in the countryside or in a house with a garden. She emphasised the child's interest in doing rather than in the finished product and believed that children should be taught to do tasks for themselves. The equipment she developed – such as dressing frames to help children learn how to fasten buttons – is widely used today. She also placed great value on everyday skills, such as setting the table and looking after animals, and believed that children should learn self-discipline as early as possible.

Rudolf Steiner
Steiner founded his first children's school in 1919 in Stuttgart, Germany, for the offspring of workers in the Waldorf Astoria cigarette factory. In such schools children between the ages of 4 and 18 are grouped according to mental rather than actual age. At nursery stage, the children are encouraged to act spontaneously and emphasis is placed on developing the artistic and spiritual side of their nature as well as intellectual and practical skills.

David Weikart
Weikart, an American, developed the High Scope curriculum in the 1980s. This is based on the belief that children learn best when they are given a choice over what they do. Children participate in a plan–do–review sequence in which they are expected to see each task through, then discuss with a member of staff what they have achieved. This method encourages decision-making at an early age to develop the child's self-confidence.

When a sibling comes along

Your special role in making a first-born child feel secure

It is often difficult for grown-ups to understand the depth of children's feelings on hearing that they are to have a brother or sister. Consider the situation in adult terms: a man who has been happily married for several years announces that he is bringing a new wife into the house. He assures his first wife that it will make no difference to their relationship and he will continue to love her as much as ever. Rare is the wife who would be happy with such reassurances. A child feels much the same way. She finds it difficult to believe that she won't be displaced in her parents' affections by the new arrival.

Jealousy of a new baby is normal; very few children show no negative reactions at all. But there is a great deal you can do to alleviate possible problems by helping her parents to prepare your grandchild for the new baby and by being a friend and ally in the weeks after the birth.

The pregnancy

One mistake people often make is to talk about the impending birth too soon. Children under five have little concept of time and become impatient if they are told what is going to happen eight or nine months before the event. Discuss with the parents when it is reasonable to start talking about the new arrival – it is often best to wait until the baby is becoming physically evident, although even then young children do not necessarily notice that mummy is looking different.

Refrain from talking about the baby as a new 'playmate' – your grandchild will be bitterly disappointed when the tiny bundle can't immediately join in her games. Find out from the parents the terms in which they have described what is happening and answer questions as honestly as possible. The days of fobbing children off with stories about storks and gooseberry bushes are long gone. There are a number of good books which can help children understand how a baby grows in the womb.

Avoid talking about difficulties with the pregnancy, however minor, within earshot of your grandchild. Children can easily misinterpret what is said, be unable to fully understand the implications of problems and may become unnecessarily anxious. As the date of delivery gets nearer, and perhaps her mother gets increasingly tired and uncomfortable, take your

A baby doll may help your grandchild to get used to the idea of a new baby in the house. It also enables you to prepare her for the fact that babies are not able to play the moment they arrive, but spend most of the time asleep.

grandchild shopping for items for the new baby. Even a three-year-old can help choose something to wear and a special 'welcome to the family' gift for the baby. If you can, make it a treat for her too by having lunch out or going to see a film.

After the birth

Once the baby has been born, apart from helping out with the additional chores, you should put your relationship with the baby on hold to spend as much time as possible with your elder grandchild, giving her the attention she may feel is lacking from her parents. While her mother is in hospital and in the first few days after the birth, it may be best if your grandchild remains at home. If she comes to stay with you, she may feel more rejected – and worry about what is happening in her absence. (She may, of course, feel especially grown up; if so, let her come to stay.)

It may help if you are on hand when your grandchild first meets her new brother or sister. The baby should be lying in a crib or in the arms of another person, so that your grandchild's mother is free to cuddle her. This is the time for gift-giving.

If you live close by and her parents are willing, be available for a few days so that there is someone on hand to give the first-born their full attention. A new mother may find it difficult to make sure that your grandchild's bathtime routine is not cut short and that her bedtime story is uninterrupted by the baby's crying, for example. If it is not feasible for you to be around in the evening, offer to help in another part of the daily routine – getting to playgroup in the morning, for example (tell staff about the new baby), going to the park or snuggling together to watch a favourite TV programme.

However sensitively you and her parents handle this period, be prepared for some difficult behaviour. Jealousy of a new baby is likely to arise whatever your grandchild's age. Older children are often more difficult

Expect your grandchild to have mixed reactions towards his new sibling – a child of three or four has no way of knowing what to expect, and cannot understand that you and his parents can love the new baby without loving him less.

than younger ones, simply because they have had their parents to themselves for so much longer and they have greater cause to resent the disruption to their routines.

You may experience some rejection – despite your best efforts, there will be times when only her parents' attention is good enough. If she regresses for a while – wetting or soiling again after months of being clean and dry, for example – offer to help with extra laundry. Go along with her wishes if she wants a bottle or feeding cup – it is understandable to think a baby's life is more appealing than hers at the moment. Help correct this misconception by emphasising all the things she can do and all the activities you can share which the baby can't. Arrange a couple of 'grown-up' outings to reinforce this point.

When a sibling doesn't come along

Being positive about the prospect of having only one grandchild

It is not unusual today for people to choose to have only one child. If your adult child and his or her partner have made this decision, you will have to learn to live with it, however keen you are for more grandchildren. Although in some cultures it is acceptable for grandparents to put pressure on their children to enlarge the family, it is generally wise to resist the temptation to question whether they plan to have a second baby and risk damaging the relationship between you.

There are many reasons why couples decide to restrict the size of their family. Some wish to have the experience of being parents but accept that the alternatives of a career break or prohibitive childcare costs make having more than one child unworkable. Despite the apparent ease with which a first child is often conceived, some couples can develop physiological problems that make having a second child difficult. And, while most of us find the idea of the state imposing limits on family size abhorrent, many people do choose to limit their family to a single child from concerns about overpopulation. Whatever the reason, throughout the Western world the one-child family is becoming more common.

If you have had several children yourself you may find it particularly sad that one has chosen not to replicate his or her own childhood. Don't look for implied criticism of the way you raised your family, but accept that your child wants something different. Eldest daughters of large families, in particular, often feel that they have done enough mothering already and do not wish to have several children of their own.

If your only grandchild is a daughter, her parents may feel under pressure to produce a boy – in some cultures the birth of a male child is welcomed more enthusiastically than that of a female. You, too, may feel that a family is incomplete without a 'son and heir' or someone to continue the family

In her preschool years, one of the most important things you can do for a grandchild without siblings is to broaden her social circle and give her a wider experience of people. Since they are used to playing alone, only children may have difficulty in relating to others and learning how to share. By helping in this way you can play a pivotal role in preparing your grandchild for the later demands of school.

Because they have no siblings to play with – or to interrupt them constantly – only children often have the concentration and patience to amuse themselves for quite long periods.

name. In these days of equality, however, many women choose to keep – and give their children – their family name.

If you suspect that there is a physical reason why another child has not appeared, don't pry. It may be that the parents themselves are desperately upset that they seem unable to conceive their longed-for second child. If it is your daughter who is having fertility problems, she may confide in you when she feels the time is right, and you can offer her love and support. If your relationship with your daughter-in-law is less easy, she may feel embarrassed to discuss such matters with you. It is important to respect her wish for privacy. Equally, don't always assume that it is the woman who is having problems – and accept the fact that your son or son-in-law is probably even less likely to want to discuss a fertility problem with you.

Your special role
However disappointed you may feel, be as positive as possible about the advantages of being an only child. Your only grandchild will never have to compete for her parents' attention or feel that she has any rival for their love. She will never experience the feelings of rejection, however unfounded, and jealousy when a little brother or sister comes along. Only children, along with first-borns, tend to be high achievers at school and work, demonstrating strong leadership skills. Used to playing alone, they are likely to be more self-sufficient and inventive, qualities which stand them in good stead in later life. They also tend to relate well to grown-ups since they live in a family of adults.

Your only grandchild may, however, be self-centred, find it difficult to share and experience a sense of loneliness. She may also be hindered by her parents' reluctance to accept her independence, or be 'pushed' into behaving like a little adult before she is ready to do so. Only children can also make enormous demands on their parents: they may expect to have constant attention, with the result that parents have little time to be alone together. Parents, in turn, can also make too many demands on an only child, investing all their hopes and aspirations in her.

As a grandparent you can take positive action to counteract some of this pressure. Because your grandchild's immediate family is limited, contact with other relatives is important. Cousins, particularly those of a similar age, can be very special to an only child and are an excellent substitute for brothers and sisters.

If you have grandchildren from other family members, include them in your plans. If cousins are not available, invite a neighbour's child when your grandchild comes to visit or team up with another grandparent and child for outings. Whatever you have planned, your grandchild's parents will probably be delighted if you take her off their hands for a while and allow them time to themselves.

Shared skills: cooking

Introducing your grandchild to preparing food

It is surprising how much a preschool child can do in the kitchen – under your supervision, of course – and how many new skills she can acquire in the process. To begin with, you are laying one of the foundations for independent living as a young adult. In addition, the weighing and measuring involved in cookery are a good introduction to maths, and the way in which heat transforms basic ingredients into different shapes and textures prefigures later experiments in science.

Working together in the kitchen also offers an opportunity to discuss what constitutes healthy food and the importance of thinking carefully about what we eat. And, perhaps even more valuable, offering your grandchild small responsibilities will boost her self-confidence. It is for these reasons that cooking is a favourite activity at playgroup and nursery school.

Allow plenty of time for your cookery sessions so that you both feel relaxed. If your grandchild takes a long time to complete a task, resist the temptation of taking over or hurrying her along. And leave time at the end of any session for her to help you to wash up and clear away, leaving the kitchen in perfect order. You may even be able to instil a habit that will last a lifetime.

What to make

There are a lot of simple dishes that you and your grandchild can make together. Anything that involves pastry is bound to delight her. At first she may treat it as if it were playdough, so make the point that if the pastry is to become something edible it needs careful handling. Children as young as three love rolling it out – buy your grandchild a small rolling pin and plenty of cutters of all shapes and sizes. An older

Clean hands that are not too hot and sticky are important when you are making pastry. Encourage your grandchild to wash and dry them frequently. Once you have rolled the pastry out to your satisfaction, cut it into any shape you like and add flavourings and toppings.

As an alternative to pastry, try biscuit dough which even young children can knead, divide and then shape.

Spending time in the kitchen does not necessarily have to mean cooking at every session. Preparing foods and decorations that are an integral part of a festival – such as the pumpkin at Hallowe'en – is another activity which you can share with your grandchild.

child can make jam tarts almost all by herself, although you should put them into the oven and take them out, and warn her not to take a bite while the jam is hot.

For special occasions, you can roll out and shape marzipan. If you have some small cutters and different food colourings you can produce exciting-looking sweets, which make an ideal gift for your grandchild to share with her parents and friends.

Preparing her own food

Children take great pleasure in making their own desserts. Powdered instant puddings that involve adding milk and then whipping are good since even very young children can manage almost single-handed if you check that all the powder has dissolved.

Making jelly is a satisfying occupation as long as it is you who pours the hot liquid into the jelly moulds. Traffic-light jelly is very popular. Make a green jelly and pour it into a large bowl. When it has set, add an orange jelly, then repeat with a red one. Try to make all the layers the same thickness.

Your grandchild can also play an important part in your cake-making sessions. She can sift flour, beat eggs and mix ingredients (do the final whisk yourself to ensure that everything is mixed); she will also love icing the cake once it is cooked and adding other finishing touches.

A child who is reluctant to eat fresh vegetables or salads may attack them with relish if she has played a part in preparing them. Something as simple as learning to pop the peas out of the pod may encourage her to eat them, especially if she has only tried frozen ones before.

Preparing a basic salad – washing and tearing lettuce and arranging tomatoes, cucumber and hard-boiled eggs – should be within your grandchild's capabilities. She may also be able to whisk together the ingredients for the dressing.

Another idea that helps to encourage healthy eating is to help her to scoop out the insides of baked potatoes and mix them with tuna, cottage cheese or scrambled egg, then return the fillings to their jackets. Allowing her to put food out on plates, perhaps arranging it in a special way, may also make her more enthusiastic about eating the finished results.

Regional specialities

Spending time in the kitchen with your grandchild can also give you the opportunity to introduce her to your culture's culinary specialities. It's a sad fact that convenience foods have meant the loss of many traditional ways of cooking. You can begin to familiarise your grandchild with the vegetables and fruit essential to re-create the meals of your homeland or childhood or let her sniff and taste the spices and herbs she may not encounter in her everyday eating. By passing on this culinary knowledge you may help to restore enthusiasm for these traditional dishes.

Pacing yourself
Making the most of limited physical abilities with active children

If you have a disability or chronic illness, or perhaps became a grandparent late in life and have less stamina than you once did, you may feel reluctant to spend time alone with your grandchild, fearing that you won't be able to keep up. If you found the physical demands she made as a baby and toddler too much to cope with, be reassured: older children do not require the concentrated care that younger ones need.

There is no reason why you should not do lots of things together. Be positive: being unable to take your grandchild to the playground or kick a ball around with her in the garden does not mean that you have nothing to offer. You can give time and interest – both of which are invaluable.

It is important that you are aware of your limitations and are prepared to admit when you feel tired. Keep periods alone limited until you are certain what you can do. Even young children are capable of understanding that you are not as energetic as they are or that you have to rest. They will probably be kind and sympathetic. Your grandchild may ask questions about your health, particularly if you are in a wheelchair or have to spend a lot of time in bed. Be as honest as possible without making her unduly anxious. A close relationship with a disabled or elderly person may make her a more tolerant and caring adult.

Remember, too, that time with a child does not have to mean endless physical activity. With a little thought and planning, you can provide your grandchild with lots of stimulating activities you both enjoy.

Quiet activities
Reading together is obviously one of the most accessible activities if your problem is mobility, but if your sight is not good,

Being outdoors with your grandchild does not have to put undue physical strain on you. Depending on the time of year, suggest that he hunts for pine cones or birds' feathers and brings them to show you. See if he can find the first flower in spring (he must not pick it but should call you to go to look at it), or how many different leaves he can retrieve from the ground.

invest in a cassette player and start collecting tapes of children's stories and rhymes. Don't play the stories straight through but stop the tape every so often to discuss what is happening and give her time to ask questions, as you would if you were looking at a book together. If you are playing a selection of songs and rhymes make sure you join in. Even better, sing together and record yourselves – children love hearing a recording of their own voice.

You can also use a cassette player to introduce your grandchild to some of your favourite music. Ask her to tell you how the music makes her feel, to enhance her understanding. You can extend this by drawing happy, sad, angry and worried faces and asking her to point out which one best suits the mood of the music.

The memory game Being able to memorise is an important pre-reading skill so this game is not only fun but also aids learning. Put, say, ten different items on a tray – everyday household objects are fine. Ask your grandchild to look carefully, then cover them with a cloth and see how many she can remember.

This can be extended by asking her to turn her back while you remove something. She then has to look again and decide what is missing. She will enjoy it if you play as well, even if you have to pretend hard that you have forgotten what was there.

Make a feely bag Hide lots of different unbreakable objects in a fabric bag – a pillowcase will do – and let her feel them and try to guess what each shape is.

Games By the age of three most children can manage a simple card or board game, although the amount of time they can concentrate does vary. Don't expect a preschool child to spend more than 20 minutes playing this type of game. Old favourites – Snap, Lotto or Snakes and

Ladders, for example – which have entertained generations of children seem to work best with young children, so you don't need to spend money on apparently more sophisticated modern options. It is worth buying good-quality games with thick cards and bright, clear illustrations which will stand up to repeated use.

Jigsaws The age guide on a jigsaw puzzle is only approximate, so ascertain for yourself the level of difficulty that is appropriate for your grandchild. Jigsaws are valuable tools for developing manipulative skills but as many children loathe them as love them. Be guided by your grandchild's response.

Letting off steam

Of course small children can't be expected to sit still for long periods and your grandchild will sometimes feel the need to let off steam. This should not be a problem, since there are physical games you can play while sitting in your armchair.

A 'ball' of screwed-up newspaper is a good substitute for the real thing and is less of a threat to the ornaments. Make several of these, place an empty wastepaper basket in a strategic position and see how many you can pot while sitting together on the sofa. Move the basket farther away, or get her to do so, as her skill improves.

Alternatively, line up some empty plastic bottles on the floor and see how many you can knock down by rolling a foam rubber ball along the floor. Put your grandchild in charge of standing them up again.

When she tires of these games and still has energy to spare, bring out the cassette player and tapes again and play statues. She can dance and skip and jump as much as she wants and you can 'turn her off' (when she must stand still) whenever she becomes too exuberant.

Books for young children

Choosing and reading books with your preschool grandchild

Preschool children need access to books of all kinds – stories, poetry and nonfiction titles which explain the world about them. You have probably been sharing cloth and board books with your grandchild since her babyhood, but it is around the age of three or four that children learn that books are both a means of communication and a way to extend their knowledge and imagination. As well as encouraging your grandchild to want to read, a good storybook can help to develop social, personal and language skills.

Books for the young traditionally combine pictures – which should enhance a story and be full of detail to encourage observational skills – with minimal text. Your grandchild will also enjoy alphabet books, picture word books and those that involve some counting. Novelty books, such as those with pop-up pictures, lift-up flaps, pull-down tabs or buttons which, when pressed, produce a sound, have lots of appeal because they involve anticipation and participation.

The drawback of such books is that they are easily damaged and have to be handled with care.

Don't avoid stories that deal with subjects like starting school, illness, a new baby in the family, bullying or even the death of a relative. Buy or borrow these books from the library at appropriate times – they can be useful in helping a child to talk about any anxieties she may have.

It is important to choose a book you like so that you can communicate your enthusiasm to your grandchild. Make sure it is appropriate to your grandchild's age, too: it is easy for adults to get carried away by beautiful illustrations.

Reading with your grandchild

Always choose somewhere comfortable to share a book together. Most children prefer to sit on your lap or snuggle up close to you. Show your grandchild how to hold the book properly and to turn the pages in the correct order. Follow the sentences with your finger sometimes so that she learns which way language reads. Put some expression into your voice, or adopt a tone for each character. If while you are reading she stops you and wants to take over, let her. A young child can learn a favourite story by heart and want to feel grown up by 'reading' it to you.

When a story is too long or complicated, she will start fidgeting or be obviously uninterested. Put the

If you are reading to more than one child, make sure they are in close contact with you and can see the book clearly. Be prepared for more discussion of the story than usual with two or more children.

book away for the time being and bring it out again in a few months' time.

Resist the temptation to introduce a new book if your grandchild insists on an old favourite. Having read a story many times before, you may be bored, but hearing again a tale with which she is so familiar that she could recite it to you while snuggled up against you gives her a wonderful feeling of security. A favourite book is almost an alternative to a comfort blanket. If you have kept some of your own child's books, introduce them too. They may look old-fashioned and tattered but your grandchild will love having a book her parent enjoyed and you will like the sense of continuity that reading it brings.

Sharing books with your grandchild can be one of the most pleasurable activities of your times together. By supplying her with books you are giving the tools that will encourage her to become a reader herself. And if she sees her family enjoying books as well as newspapers or magazines she, too, is likely to develop a lifelong love of reading.

HOW TO CHOOSE A BOOK

Ask yourself the following questions before you select a book for your grandchild.

• Does it have an overall attractive appearance? A dull-looking book will not inspire a child to examine it more closely.

• Is it well written?

• Are the illustrations clear and detailed?

• Are the story and the language used appropriate for her age?

• Will your grandchild be able to sympathise with or relate to the characters?

• Does it reflect the world in which she lives or teach about other lifestyles and cultures?

• Does it offer positive images? Are the people depicted from a range of cultures? Are characters free from stereotyping – are girls and women shown in active roles, for example, as well as boys and men?

• Does the story involve lots of repetition? Children love familiarity and the sense of control given by knowing what comes next.

Storytelling
Maintaining and reviving the oral tradition

Telling stories to your grandchild, as opposed to reading a story, will enthral her and offers more intimacy than almost any other shared activity. If you hold her close to you as you talk, there is nothing to disturb your concentration – not even the turning of a page. This can be particularly soothing when she is tired or fractious since telling your own stories allows you to adapt themes and storylines to suit the mood or the moment. It is also entirely personal – nobody else will ever tell your grandchild the tale you tell in the way you tell it.

Storytelling may come easily to you, particularly if you are from a culture with a strong oral tradition and can easily recall the tales you were told by your parents and grandparents. Nevertheless, your own child may have shown little interest in this time-honoured skill: the appeal of television has often proved unbeatable. There are signs, however, that this is changing as people become disillusioned with the passive nature of watching television and seek a leisure pursuit that enables them to interact with other people and to share experiences. Storytelling groups are becoming more popular, and a professional group may well visit your grandchild's nursery school or local library at some time.

Don't feel that you require special talent to enchant your grandchild with your stories. You do not need great acting skills or special fluency, although it does help if you can attempt a few different 'voices' – perhaps a gruff one for the baddy, or a high one for the princess or heroine.

Old favourites
If you don't have a specific cultural oral tradition on which to draw, think of the numerous fairytales many of us know by heart. Generations

When you tell a story, sit close and turn a prop around and around so that your grandchild can see it from all angles and appreciate its pivotal role in the story. If you are not using props, maintain eye contact so that you can gauge if the pace is flagging. A high level of skill is not necessary; more important is your enthusiasm for the tale you are weaving.

of children have enjoyed stories like 'The Three Bears', 'Little Red Riding Hood' and 'Cinderella' and will continue to demand them. These stories are valuable because they involve basic concepts of good and evil and frequently present simple moral dilemmas which you can go on to discuss with your grandchild.

The great advantage of telling – as opposed to reading – a well-loved fairytale is that you can adapt the story to suit your grandchild, omitting sections she might find frightening, changing the ending or giving one of the characters her name to make it extra interesting. These stories can develop with your grandchild's participation. Encourage her to think of different endings to traditional tales. What would have happened to Cinderella if Prince Charming hadn't found the slipper?

Small children also love to hear stories about your childhood and about when their own parents were small. These can be the simplest accounts of a trip on holiday or a memorable birthday party. Such tales may well pass into your family's folklore and be handed down to your great-grandchildren some day.

Helping the story along

If you find it difficult to conjure stories from memory or imagination you can always use props. Stories about your own child's early years are easy to evoke by getting out the photograph album and talking about the people in the pictures and what they are doing. But other visual material can also stimulate stories. A book of famous works of art, for example, can prompt a conversation about the people featured and lead to your making up stories about them

and what they were doing before they were frozen in time by the artist. Choose pictures that appeal to you but will also be comprehensible to a young child: portraits, landscapes, or still lifes of familiar objects.

If you prefer three-dimensional props, choose a couple of objects and weave a story around them. Keep the objects and stories simple to begin with – a shell may evoke a story about a girl finding it on the seashore and the magical sounds she hears inside it, for example – and make them more complicated as you gain in confidence.

You could also consider using dolls or puppets as aids to your imagination. Shop-bought puppets, although the result of someone else's imagination, can be useful. Choose hand or finger puppets – those on strings look appealing but are almost impossible to manipulate unless you are a skilled puppeteer. Finger puppets are easy to make at home but there are other simple ways to create characters. Drawing faces on plain paper plates and taping a drinking straw or thin stick to the back gives your grandchild several puppets with which to act out a story as you tell it. She will also enjoy colouring the faces.

Many people find talk of storytelling as an 'art' off-putting, but this is a skill which is relatively easy to acquire. You can have a lot of fun stretching your imagination in this way. And remember that your grandchild will be there to prompt you if your mind ever does go blank.

When to intervene

Identifying and reacting to signs of neglect or abuse

There will inevitably be times when you disagree with the way in which your grandchild is being brought up. You may think that her parents are too lax about table manners or too strict about bedtime. It is usually better to bite your tongue and accept that the parents have the right to set their own family agenda.

More serious, however, are situations that make you suspect that they are being overly harsh with the child. Perhaps they are physically cold with her, pushing her away when she wants a cuddle. Or they might seem to expect too much of her and be unreasonably irritated by aspects of her behaviour. You might notice bruising or sores which can't be explained. Any of these observations could indicate that your grandchild is being emotionally or physically abused.

Even more unpalatable is the suspicion that your grandchild may be experiencing sexual abuse, a term that covers fondling and kissing her genitals through to full-scale penetration of her body. Remember that boys also may be sexually abused.

It is a sad fact that most child abuse is carried out by someone known to the child, despite the emphasis we place on the danger of strangers. It also happens in families from all cultural and social backgrounds.

If you suspect that your grandchild is being neglected or abused, you cannot ignore it. Your first approach must be to the parents. If they are the culprits they will no doubt deny it, but if someone else is the perpetrator you will have alerted them. If they cannot explain what you have seen or heard, think about enlisting the help of the other grandparents. They will be as concerned as you are and together you may be able to resolve the situation.

If the signs of neglect or abuse have become apparent since the birth of a new baby, your daughter or daughter-in-law may be suffering from postnatal depression; do encourage

If your grandchild is being abused, you can help by being her ally. Abuse thrives on secrecy, with the result that she may not tell you directly what is happening – she may be too young even to put into words what is going on. But her behaviour and the way she reacts when she is with you may be enough to arouse – or confirm – your worst suspicions.

CASE HISTORY

My daughter Diane and three-year-old granddaughter, Louise, live a long way away and I don't see them often, so I was delighted when Louise came to stay while her mother was on a course. She seemed a bright, if quiet, little girl. But one thing worried me: she had extensive bruising on her back. It was so bad that she flinched when I tried to dry her. And she was vague when I asked how it had happened.

I could hardly bear to think about it, but wondered if Diane had been hitting Louise. Her marriage had recently broken up and she was stressed. She had taken on a full-time job and had had to find someone to care for Louise – I knew that Diane had been delighted when a neighbour who was also a childminder had agreed to look after her.

When Diane arrived to collect Louise, I asked about the bruising. Diane said that the injuries had happened at the childminder's – another child had punched Louise. The childminder had promised that it wouldn't happen again. I was uneasy that such bullying appeared to be tolerated and I sensed that Diane felt the same, but when I tried to push her further, she became angry and told me that I had no idea how difficult it was to find convenient, affordable childcare. Being able to leave Louise a few doors away made things easy.

I knew that Diane had been too busy to do a great deal of research into childcare in her area and offered to return with her for a week or so and see if together we could find somewhere more suitable. To my relief Diane agreed. I had a lovely time visiting nurseries with Louise and was delighted when there was a place for her at a childcare centre where the staff had been very friendly and had taken a real interest in Louise. It cost more than the childminder, but I offered to pay a small sum into Diane's bank account every month to cover this and Diane accepted. Louise has settled down well and Diane is delighted with her progress.

We didn't challenge the childminder, which we regret – a few months ago she was charged with assaulting a little boy in her care.

If a normally outgoing child suddenly becomes withdrawn she may have experienced some trauma. Ask her parents if they can explain her changed behaviour.

her to seek medical advice. If the parents have financial or marital problems and you suspect they might be taking out their frustration on their child, you may help by offering to babysit or have your grandchild to stay while they sort out their difficulties.

If you cannot resolve the problem in these ways, report your fears to your grandchild's doctor or the police – the child's health and happiness must be paramount.

The warning signs
• Your grandchild may be suffering from neglect if: she is smelly; she has dirty hair; her clothes are unwashed; her skin is dull and lustreless; she has noticeably lost some weight.

• She may be being abused if: there are unexplained bruises and sores on her body.

• She may be being sexually abused if: there is soreness around her genitals; she refuses to let you wash and dry those parts of her body; or she demonstrates precocious sexual behaviour, like insisting on mouth-to-mouth kissing, or putting her tongue in your mouth when you kiss her.

CHAPTER FIVE

The Younger Schoolchild
5 to 8 years

At about the age of five, your grandchild takes one of the most significant steps of his life – he begins his formal education. School opens many doors for young children, broadening their view of the world, their social skills and intellectual abilities almost beyond recognition in a few short months. If you are not in close contact with your grandchild you may be surprised at how quickly his understanding of the world matures.

During the years between five and eight, your grandchild will become a fluent reader, be able to write you a legible, well-constructed story and be capable of simple arithmetic. He will have questions on subjects of which your knowledge may be rusty or non-existent. Equally important, he will become more independent – deciding when he wants to come to see you, for how long and what he would like to do while he is with you.

Sharing the discoveries of these years with your grandchild can make this a hugely satisfying period of your relationship.

What 5 to 8 year olds like doing

Fun games and activities for your young grandchild

School helps to strengthen children's concentration skills, with the result that once absorbed in an activity, your grandchild is likely be happy with it for some time. This increased concentration also makes it possible for you to make familiar games more difficult and enables you to introduce some new ones as well. School will open his eyes to the world around him, and he will start to take a real interest in everyday things, commenting on shadows and rain, trucks and planes, birds and flowers. In fact, simply chatting together is one of the activities your grandchild is likely to enjoy most.

Gardening instils in children a respect for the natural world, fosters a love of beauty, introduces the concept of life cycles, and makes them aware of the changing seasons.

Indoor activities

Five to eight year olds retain their love of the familiar and like to watch a favourite video again and again. And they will enjoy it all the more if you are there to watch too. Watching does not have to be passive (which is parents' major complaint about this pastime): talk about the bits you like best (see if they differ from your grandchild's preferred sequences). Freeze the frame once or twice – not too often or he will get annoyed – and ask your grandchild to tell you why a character behaved in a certain way (to show you are as involved as he is). If you want to make the occasion special, pretend you are at the cinema: make some popcorn and serve bottles or cartons of juice with straws.

As they practise writing and drawing, children make innumerable lists and write endless stories. When your grandchild comes to stay, provide plenty of paper and pens. Although this can be a private activity, he is likely to have lots of requests for help with spelling. It's tempting to provide the answer all the time, but in fact in schools certain pieces of work are done without the use of dictionaries or teacher input, in favour of educated 'guessing'. You can do this by sounding out a word, or asking your grandchild how he thinks it should be spelled before you give the answer.

The love of books you fostered in his growing years will pay dividends now. He is likely to want to demonstrate his reading skill, which is a good idea, but he may get tired or bored if he has to read a long story. A way around this is for you to read one page and him the next. A trip to the library to choose a book or to the bookshop – perhaps to pick one to leave at your house for future trips – will also give him pleasure.

Now is the time to introduce your grandchild to some old-fashioned games; some five and six year olds can master draughts with a patient partner; pairs is still popular; and start playing word games

By this age, many children have the patience and dexterity to enjoy playing with model trains, helping to make station buildings and choosing figures to complete a realistic scene.

such as junior Scrabble. If he didn't like them when he was younger, your grandchild probably won't start to like jigsaw puzzles now. But for those children who took to them, these are great family fun. Card games and dominoes are also entertaining.

Finally, children in this age group are constantly busy making or doing things. Many of the gift suggestions for things to do on pp. 102–3 do not involve a large financial outlay – or can be improvised – and your grandchild will love them.

The great outdoors

Adventure playgrounds with rope ladders and swing rings come into their own at this age; children have learned a little caution so your grandchild is unlikely to be at the top of a scramble net before you can stop him. Swings and slides are still fun for those at the lower end of the age group. In the park, your grandchild will continue to enjoy activities from his preschool years such as collecting pine cones. And introduce him to such games as boules and

skittles (use a beach set for this). Miniature or 'crazy' golf is also good outdoor fun for family members of all ages.

Model-making is hugely popular with five to eight year olds. If you have plenty of space, model aeroplanes are a good choice; and if you are a model train enthusiast, this is the age when your grandchild is likely to become interested, if he is going to. With all these activities, look out for local events, or local societies with a junior branch whose meetings you could attend.

The early years at school are also those when children start to take a real interest in the growth of living things, making gardening an ideal activity. If you don't have a garden, buy some quick-growing herbs that your grandchild can plant in a small trough; or choose some indoor bulbs and help him to plant them in time for a table display at Christmas, or whenever else your family gets together. If you have a garden and your grandchild is a frequent visitor (or accepts your help in his absence), give him a small plot that is his alone.

Look through books on flowers together to find suitable plants that will grow in your area. To avoid disappointment, suggest that he select the colours and leave the choice of suitable varieties to you.

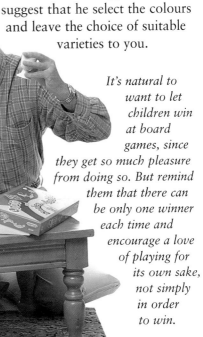

It's natural to want to let children win at board games, since they get so much pleasure from doing so. But remind them that there can be only one winner each time and encourage a love of playing for its own sake, not simply in order to win.

Gifts for 5 to 8 year olds

Birthdays, Christmas and 'spur of the moment' purchases

Christmas and birthdays are still magical for five to eight year olds. But over-excitement can easily lead to tears if your grandchild considers a gift 'too babyish'. Choose according to personality, not the age on the box.

Children develop a great deal once they start school, and their interests and ideas change under the burgeoning influence of their peers. This can be difficult if you are a long-distance grandparent – a child who is quite immature on one visit may seem very grown up on the next. All these factors can make choosing appropriate gifts tricky.

It helps if you keep in contact through letters and phone calls. In this way, you will hear what he has that is new and what he has given his friends for their birthdays (often a good indicator of what he might like for himself). You will also be able to keep up to date with his developing interests and hobbies.

You may – unwittingly – tend to err on the side of caution, keen to buy gifts that 'last'. Obviously some 'useful' presents (additions to construction sets, for example, or collectables such as stamps, coins, dolls or minerals) are a good idea, but give your grandchild toys (including soft toys) and fun items occasionally. There is no point in buying something indestructible if he not going to play with it, or get any fun from it. Try to see the world through his eyes when choosing a gift.

Large purchases

Always discuss these with your grandchild's parents first to ensure that the gift is acceptable – you may see nothing wrong with buying a seven year old a TV for his room, for example, but his parents may have serious reservations.

Suitable items in this category include computers or audio equipment; bicycle; sports equipment; and toys for the garden.

Origami is an ancient art, well worth reviving with your grandchild. You can buy a simple 'how to' kit which will provide everything you need including instructions. Alternatively, borrow a book from the library and buy a selection of paper. Your grandchild might like to fold place settings for a special family meal.

CRAFT GIFTS AND KITS

These are the ages at which manual dexterity improves by leaps and bounds – which is why children's handwriting becomes increasingly legible. In many ways this gives enormous scope when you are considering 'things to do' gifts for a child.

Paper
Kits to enable you to make things from paper, such as flowers or buildings; stencil sets; blocks of different-coloured papers; kits to make paper itself.

Jewellery
Sets of beads from which to create necklaces, bangles; kits to make hair slides and badges; hair-braiding kits.

Models
Either pre-formed kits for such items as dinosaurs, boats, cars and planes, or – especially for children

who were keen on playdough when young – modelling clay. Some sorts air dry, others need baking in the oven; some make such items as fridge magnets, brooches or hairslides.

Wool and fabric
Simple tapestry pictures; learn-to-knit kits; making finger puppets (this may not involve sewing – many can be glued together); friendship bracelets; small weaving loom; kit to make peg dolls.

Art
Watersoluble crayons, which come in packs with a paintbrush: they can be used as coloured pencils, but when brushed with a wet paintbrush they react like watercolour; a beginner's watercolour set; felt-tip markers; glitter pens; sand art (a pack of coloured sands which stick on to precut designs).

Videos, books and tapes
Much-heralded new video releases are obvious gifts for children in this age group, but they are usually acquired fairly quickly so check with his parents in advance. Older stories, although apparently less in demand, may prove as popular in the long run.

By this age, children are able to take care of books, which makes hardcover editions a more special gift. As well as perennial favourites, many of which are regularly reissued with new illustrations, you could also consider simple, repetitive stories with lively illustrations for children to read alone; and longer tales, perhaps with chapter breaks, for an adult to read over several nights at bedtime.

Story tapes are useful on car journeys and can be a good introduction to classic children's literature, which is too difficult for five to eight year olds to read alone.

And don't ignore music tapes. Children this young may enjoy listening to music channels on the radio, and some CDs or cassettes that are 'theirs' can be special.

TV power
At this stage TV advertising ceases to be of passing interest and becomes a trigger for a constant cry of 'I want'. Parents suffer more from this than you will, but if you ask your grandchild what he would like as a present, you may get an answer that you don't understand (unless you watch children's TV too), or a request that you are unhappy to honour. Keep a sense of proportion. What to you is an ugly piece of plastic may give your grandchild hours of imaginative play. But don't compromise your principles. Many people are worried about the effect on children of toy weapons, for example, or physically 'perfect' dolls.

Outings with 5 to 8 year olds
Special days out with your young grandchild

You have several advantages over parents when planning outings with your grandchildren. You can take them places during school holidays when their parents may be working, you can probably devote more time – both to choosing a suitable destination and visiting it – and you may get concessionary entrance fees because of your age.

Choosing a venue
Try to think of something that will be out of the ordinary for your grandchild. All children like theme parks, for example, but they may have been several times with their parents or friends already. And while the cinema is always popular, they may go sufficiently regularly for this not to seem special. Live action, however, is different – ice shows, children's theatre, puppets and magicians are all treats.

Most children love animals. Some are keen to join in any activity on offer, holding, feeding and being photographed with exhibits (below). Others prefer to watch from a more measured distance (right).

Plan ahead and to avoid disappointment don't mention it to your grandchild until you have the tickets.

The natural world
Most city children like farms but check whether there is anything of specific interest – such as sheepshearing, baby lambs or new chicks that a child can hold. A child who has not been around animals much may be wary of having a lamb or kid chewing out of his hand, so don't force it. And, no matter how interesting you find the animals, be prepared for him to spend time in a regular play area, if there is one.

Many zoos no longer keep large animals in cages but may have safari rides or fenced-off areas where they can be viewed. Or you could go to a national park. Check how far you may need to walk: five or six year olds tire easily. If you have to stay in your car, make sure you take binoculars that are suitable for a child; yours may be too heavy for him to hold for long. A child keen on animals may also like a nature trail.

Aquaria, too, are worth a visit. You may be surprised that many children do not choose to watch the tropical fish. They prefer the 'scary' ones such as sharks and the 'odd' ones such as sting rays and octopuses.

Museums and collections
The days of stuffy museums patrolled by humourless curators are long gone. Most museums today are friendly, child-oriented places. The scope is endless – science and technology, toys

Trips for all the children in the family tend to be less successful as they get older and their interests begin to differ. It is often best to arrange an outing for one child at a time; if you want to take two or more of your grandchildren, take those of a similar age, rather than brothers or sisters unless they are very close. Both younger and older children will get bored.

and games, clothes, natural history, transport. Ask what your grandchild is doing at school and choose a venue that complements or expands his current activities. If you are not sure whether something is appropriate, ring the museum, give your grandchild's age and interests, and ask for advice.

Check in advance what subject areas the museum covers and whether it has any literature that might help you decide what to look at – a trail to spot different animals or certain clothes around the collection, for example, or puzzles and quizzes relating to it. If the collection is large, pick a few areas that you know will be of interest, and leave some time to return to something that really appeals. Expect the unexpected: he is likely to glance over what you think he will find fascinating and spend a long time on something you find mundane. Particularly with science, technology and transport, opt for areas of the collection that are 'hands on' – children like to be able to touch and to discover that pressing a certain lever releases a spring or sounds a horn.

You can include art galleries, but again choose with care. A room in which there are paintings of children or animals may appeal, as will one in which most of the exhibits are colourful. But many five to eight year olds don't have the concentration or artistic appreciation to gain an enormous amount from art collections: be prepared to keep the visit short.

Places of interest

Historic houses tend to be of little interest to young children unless there is something specific that has inherent child appeal, such as a collection of old toys. Reconstructions or model communities, however, can fire their imagination, especially if you are able to explain the day-to-day workings of the community. Your grandchild is likely to be most interested in where the food was cooked and the toilet arrangements, but it is worth trying to get him to think about the differences between what he is seeing and what he is used to – such as how small living spaces were, and the fact that there was no TV.

Finally, ships appeal to many children. Again the eating, toilet and sleeping arrangements are likely to hold their attention for longest, but they may be interested in the stores and rigging, and in any guns or cannons on deck.

MAKING IT PERSONAL

Your grandchildren are likely to be captivated by anything to do with you, so if you played a sport when you were younger, one of them might like to go with you to a sporting collection or hall of fame; if you worked in the motor industry, he may be interested in a museum or collection devoted to cars or motorbikes, for example; if you drove a train, a collection of model trains may spark enthusiasm.

Younger five to eight year olds don't really have much concept of the past, so your grandchild may be unable to differentiate the recent past (when you were his father's age, say) from 100 years ago. Nor do most children now study history chronologically. If you are visiting something to do with your past, be prepared for misunderstandings over exactly how long ago it all happened.

Then and now:
Attitudes to discipline

After generations during which many adults believed that the best way to discipline children was with physical punishment, attitudes have changed radically. Smacking is now against the law in many countries and parents can be prosecuted for using undue force against their children.

THEN

Many parents today do not physically punish their children, preferring to find other ways to cope with unacceptable behaviour. The best that can be said for smacking is that it sometimes (temporarily) shocks a child into doing what you want.

But the arguments against it are far more persuasive. Smacking (whether with hand, belt or stick) reinforces the view that 'might is right'. And it raises the question of how much violence is acceptable: when do you know that you have hit hard enough? If you smack in the anger of the moment, you risk injuring a child; if you leave it until you have cooled down, the punishment is unrelated to the crime – and in fact seems even more callous.

Smacking does little good. Children who are physically punished for a misdemeanour remember their anger and resentment at the pain inflicted, rather than the nature of the offence that caused the punishment. Briefly explaining why behaviour is unacceptable is more likely to lead to acceptable behaviour in the future.

It is hard when the media appears to back the perception that standards of behaviour are declining not to voice the opinion that 'I was smacked and it didn't do me any harm'. In individual cases this may be true. But parents who physically abuse their children are overwhelmingly those who were severely physically punished themselves.

Setting standards

Children are impulsive and can be thoughtless time and again. They also do things that they know they shouldn't, for a number of reasons – to get attention, because they are bored, or because they simply 'feel like it'. Every parent learns that disciplining a child is necessary sometimes.

Discipline teaches children the meaning of right and wrong; it helps them to learn self-control; teaches respect for others' feelings; helps them cope with the real world; and keeps them safe. Children respond to and like limits, but they must be reasonable and there should not be too many of them.

NOW

ALTERNATIVES TO SMACKING

These are the most common ways in which parents show disapproval of their children's behaviour. Your grandchild may behave better when he is with you than at home, but if you need to discipline him, check in advance what his parents do.

- **Time-outs**

These can be used from toddlerhood onward. The idea is that you pick a place where the child who has offended sits for a short, specified period of time. This gives him an opportunity to consider his actions. Time-outs don't work for some children, who simply go to their room and have a relaxing time reading or playing. But for a child who dislikes being away from the rest of the family, a short period in his room is a punishment. And, of course, sending him to his room even for a few minutes gives everyone time to 'cool off'.

- **Loss of privileges**

This includes such measures as withholding pocket money, cancelling specific trips or outings, and banning favourite TV programmes or computer time. These can work, but it is important to consider others too: cancelling a play visit by a friend punishes the friend, too, and calling off an outing deprives other members of the family who would have enjoyed it.

- **Task-giving**

This is a way of appropriating otherwise free time that would be spent in enjoyable pursuits. The problems are that children then associate tasks that you might expect of them – washing up, raking the leaves – with punishments and there is a time lag between the offence and the punishment.

Don't withhold affection as a punishment: disapprove of your grandchild's behaviour by all means, but not of him.

Discipline should be consistent. The children who grow up with fewer problems are those who come from homes where discipline is consistent; whether it is strict or lax is less important. If your grandchild stays with you, it is important to know where his parents set the limits and vital not to go against their wishes, simply because he is 'on holiday' with you.

At school

When you and perhaps even your children were at school, discipline began with humiliation, standing in a corner or outside the head teacher's office. More serious offences, however, were physically punished either by the class teacher or the head of the school.

Most schools today have a code of behaviour which is explained to pupils. Teachers rely on a consensus between parents, pupils and teachers to maintain acceptable standards. For persistent code violations, teachers have the right to exclude a pupil, for one or more days. The final sanction is expulsion.

When grandchildren come to stay

Ensuring a happy and trouble-free visit

Having grandchildren to stay can be fun, for you and for them. But it can also be a worrying time. Will they miss their parents? What will you do if one is sick? How can you make sure they have enough sleep? If they are familiar with your home and have stayed overnight with or without their parents almost from birth, staying alone or extending the stay is unlikely to cause problems. But if your grandchildren have not spent the night before there are some factors to consider.

Recalling parents

Establish with your child the circumstances under which he or she wants to be called back to your house, but be guided by your instincts. If your grandchild is staying on his own and becomes genuinely distressed, you must call his parents. If you have more than one child staying, peer pressure may help the one who is least happy to settle, but don't let the situation escalate so that you have three unhappy children instead of one.

Don't put yourself in the position of being unable to get hold of parents for more than a few hours until you have had several practice runs, gradually increasing the time the children spend with you. If the proposed first visit to you is an extended stay while the parents are away, you may prefer to refuse, rather than run the risk of having inconsolable children for several days.

Bedtime

Talk through in advance what you might expect at bedtime – some children protest vehemently at the thought of going to bed, but settle once they are actually there. Agree with their mother or father in front of the children what time they should go to bed. Take into account that they might be excited at the thought of staying at your house and be prepared to be a little flexible, but don't override parents' wishes.

In the half hour or so before they go to bed, make sure children are calm and relaxed, rather than running around getting

Most five to eight year olds view sleeping away from home without their parents as a sign that they are 'grown up' and may look forward eagerly to the day their parents leave them at your house. After a couple of short trips, staying with you can become an integral part of some of their school holidays and provide an ideal opportunity to catch up on what you have all been doing.

EMERGENCIES CHECKLIST

- Keep a first-aid box on hand, and make sure that supplies are replenished regularly.

- Attend a first-aid course or study an illustrated book on first aid. You may be happy to deal with cuts and 'foreign bodies', but it is essential to know how to react in an emergency – a child choking, losing consciousness, suffering acute burns or severe bleeding, for example. Your prompt action could save your grandchild's life.

- Adapt the home and garden safety procedures on pages 66–69 to suit the ages of the children but err on the side of caution.

- If a child is unwell while at your house, be guided by your instincts. Remember that childhood illness comes on very quickly. Monitor his temperature and if it goes over 38.6°C (101°F) call the doctor. If in doubt, call the doctor and his parents.

- If you can't reach a doctor, ring for an ambulance, giving details of your grandchild's age and symptoms.

overexcited. A suitable short video or television programme, a book or a quiet game with you, may calm them down. When it is time for bed, turn the television off – even if you intend to watch later – so that they don't have the excuse that they might be missing something.

Check whether the children have a set bedtime routine but again be prepared to be flexible. If you are telling, rather than reading a story, for example, novelty value may mean that they want you to tell another. Once you have finished, however, settle them down, say goodnight and leave the room. Find out in advance whether they are used to a nightlight or leave a light on in the hallway so that they can find the bathroom or you during the night.

If a child gets out of bed again, take him back straightaway. Settle him down, perhaps sit with him for a while, but be firm. It is past bedtime and he should be in bed. Requests for food or drink – or a wish to go to the toilet again – are likely to be delaying tactics. Let him go to the bathroom once and bring him a drink of water in case he is genuinely thirsty, but refuse subsequent requests. Leave the room, but say that you will be back in 10 minutes to check on him. Make sure that you return after the set time.

A child who sleepwalks may worry you but is unlikely to come to any harm. Don't wake him, but gently guide him back to bed. If a child wets his bed, don't make a fuss. Change him and the bed as quickly and quietly as you can and settle him back down to sleep.

Saying no

Some people find it difficult to say no to anyone and it is doubly hard to say no to a loved grandchild. But most children like bounds and respect those who set them.

- If you genuinely can't agree to a request, say no calmly. You don't have to give a reason; in fact, doing so may embroil you in an argument. Simple reasons that don't invite a reply – 'It's too late', 'Nobody plays football indoors here' – are best.

- If he shouts or cries, let him. Remember that you are probably getting a diluted version of how he manifests annoyance at home. When the temper fit has passed, hug him and remind him that you love him, but don't change your mind over the issue that caused the problem.

- If he still won't accept your decision, leave the room for a short time so that he has a chance to reassess the situation and you are not tempted to give in.

- When you return, change the subject, suggest something else to play, or talk animatedly about what to do tomorrow. Don't mention the disagreement again.

Making your home a haven

Providing a welcome environment for your young visitor

When your grandchildren come to stay, they leave familiar toys and games behind and enter an adult environment. It is important, therefore, that there are some child-centred areas of the house and some toys that they can remember from one visit to the next.

A room of their own

If you have the space, it is a good idea if children have their own room at your house. It isn't necessary to decorate it especially for children – they will outgrow it too quickly – but try to make it light and bright. Add some pictures on the wall and choose lights and bed covers that will appeal to them. Make sure that there is at least one drawer for each child to put clothes in and somewhere to hang things.

If your guest room is shared, put away the adult trappings before your grandchildren arrive. Keep some children's books to replace the adult ones on the shelves and swap some of the pictures on the wall for ones more suitable for children. Don't worry too much about furniture but put away any ornaments and make sure that there are no sharp corners or other hazards on furniture.

Keep a small toy cupboard especially for your grandchildren. Remember that variety is important: if you have only what they have at home, there is less point in coming to play at your house. Some sort of construction set, plenty of paper and crayons or felt tips, with perhaps some small dolls or cars and something to play with outdoors, such as a ball, will be enough for a first visit of a couple of days – if they are to stay longer, make sure they bring favourites from home.

If more than one set of children play with toys, some breakages are inevitable. One way to minimise potential distress is to buy one small

Staying with you often gives your grandchild an opportunity to be younger than her years and indulge in favourite games and pastimes from her preschool days. If you have a box of dressing-up clothes – especially if they belonged to you or to her mother – you and your young grandchild will have hours of fun.

Your home is perhaps the only place where your grandchild can enjoy old-fashioned games. You may find yourself involved in endless games of snakes and ladders, for example.

new toy or game each time a child comes to stay. In this way, all the children have the excitement of opening something new before they realise that a former favourite is no longer there. Children also find toys that their parents owned fascinating, so if you managed to hold on to some of those, produce them as a special treat.

Telling tales

If the house in which you live is also the one in which your son or daughter grew up, your grandchild is likely to be captivated by stories of his or her young life there. Don't limit your tales to particular exploits – the time he climbed the tree in the garden and couldn't get down, for example – but include his habits too, such as where he kept his toys, which were his favourite hiding places and how his room was arranged. If you have photographs or even film of your child, so much the better.

What to play

If you have not been around children since your own were young, you may be tempted to try to organise an activity for every minute they are with you. Most children in this age group, however, are happy playing alone for some of the time and easily tire if they never have a quiet moment to sit with a book or watch a video. Some only children are very keen on company and will happily chat to you for hours, others are far more self-reliant, but they will all want time alone.

Organise some games and join in their play when they ask you to (or offer to do so if you think they would like it), but don't be afraid to include your grandchildren in some of your daily activities such as shopping or dusting. Arrange one or two outings over the course of their stay and if they complain that they are bored, be ready to improvise – go to the park, bake some biscuits, make glove puppets out of old socks, buttons and scraps of wool.

CASE HISTORY

As soon as we saw the house, I knew which room was going to be the one I set aside for the 'babies'. It was lovely and light and just across the hall from the bathroom. I didn't decorate it to appeal to children, but I had a patchwork quilt that my mother had made and a lovely rug a friend had brought back from a trip, so they immediately gave the room some colour.

I still had a few of my own toys, including a very bald dog and a rag doll that my grandmother made when I was born. I also had quite a few of my daughter's toys that she had long forgotten – a tea set, some building blocks and a couple of cuddly toys.

I've always liked children's books and already had quite a collection, but once my daughter had children, I started adding to it so that now there is a whole bookcase full of things to read that are special to Granny's house. Every so often, I buy something new to take account of the fact that they are growing, but usually the children can't wait to get up to 'their' room and find all 'their' toys when they come to stay.

Family holidays

Special days and weeks with your children and grandchildren

Spending a week or two with your grandchildren and their parents is an appealing prospect and obviously stands most chance of being successful if you know that you can live together amicably – if you often spend weekends at each other's homes, for example. It is a good idea to have this sort of 'dry run' before you embark on a costly trip.

The other factor that contributes to success is to recognise that you all have different needs. A holiday on which you are all expected to do the same thing is less likely to work than one on which you please yourselves, going off in ones and twos when you feel like it, and gathering as a family at other times.

On whose terms?

If your child has asked you to join the family holiday, check in advance what your role is going to be. If you suspect – or know – that you are being asked to serve as babysitters, agree to go only if you are prepared to act in this capacity. Of course you may be happy to sit once or twice if the parents want an evening out, but you want a holiday for yourselves too. Also, don't assume that your child's reasons are altruistic and their partner's manipulative: all parents can be quite thoughtless in these circumstances.

Areas of conflict

Even the best relationships can start to crack once you are all under the same roof. There are three potential minefields in a family holiday – who does what, who pays for what and arguments about the children.

If your family is doing its own cooking, discuss in advance who will do which chores. It is obviously unfair if one person does all the cooking or all the cleaning. Although it may seem rather formal, it is probably worth compiling a roster for the major chores (include over-fives – they can help wash and dry dishes). Otherwise the most houseproud – possibly you – will do more than a fair share. If you think that you are being expected to do too much, say so calmly. Don't wait until you feel resentful or allow yourself to be a martyr. If

A week or two away from the domestic routine in beautiful or interesting surroundings can be idyllic. Make sure it works for everyone by discussing areas of potential conflict in advance.

If you are clear about the ground rules, special family occasions such as anniversaries can be wonderfully happy days that your grandchildren will remember for years.

the worst happens and you have a major disagreement, don't let it spill over and ruin your grandchildren's holiday.

Discuss the financial arrangements well in advance. Also check expectations: if the family intends to eat out each evening, do you want to go along too? How much is that likely to cost? If you can't afford to do as they do, say so. Conversely, if you are considerably better off than they are, don't insist on treating at every turn. Simply offer to take them all out for a meal, for example, or perhaps take the children somewhere special.

When they are on an exciting holiday, even the best-behaved children can lose all control. But discipline is a matter for their parents. If you are in charge, follow the parents' guidelines – giving children two sets of rules to live up to is not fair.

Family occasions

Getting the whole family together for religious festivals or public holidays – especially when you don't live close – can be an occasion to treasure. On the other hand, it is worth remembering that such gatherings can be very stressful for many people. Family members often speak to and treat each other in ways they would never dream of repeating with their friends.

If you are the host

• Usually you will be in charge of menu planning, so it is up to you to decide how much you want others to do. You may like to ask for suggestions or contributions of particular dishes from different members of the family. Think in advance about who you will allow to help you in the kitchen on the day, what exactly you will ask them to do, and for how long.

• Do you think there will be conflicts over the children's behaviour? If this is a potential problem, discuss with the parents what you expect. Try to be flexible in your standards – it's unrealistic to expect excited children to sit at the table until all have finished eating, for example – but be sure to tell parents that you will intervene if they don't when you feel that a grandchild's behaviour is getting out of hand.

If you are a guest

• Offer to help, but if your offer is refused, don't interfere. If what annoys you – empty glasses left unwashed, children's toys all over the floor – does not bother the hosts, let well alone. Don't assume they haven't seen them: they probably have and are genuinely unconcerned.

• If you find a grandchild's behaviour unacceptable but her parents say nothing, keep quiet. Have a word with her parents later if you must, but be prepared for nothing to be done.

• Don't compare the occasion – favourably or otherwise – with a previous year. This is unfair to your hosts. Again, be wary of any tendency to praise your son or daughter at the expense of your daughter-in-law or son-in-law.

• Don't offer advice on any aspect of the food or other arrangements. Be considerate, thoughtful, complimentary, open-minded. Your host's way of making cranberry sauce or pancakes is likely to be as good as yours. And refrain from making remarks of the 'I always make my own cakes rather than buy them from a shop' kind.

Shared skills: swimming

Making your grandchild safe in the water

Today, many schools do not offer swimming as a routine part of the curriculum for children as young as eight, with the result that unless your grandchild has lessons at a nearby pool he is reliant on his family to teach him this skill. If you can swim and are fairly fit – or if you think that you would benefit from the exercise – this is a role that you could consider taking on.

Many parents do not have the time (and may not have the skill) to devote to sports coaching of any sort. And, in many cases, children are reluctant to accept their parents as teachers. You, however, can probably devote time to the activity, may well have greater reserves of patience than his parents and are almost certainly a more acceptable teacher to your grandchild.

If he is not used to the swimming pool, it is best to go a few times before you start teaching. The sounds and smells of the pool will be unfamiliar, he has to be prepared to be splashed, for other swimmers to make waves, for his hair to be wet and his head to go under water. Encourage him to hold his nose and submerge his head. He may also need time to adjust to your new role as his instructor.

Mastering the art

Making lessons too long and tiring is likely to be counterproductive: little and often is the best way to learn. Leave some time to play before and after your lesson and have a drink and snack afterwards, perhaps while you watch other swimmers.

The steps that follow cover the basics that should be mastered in learning to swim. It is worth contacting your local pool or national swimming association for advice on the best ways to teach a child (or read a book on the subject), but what suits one child may not work for another. And be patient – some children learn quickly; others take many months to become proficient.

It is sensible to have one adult to look after each child at this age. By turning a trip to the pool into a family occasion, you can keep an eye on children with different levels of expertise. You will probably find that you enjoy the exercise, too.

Knowing she has something to keep her afloat increases your grandchild's confidence in the water. Make sure it is safety approved. An inflatable ring will still be fun to play with when she can swim competently.

A child who is having fun is likely to master this skill more easily than one who finds it a chore, so make sure your grandchild keeps up other activities too: he will soon become bored if he has no other outlets for his energy and enthusiasm.

Use a flotation aid your grandchild finds comfortable – armbands are the most popular – and start by supporting him while he floats, so that he gets used to the feeling of not having his feet on the bottom of the pool. Next, try to get him to move through the water with his feet off the bottom. This is more difficult than it sounds. You may find it helps to hold his hands and 'pull' him along as he paddles with his feet. Show him how to kick his feet.

When he can do this, let go of one arm, then the other. Encourage him to paddle his hands, while keeping up the movement with his feet. Work towards a good overarm movement. Gradually increase the distance he paddles. The easiest way to do this is for him to start at the side of the pool and swim to you – you, of course, are standing farther and farther away as his confidence grows. The next step is to reduce his reliance on the armbands. Either gradually decrease the air in them, or encourage him to try for increasing periods without them.

Non-swimming grandparents

If you can't swim yourself, you could consider enrolling both yourself and your grandchild for a course of lessons (many pools offer pre-holiday crash coaching for adults and courses for children during the school holidays). Or offer to take your grandchild to lessons: courses at weekends are often over-subscribed, so if you are free during the week, you will be doing his parents a favour.

If you can't swim, you may have to rule out trips to the pool unless a swimming parent comes, too. Although the water is shallow in children's pools and you may never be out of your depth, you must be able to cope in an emergency. But once your grandchild is older and can swim confidently, you could invite one of his friends along and watch them, initially from the poolside, then from the spectators' gallery. Make sure that you do watch – your grandchild will expect you to notice everything he does.

Shared skills: handicrafts

Teaching your grandchild to sew and knit

In the past most girls – in particular – learned to knit and sew through economic expediency. It was cheaper to knit school sweaters than to buy them; a dress that could be let out or rehemmed might last another summer; darning socks gave them a few more weeks of life.

Higher living standards and a shift towards a more disposable society have meant that this is no longer so crucial and as a result it is easy to forget the many benefits of learning to knit and sew. Both build on children's manual dexterity: manipulating knitting needles or a needle and thread are completely different from manipulating a pencil or moulding clay. They give children the satisfaction of producing something, whether a finished tapestry to frame as a gift or a scarf to keep a doll or teddy warm in winter. And they offer a means of expressing

individuality (two children who start off with the same pattern and colour wool will still produce individual pieces of knitwear).

If you are a knitter or skilled in needlecraft, it may be second nature to try to pass these skills on to your grandchildren, boys as well as girls. (After all, traditional fishermen's sweaters were produced by men, and many of the world's renowned names in knitwear design are men.)

A child who has grown up seeing you occupied with either of these crafts is more likely to be eager to have a go and may ask for your help. But don't rule yourself out if handicrafts are not a special hobby. As long as you know the basics, are keen to pass them on, can remember some of the frustration involved in learning and have plenty of patience, your grandchild will find that you are an acceptable teacher.

Once she has mastered the basics – casting on and off, knit, purl and perhaps increasing and decreasing – the scope for knitting projects is enormous. If she is enthusiastic, look for simple patterns – something for a baby, for example – and pass on the skill of reading them, too.

Where to start

Set aside a time when you are not likely to be interrupted. It is often easier, with knitting in particular, to sit your grandchild on your knee so that you can help him position his hands correctly. But if he is too big or reluctant, sit next to him.

You can buy starter kits for knitting, embroidery and tapestry. Aimed at children, these are ideal if you are unsure what size needles to use, for example, or perhaps don't know what your grandchild might be able to achieve without getting bored. But they are not really necessary. If you have a full sewing basket or knitting bag you are almost certain to have something suitable for a beginner. Short, thick knitting needles are easier for children to handle; with sewing the longer and thicker the needle, the better. Bright threads and wools are more popular than sombre colours.

What to knit

Scarves for teddies and dolls are an obvious, easy place to start. You can knit a whole scarf in one colour, or teach him how to join colours in stripes. An older child in the five to eight age group may be able to knit a scarf for himself, as long as he really wants to try. Knitted squares and diamonds can be sewn together (you may have to do this) to make pram covers and blankets.

A child who shows a real interest can probably manage mittens: use a circular needle and be prepared to do the shaping yourself if he runs into problems. There are also many patterns for knitted soft toys.

What to sew

Tapestry pictures are a good place to start; choose one that is appropriate for his age and which will make a picture he likes. Alternatively, try a simple stencilled embroidery design that can be filled using only one or two different stitches.

Curtains or bedcovers for a dolls' house are easy for beginners. A simple skirt or a dress for a large doll are also good projects

You may have to offer to sew on badges for sporting prowess yourself, even after your grandchild is proficient with a needle: the fine stitches needed require greater control than many eight year olds can manage.

to start with. And for older children a drawstring bag can hold anything from small pieces of jewellery to dolls' clothes, depending on size (make this extra special by helping to glue on beads or sequins, or applying an iron-on appliqué design).

Tips for success
Do:
• Be prepared for mistakes: dropped stitches, knotted thread, crinkled backgrounds
• Give help when he asks for help
• Resist the temptation to take over or 'do a few rows – or a bit of sky – to make it grow' unless he specifically asks you to.

Don't:
• Criticise his choice of project
• Suggest a long-term project: he will be bored by his slow progress
• Give up too easily: if he doesn't like knitting, try crochet; if tapestry doesn't appeal, suggest patchwork or appliqué
• Pressurise him if he really isn't happy; put it all away for a few months until his hand-control has improved, then try again.

Common dilemma: Am I jealous?

When the other grandparents seem to have it all

A good relationship with your grandchild's other grandparents can prevent slightly awkward situations developing into real problems. If they are your friends, it is often easier to remember that they are not trying to 'upstage' you: they are simply acting in what they believe to be your grandchild's best interests – as you are.

It is a common occurrence: you buy your grandchild a book you are sure he will enjoy, only to find his other grandparents have bought a bicycle; you take him to the cinema for a treat, his other grandparents spend a couple of days at a theme park with him. You see your grandchild for a couple of weekends a year, while his other grandparents are frequent visitors. How you cope with such inequalities can be the difference between happy and uncomfortable family relationships.

Financial concerns

If differences in your financial situations bother you, talk to your child. He or she may be unaware of your feelings. A word to his or her partner who can mention the matter to the other grandparents may make you more comfortable. They may simply be unaware that their generosity is embarrassing you or making you feel awkward. It is important to remember, however, that all grandparents want the best for their grandchildren and to some people that includes the best materially. If they can afford it, why shouldn't they give now? It is a persuasive argument.

Also bear in mind past circumstances. Age may be a factor here: perhaps you helped your child and his or her partner when they were setting up their home, when the in-laws were still educating younger children; now that you are retired and they are still working, it is their 'turn' to give. This does not mean that your contribution was or is any less valuable.

Your grandchild's perspective

Children tend to take things at face value. Just as some grandparents are more active than others (see pp. 90–1), so one set may take them on different sorts of outings and offer different kinds of gifts. Five and six year olds also have a limited concept of the value of gifts – if they consider the question

CASE HISTORY

My granddaughter's other grandparents were overgenerous to her – to my mind – right from the start. One of the first things they did was pay to have her professionally photographed when she was a few weeks old. They are lovely photographs but at the time I rather resented it. And so it went on: they took the whole family on holiday each year and bought our granddaughter expensive presents. I tried not to be uncharitable, but Charlotte didn't play with many of the things they bought – the toys needed more manipulative hands than hers, or the batteries kept running out, or they took too long to set up and she got bored waiting to play. I talked to my daughter, but her attitude was 'They can afford it. Where's the harm?'.

Matters came to a head one Christmas when we all shared a cottage by the sea.

We'd bought Charlotte a kite. Her other grandparents bought a rocking horse which of course bowled Charlotte over. She'd have eaten her meals sitting on it if we'd let her. But a day later, she was bored with 'Black Beauty'. The sun came out and my husband took Charlotte down to the beach to fly her kite. They were gone for hours and came back exhausted but with very rosy cheeks.

The night before we left I heard my daughter and Charlotte talking and couldn't help eavesdropping. My daughter asked what she had liked most about the holiday. Charlotte replied with no hesitation: 'Flying my kite with Granddad. I like that Granddad.' I realised how foolish I had been all these years – it was the time we spent with her that she valued and I should have been doing the same.

at all. For this reason, a gift that costs a little will be as welcome as one that costs a lot if it is something your grandchild wants. It costs nothing to listen to him and decide on the perfect present.

A lot depends on his parents' attitude. If they treat all gifts the same – to be received with thanks – your grandchild is likely to do so as well. The same goes for outings: if your grandchild looks forward to a day with you, where you go and what you do are secondary to the fact of your company. He is unlikely in any case to know who pays for what. He knows that he goes to a holiday resort with his other grandparents for a week, not that they foot the bill.

It is also a truism that money doesn't buy affection. Your grandchild loves you for who you are, not the material things you give him. In later life he is as likely to remember an afternoon when you took him on a picnic as he is that he had the best seats at a children's play each Christmas or

went to a theme park before anyone else in his class.

Give what you can. If this is time rather than money, don't undervalue yourself. No parent gives their child as much time and attention as they feel they should, and these are commodities that are priceless.

Time constraints

If you are grandparenting at a distance and the others live close – or have a large house that makes extended stays more practical – don't waste time and energy bemoaning your situation. Make the most of the time you spend with your grandchild and find other ways of being close. You may find that you know as much about what he is doing from a scheduled weekly chat on the telephone as the grandparents who see him a couple of times a week: he may be less likely to interrupt his routine – playing with friends, going to sports practice and so on – for their more frequent visits.

Understanding the jargon
Computers and computer technology

Computers are a fact of your grandchild's existence. He may have one at home and is likely to have used one at nursery school. Now that he is at school he will be more than familiar with how to switch one on, load a program, use the mouse, play a game or type a short story and shut down when he has finished. And he may well have a console which can be used with a TV or computer monitor for games at home or a portable machine so that he can play games in the car or on the bus or train.

If you use a computer every day, you will probably consider this early introduction to new technology an excellent idea; if you are unfamiliar with them, you may be baffled by his enthusiasm and some of the jargon.

Whatever you think of the desirability of your grandchild sitting for long periods in front of a computer screen or battling against himself on a portable mini-games machine, it is worth making an effort to understand at least the basics of computing if you want to be able to communicate with him. There are several ways in which you can keep up to date with developments.

• Hands-on experience
If your grandchild is more knowledgeable than you, ask him to show you what he is doing. Although you might feel reluctant to admit your ignorance, he will be delighted to know something that you don't. But if you think that he will be too quick for you, and you prefer to grasp at least the basics in advance, enrol on a course at a local school or college. Or visit a computer show, and perhaps take your grandchild along to show you the ropes. (Ring in advance to check which days and times are likely to be the least busy.)

• Books and magazines
Some computer books are too technical for beginners, although many of those aimed at absolute beginners are fine. The problem with books, however, is that by the time they are produced technology has moved on. Magazines can keep you up to date with what is happening, but some of them assume a basic knowledge. You may need to browse through several before you find one that meets your needs. Alternatively, ask for help in a specialist shop or specialist department of a book shop.

Some non-specialist magazines aimed at younger readers review new games and programs for computers and consoles. Some newspapers have weekly computer supplements; check the children's page of the newspaper for reviews of games.

If you are considering a purchase – either for yourself or as a gift for your grandchild – ask around to find out which store or warehouse is best in your area. Pick a time when the assistants are not too busy and when an enthusiast can demonstrate exactly what a machine can do.

COMMON TERMS EXPLAINED

CD-ROM An optical disk read by laser that stores words, music and animated pictures. This cannot be altered or wiped by mistake.

E-mail A method of sending messages from one computer to another.

Format To prepare a disk so that information can be written on to it or read off it.

Games console A machine that plays CD-ROMs containing games programs. Most consoles use the TV screen or a computer monitor.

Hardware The pieces of the computer itself: the screen or monitor, hard drive, keyboard, mouse and printer.

Interactive A program that allows you to control it by changing the story. Many children's games are interactive.

Internet A very large worldwide computer network, consisting of smaller networks and computers linked together so that they can communicate and exchange information.

Modem A device by which a computer is linked to a phone line, necessary for sending e-mails or connecting to the World Wide Web.

Mouse A plastic device, connected to the computer by a cable, which enables you to move around the screen, draw an image or select a course of action from a menu.

Program A set of instructions that tells a computer how to do a particular task.

RAM This stands for random access memory and describes the temporary memory in which data and programs are stored while the computer is using them.

ROM Read only memory: a permanent memory that stores data even if the computer is switched off.

Software The programs and instructions that allow you to use the computer to perform various tasks.

Virtual reality Technology that creates the illusion of a three-dimensional world in which you play a part and are able to influence action.

World Wide Web The largest of the Internet services, containing a vast quantity of information. Advertisers and others wanting to make information available to the public set up what is known as a web site.

● **TV, video and radio**

Many children's TV and radio programmes feature reviews of new games, often compiled by young players. These will give you some idea of what may be worth buying or renting to play with your grandchild. Some interactive CDs are 'trailed' on videos that your grandchild may see. These are likely to be extensions of or related to feature film releases.

Buying software

Some computer games have a short life, but others are played over and over again, so it is probably worth asking what he would like before you buy. Games usually work with only one make of computer or games console (although some are produced in different formats), so check compatibility.

Depending on your grandchild's interests, consider some of the more enduring games you know, many of which have now been produced for computer. Simple games like hangman (for younger children) and solitaire exist for computer, as does chess (for older children in this age range). You can also play tennis, golf or soccer on screen. Try a special games shop, computer warehouse or a large toy warehouse.

More educational CD-ROMs can make good gifts, but check with his parents or with your grandchild which ones he uses at school (some like to have them at home too). Many bookshops have good multimedia departments, where you may be able to try out a CD-ROM you are considering buying. The range here is usually limited to reference rather than 'fun' titles.

From a distance
Keeping in touch with a schoolchild who lives far away

It gets easier to be a long-distance grandparent as children get older. You can encourage parents to keep on sending you photographs and videos, but your grandchild himself is now better able to take the initiative and keep you in touch with what is happening in his life.

The telephone
Although you can communicate by phone with your grandchild as soon as he can talk, 'conversations' are largely one way. These develop over the years – as your grandchild's vocabulary and understanding of language improve, and as his horizons widen, he has more to tell you about. A child of five has a vocabulary of 3,000 to 5,000 words and you can expect to have fairly lengthy conversations with him.

Let him tell you what he has been doing. Even if you know something exciting has

A child can record the minutiae of a day at school on a single-use camera, giving you an ideal insight into her daily life.

happened, allow him to fill you in on the more mundane parts of his week (they are interesting to him) before you ask. If possible, wait for him to call you, so that he does so at a time when he wants to talk, rather than play or watch TV. Encourage him to ask permission before he uses the phone – asking to speak to Mum or Dad after you have spoken to him will prevent him from running up large bills without their knowledge. If cost is a problem, keep the conversation reasonably short.

Writing and drawing
As they move through their first couple of years at school, children's ability to write improves and many happily spend time practising their handwriting, either by writing stories about themselves or others or by spelling out words. Encourage this by asking your grandchild to send you any stories he has written of which he is proud, lists of his friends, who was at a certain party, any new books or videos he has been given and so on. Until his writing is proficient, he might like to complement these pieces with drawings or paintings.

Try to avoid 'one-way traffic'; write letters to him. Keep them short and simple to begin with, and gradually increase their length and the complexity of the words you

You can encourage your grandchild to write letters by sending him stationery and pens, and perhaps – if you live in the same country – adding a few stamps so that it is easy for him to mail you a letter as soon as it is finished.

use. Telling him what you have been doing is an excellent way to get him to reciprocate.

Technological developments mean that it is possible to write a letter on a computer and send it to another computer (this is more expensive than conventional mail but cheaper than a telephone call). If you and your grandchild have access to computers, investigate the possibilities of e-mail.

Recording daily life

If your grandchild has a cassette recorder, try sending him cassettes on which to record his activities, or make up stories for you. Again this need not be one way: tell him what you have been doing on tape, too.

If you want visual reminders of important occasions – or even simple daily routines – send him a single-use camera every so often. You can make specific requests, like asking him to take it to school, if his teacher agrees – it could be a good activity for the end of term – or leave him to decide what to photograph. Expect a few shots of the sky or ground until he is competent with the camera. It's unfair to ask him to document his own birthday party, otherwise he'll be too busy to enjoy it, but he could take pictures when friends come to play, on a day out, or of his pets or the garden. Keep his photographs in a separate album or box so that when he comes to stay he can look through them with you.

LINGUISTIC BARRIERS

If you speak a different language from your grandchild, you may face problems. When you live close by, it is easy to talk to a child in more than one tongue from birth: children brought up bilingual rarely have problems telling their two languages apart. If you live at a distance, however, you are unlikely to be able to communicate enough to allow a child to pick up your language.

There are no easy solutions. You may feel, justifiably, that you should preserve your own language and culture, and that learning a new language in middle age is not an option, even if it is the official language of the country in which you now live. You may also feel resentful that your child no longer uses your native tongue and has not passed it on to your grandchild.

Try not to criticise: your son or daughter has almost certainly taken the decision not to speak your language to your grandchild in what they consider his best interests. Perhaps your child has moved to a different community or to a new country and is trying to fit in – and wants to ensure that your grandchild does too. You could, however, try pointing out what that will mean for your relationship with him. His other grandparents may be allies for you here.

You could suggest that your grandchild might learn your language, and perhaps in return learn some words of his tongue so that you can communicate by telephone. If you don't, keep in touch with photographs and videos, and – with his parents' permission – perhaps send stories or songs in your language to your grandchild so that he does not grow up unaware of his heritage.

CHAPTER SIX

The Older Schoolchild
8 to 12 years

This is likely to be one of the most enjoyable and satisfying stages in your grandchild's life. She has passed through the physical struggles of infancy, grasped the fundamental differences between right and wrong, and learned to communicate clearly. Although she is on the road to independence, with her own ideas about who she is and what she likes, she nevertheless retains much of her childish enthusiasm and innocence.

This is the time to enjoy taking your grandchild on outings, choosing gifts for her, showing her skills which will stay with her forever, talking about and, more importantly, listening to what she is interested in and what she has found out about life. A child's developing mental capacities are thought to be most active at this pre-puberty stage. Your grandchild will be articulate, appreciative and challenging. Whatever you do and say to her now, she will remember in the future. This is the beginning of her real friendship with you.

What 8 to 12 year olds like doing

Making the most of your grandchild's unbridled new enthusiasms

Between the ages of 8 and 12 children acquire strong views on how they want to spend their leisure time. They may play games their parents have never played; become passionate about subjects of which the adults around them are more or less ignorant; or take up a new hobby simply because their peers are interested. Such steps are part of the child's growing independence. As a grandparent you can support and enjoy the untrammelled enthusiasm with which children of this age approach new interests.

You can encourage and share in your grandchild's newly discovered activity when her interest might otherwise dwindle due to lack of parental involvement or input. You may remember from your own parenting – and constantly witness now – that there can be days, even weeks, when all that parents can cope with are the basic necessities of childrearing, work and housekeeping. But you may be able to participate fully in your grandchild's chosen pastime and make the most of this rewarding phase of her life.

Sports

A grandchild who shows a keen interest in sport can be introduced by you to games she may never have considered before. If football is her current enthusiasm, taking her along to watch professional games will stimulate her interest, but consider spending time on other ball games too. Your local library or leisure centre should be able to provide information about courses available, especially during school holidays, to improve ball skills and teach different sports. You may be lucky enough to find some which allow you both to play.

Make your role one of learning as well as teaching and encouraging. It will please your grandchild enormously if she can teach you as well as receive knowledge from you. Learning how to play a game or sport together will be an experience both of you will always remember, and it will bring an extra closeness to your relationship.

Before you offer to enrol your grandchild on a course, consult her parents. They may have plans for her to learn what you had in mind at another time, or for her to learn something different. In the majority of cases, the parents will be delighted that you are willing to give your time to their child. However, it is equally important, before you get carried away by the idea of beginning yoga or sub-aqua classes together, that you know the child's true feelings on the subject.

If she is only trying to please you when she says she is happy for you both to take a course, hesitation or lack of eye contact

Young muscles are easily strained. With high-impact sports such as tennis, badminton or squash, check that the playing surface is suitable and include some gentle warm-up and cool-down exercises before and after coaching.

Most weekend teams lack volunteers to fulfil every role, so don't let the fact that you can't play rule out your participation. Her parents will be delighted if you can ensure that your grandchild gets to and from a venue safely with all her kit.

when she is speaking will give her misgivings away. Don't question her – that will make her feel uncomfortable. It is simpler to book a course for her to participate in by herself and to accompany her there and take an interest in how she gets on. Although children of this age are usually still keen on adult participation, she may fear her friends will behave insensitively towards her if you were actually to take part.

If your grandchild is already involved in a team or group activity, extra adult help is almost sure to be welcome, whether in the form of coaching, setting up nets and providing refreshments or driving children to and from the venue. At this level, involvement can be addictive, and after running along the sidelines for a few weeks you will be amazed at how much fitter you feel. While support and encouragement are always valued by children, don't become

too loudly partisan – this is the age at which children are easily embarrassed by the adults around them.

If you are keen to pass on to your grandchild your skills in a chosen sport, consult your local bookshop or library to find out how the game is taught to children. The last thing you want to do is put her off by making it seem too difficult. Put yourself in her shoes and at her height and strength and keep sessions short.

Skating, skateboarding, swimming and cycling are high on the list of physical pastimes for this age group. Although you may prefer not to indulge in skateboarding, you could take your grandchild to some good, safe sites so that she can enjoy herself. If cycling is her passion, you could take up this form of exercise yourself. Remember that adults need helmets, too.

Sedentary interests

Many 8 to 12s have boundless energy, but they also enjoy indoor pastimes. Computers feature prominently and at this age she will be more than competent. This is an area in which your grandchild may have much to teach you, or you can consider taking a course for adult beginners at a local school or college.

You should not try to become too knowledgeable, however, since this is doubtless a skill that your grandchild is proud of. Don't dismiss computer games out of hand: many encourage manual dexterity, quick thinking and problem-solving. If you enjoy chess, buy a computer chess program, since your grandchild may be more eager to play in this format than to sit at a traditional board.

Computers aside, you can entice your grandchild to play card games, board games, darts, anything you have played in the past or have always wanted to try. Children of this age love to learn new skills and providing you teach gently and do not resort to over-competitiveness, your grandchild will become your most enjoyable games partner.

Gifts for 8 to 12 year olds

Inventive presents for older children

Do not assume that buying presents for this age group involves expense: children genuinely appreciate presents that are unusual and surprising.

Along with her growing sense of independence, your grandchild will have ideas about what she would like to buy if she could afford it, so gifts of small amounts of money will be most acceptable, as long as her parents don't object. Make these gifts irregular to ensure that your giving is not taken for granted. Also, if your grandchild makes a habit of telling you about something she wants but cannot afford, don't respond by opening your wallet immediately – you will start to appreciate each other less.

If you want to give gift tokens rather than money, make sure that you choose an appropriate store. A grandchild with a passion for clothes may not appreciate having to buy her present from a computer store, for example. And remember that most children enjoy the sense of independence and power that money in their hands gives.

Gifts are particularly appreciated when they add to a special event. If your grandchild is going camping or on an overnight school trip for the first time you could buy a torch, sleeping bag, compass or other equipment. Children of this age like the idea of 'adventure'. Build on this by buying a map of the area she is going to visit, a book about the area's history, rations or a survival kit (from good camping stores). This sort of gift will add to her feelings of independence and excitement.

What you give can also trigger new interests. Many 8 to 12 year olds love collecting things. If your grandchild has started a collection of model cars or horses, for example, you can add to it, but if you listen to her conversation you may discover other items she could collect. Children of this age collect anything from baseball hats to reproduction Egyptian artifacts, and any additions you provide are likely to prove a success. Do not feel aggrieved if, on your next visit, one collection has been terminated in favour of a new subject; passing enthusiasms are common.

If you live far away, items received through the post will be some of the most exciting gifts of all for your grandchild, especially if they are unexpected. Things which will add to her collections – books in a series, coins, stamps, badges – will all brighten a mundane day for her, but so will gifts which let her know you were thinking of her: a coin purse you saw while you were shopping, a headband, sunglasses or cap you know would suit her. It's not the expense of the items that makes them appealing, but the concept that she is always in your thoughts.

Pets awaken children's ability to look beyond themselves and care for creatures that are smaller and more vulnerable than they are. Knowing that an animal depends on him for survival will enhance your grandchild's sense of responsibility.

twenties', in which case, gather together some appropriate outfits and organise a photo session at your local studio to indulge her fantasies.

The important thing is to give graciously and in a spirit of generosity. Give what you feel your grandchild would like and not what you think she ought to have.

The purchase of a dog or cat requires parental approval, but if you can offer holiday accommodation and live close enough to take the dog for walks when family members are busy or sick, you could give your grandchild the best present he will ever receive.

Ideas for collectables abound: writing to penfriends could provide the basis for a stamp collection; an interest in a historical period could be enhanced by some coins. Keeping abreast of her current enthusiasms will give you the inspiration to find the perfect gift.

Special occasions

For birthdays and other special occasions you may need to consult her parents to discover what is on your grandchild's 'wish list'. If she can't decide between a personal stereo and new skates, you could help her parents by offering to buy one of the items and, if necessary, sharing the cost with the other grandparents.

Children derive special pleasure from gifts they can keep and remember you by. This usually means jewellery, watches and ornaments, but at this age they are still quite young to look after valuable items. If you think that the loss of your gift would be really upsetting for you (and her), wait until your grandchild is a little older – the last thing you want to do is create guilt and stress over a gift you have given.

Children often can't think what they would like for their birthday other than the obvious 'big' items they have asked their parents for. Be inventive. If your grandchild has expressed a desire to learn to ride, consider booking a course of lessons. If this new hobby takes off you will be spoilt for choice when it comes to future gifts – hat, boots, books on horses and so on. Or perhaps she has developed a passionate interest in the Victorians or 'roaring

PRESENTS THROUGH THE POST

If you live at a distance and want to find an appropriate gift that is also easy to post, consider the following options:

• A subscription to your grandchild's favourite comic/magazine.

• Membership of her local sports centre or club.

• Adoption certificate for a dolphin/whale/wild duck (or any animal she loves that can be sponsored in this way).

• Humorous newspaper cuttings containing spelling errors or describing funny incidents made up into a book.

• Souvenirs from places you have visited without her, including postcards, little gifts and interesting information.

• A formally laid out itinerary of events planned for her next visit to you (you have to be prepared to adhere to the plan).

• A collage or photo album of the places you have been to together, the people you met, things she liked best.

Outings with 8 to 12 year olds

Exciting 'grown up' venues for your special days together

Going on outings with a child of this age is a less stressful experience than with younger children, who need so much intense supervision, or older ones, who are far more difficult to please. This should be a time when you can both thoroughly enjoy yourselves and have some memorable excursions.

Listen to what she tells you during casual conversations to gain an idea of the type of places she would like to visit. Almost all children of this age adore animals but many are opposed to zoos on moral grounds. Children who seem never to be without their football will not necessarily enjoy being a spectator as much, though many will have a favourite team and relish the opportunity to see them play. Also, by this stage your grandchild may have visited the local aquarium so many times that she is less than enthusiastic about going again. Collect ideas for outings even when one isn't imminent. Visit your nearest library, peruse local newspapers and entertainments listings to keep abreast of anything interesting that is on offer.

If sport is a shared passion, going to watch a match together provides the obvious opportunity for an outing. Such excursions should be accompanied by a trip to her favourite pizza palace or burger bar to give you time to talk about the game or answer any questions, particularly if you have chosen a sport that is new to her.

Trips to places that children may never have considered interesting are often unexpectedly successful. If her class is studying a particular historical topic you could take her to a relevant museum or exhibition. Seeing the artifacts, paintings or costumes for herself could help her school work and spark a desire for more excursions of this kind.

If you feel you have exhausted the possibilities of public transport, think again: vintage cars or buses, and steam or diesel trains are all popular. Check in advance for special excursions to make the occasion even more magical.

A picnic or twilight feast in the open air will appeal to children of this age, and if she lives in a city she will relish a trip to the country or to the beach. You can give the day a flavour of adventure by marking out a route on a road map and letting her direct the way or including a special walk to a point of interest, with plenty of rests and refreshment breaks along the way.

If your grandchild spends a great deal of time being transported by car, you could simply visit neighbouring towns and areas by public transport and allow her to lead the way in exploring when you get there. This sort of outing requires a preliminary visit by you without your grandchild to confirm that the area is safe and interesting. You also need to consult public transport services in advance to ensure that the journey is enjoyable and straightforward.

Abiding passions

Try to complement your grandchild's hobbies and pastimes: if she loves making model aeroplanes, look out for public air shows; if horses are her passion, contact the relevant society to discover when point-to-point or dressage competitions take place. Don't be put off if you have never had any involvement yourself or do not know where such events might take place. You may be surprised at what is going on in your neighbourhood.

If the big cities with their art galleries and historical sites are too far away to reach in a day, concentrate on local history. Again, contact with any relevant societies might reveal that your town has a colourful past. You may find a walk or tour which could help your grandchild discover that there are no boring places, simply boring attitudes.

The importance of friends

Children become keen on the idea of asking a friend to accompany them on outings. This is not because your grandchild finds your company boring but because this is the age at which making and breaking friends becomes all-important. Even if your grandchild seems to choose different children for different outings arbitrarily, accept how important these companions are to her. Communicate with the parents of the friend or make sure that your grandchild's parents have done so. Do not allow your grandchild to take sole charge of making the arrangements with friends who are to accompany you on an outing, however usual this may seem to her. You need to be clear about the time the friend is expected home, where she lives, and what the contact number is in case of an emergency.

The presence of an extra young person may lay you open to more coercion than normal. But the rules you follow on outings must be adhered to, whoever comes along. Run through these with your grandchild and her friend before you venture out to avoid misunderstandings or arguments about what is and is not allowed. Remember that children this age are prone to act differently when they are with friends from when you are with them one to one.

Inexpensive options

It is important to organise some outings that do not involve financial expense and treats. If your grandchild associates everything you do together with having things bought for her, the places you visit will become secondary to what the gift shop sells, which can be demoralising. Picnics, walks, going exploring, even trips to visit relatives she may not often see with her parents, can all be mingled in with the more 'glamorous' outings.

Spectator sports come into their own with many children at this age: younger children tend to be too overwhelmed by the noise and crowd to enjoy such trips. Choose seats with care: being able to follow the action easily is important to your grandchild's understanding and enjoyment.

Then and now: Education

A working partnership between teachers, parents and pupils, in which all have a valuable contribution to make and different skills to share, is today judged the most effective means of educating our children.

THEN

There is no doubt that educational theory and practice have changed a great deal since you were at school. Even your grandchild's parents are bound to comment on how different teaching methods and subject matter are from when they were pupils.

Broadly speaking, the biggest change that has taken place since you and your children went through school is that education is now more 'child centred'. Large classrooms in which children are seated at fixed desks all facing the lecturing teacher at the front are not now viewed as the best way of stimulating and teaching children.

Today most subjects are approached through project work, and children may work cooperatively in small groups to discover facts and explore ideas, rather than be given information which they have to commit to memory. If you think back to learning a poem by rote you will be forced to acknowledge that, while you may still remember some of the lines of the poem, you probably did not understand or appreciate the language or feel inspired to try to write poetry yourself.

Present-day educators believe that the best way of understanding a subject is to experience it 'hands on'. You will probably notice that, while in some cases your grandchild may not have such a strict grasp of grammar and syntax as you had at her age, her knowledge of many other subjects is broader and far more sophisticated than yours was.

Relationships

Your grandchild's relationship with her teachers will differ from the ones you may remember. Although in almost all schools children still address their teachers as 'Sir', 'Miss' or by their surname, it is unlikely that your grandchild will feel the fear that you may remember in relation to some of your teachers. In retrospect it is easy to make light of old schooldays and think that the 'ruling through fear' approach was effective. But now most children experience far more humane and intelligent teaching methods, which are bound to lead to more effective learning – it is difficult to learn properly if you are scared of the person who is instructing you.

Physical punishment is also absent from schools today. It may seem to you that this coincides with more difficult, badly behaved children, but long-term research indicates the opposite. It is a truism that children who are beaten will in turn beat others and so, when you talk about your schooldays to your grandchildren, try not to voice too many criticisms of what is happening now.

NOW

In the past, education chiefly involved listening to a teacher impart information which had to be memorised and recalled (above left); today, the emphasis is on children exploring for themselves, discussing options and sharing knowledge with their classmates (above).

Parent participation

Another enormous change in schooling, compared to when you were this age, is that parents are expected to be far more actively involved, with most schools insisting that a child's education comes from a partnership between parents and teachers. The positive side of this is that your grandchild's parents will feel more able to talk to people at the school when your grandchild is experiencing problems, and your grandchild will not feel that school is a totally separate and alien world from family life.

In addition, parents are encouraged to spend time in the school on a voluntary basis, working on shared reading schemes or helping in other lessons, as well as attending special assemblies, plays and celebrations. This can produce added stress for working parents and it is upsetting for your grandchild if her parents are always the ones who cannot fulfil their obligations. This is an area

where you can help out if you have available time during school hours. Your presence will be much appreciated by staff and your grandchild alike, whether you go to the short, 'one-to-one' reading sessions or to watch your grandchild perform in a play or take part in a special project.

Private education

If you have not considered it before, as your grandchild approaches the age at which she changes schools (usually 11 or 12), you may feel you would like more involvement in her education, perhaps by paying for her to go to a private school. Obviously, this decision is one her parents must make, but if private education is a family tradition they may appreciate some financial contribution from you.

If, however, you are happy to pay towards one grandchild's education, you need to consider doing the same for all your grandchildren. And because you are providing funding it doesn't mean that you can insist on your old school being chosen or have a say in which school is selected.

Don't push parents towards private education simply because you can afford to pay for it. But if they are concerned about what school their child will attend and are unable to choose the one that they feel will be most suitable for her due to lack of funds, offer to step in if you have the means to do so. This will not give you the right to a greater say over your grandchild's future and you should not use your financial backing as a means to gain power over your family.

Remember, too, that the expenses involved in private education do not stop at fees – there will be uniform, equipment and all kinds of extras to pay for. Take these into account when budgeting and be sure you can afford them before you make any offers.

Shared skills: gifts for life

Introducing your grandchild to pastimes that have enriched your life

The idea of passing on some of the knowledge and wisdom that you have gained over the years so that your grandchild, in turn, can enjoy it with you and hand it on when the time comes, is appealing. Sharing some of the skills you have acquired can be a highly satisfying way of spending time with your grandchild.

If your grandchild knows you go fishing regularly or hears you practising the piano, for example, she may take the initiative and simply ask you to let her go along with you or teach her how to play. Alternatively, she may not consider it possible to do what you are doing, especially if you are a skilful musician or a particularly keen fisherman.

It is up to you to build your grandchild's belief in her ability to learn what you have to teach her before you begin any instruction. Children love to hear stories about what adults got up to when they were young, and this is a good opportunity to relate how you first got involved in your hobby, the mistakes you made and the setbacks you overcame. Be sure to keep your account lighthearted and, if possible, humorous, so as not to put her off.

Before you begin to teach your grandchild to play an instrument you will need to do some preparation of your own. She will need her own instrument, or at least ready access to one, probably yours. If you are planning to buy her a guitar or clarinet for herself, for example, avoid the impulse to invest in an expensive, new instrument. However keen she may be initially, there is always the possibility that she will give up and your money will be wasted. Opt for a good second-hand instrument or investigate hiring one until you see how she progresses. You can always graduate to something grander later.

If you are unsure how to teach a beginner, you may prefer to organise professional tuition and support your grandchild's efforts between lessons. But don't underestimate a child's willingness to learn from you. Even if you don't convey the information in exactly the same way as a professional tutor, you have the closeness of a family relationship to help you. Your grandchild may find your methods a welcome change from formal instruction. You can lace your instruction with humour,

Learning to play an instrument is a skill that will enhance your grandchild's life. Move at her pace and resist the temptation to push her from one level to another, regardless of how proud you are of her achievements. Time to consolidate her skills and simply have fun with you are also important.

Fishing has many advantages: it's an open-air activity that is not too 'sporty'; it's inexpensive for beginners; and the basics are easy to grasp.

Modelmaking can be rewarding. Don't restrict yourself to indoor models – flying a plane or sailing a boat you have made is also great fun.

go at the pace that suits you both and take pride in any progress made, since it is a credit to both of you.

If you can't remember what you did when you first began to learn, consult some books on the subject. Do not, if your grandchild is struggling to play a chord, take over and show her how easily it is done. Respect her efforts and try to recall how difficult learning can be in the early days. Never force a child to practise or persist with playing if she is tired: the idea is to give her pleasure now and for the rest of her life, not to create miserable memories.

Outdoor pursuits

If you share your love of birdwatching or fishing you will also teach the importance of observation and patience. These are desirable, useful attributes in today's fast-moving and stressful world, but you should appreciate that your grandchild's youth predisposes her to movement and noise. It may take years for her to appreciate what

is to be gained from sitting quietly for hours on end, but that does not mean she cannot enjoy shorter sessions with you, during which she can gradually become accustomed to what is required. Time begun in companionable silence is conducive to intimate chats and shared confidences on the way home.

It is vital that your grandchild is suitably dressed and that you have enough refreshments with you in order for her not to view these occasions as wet, cold and boring. Provide plenty of information about the birds you are watching or the fish you are catching. If your grandchild picks up on your enthusiasm for the pastime, you will be able to equip her with binoculars, fishing tackle and other necessary items that will make her feel part of the whole experience.

Your skill in a more energetic pastime such as horseriding may be the one your grandchild wants you to share with her. If so, you obviously have to have great regard for her safety while learning. Sessions should be long enough for her to gain confidence but not so long that she becomes overtired. You should establish regular times for teaching, once or twice a week, say, so that she can enjoy rapid progress. If you vary the lessons with grooming and mucking out, your grandchild will quickly grow used to being around horses without fearing them.

If none of these hobbies has attracted you over the years, don't feel you have nothing to offer: an energetic walk is an appealing prospect for many 8 to 12 year olds.

Finally, remember that in sharing any active skill you must make allowances for your grandchild's age so that she does not become physically or mentally overstrained.

Talking about death

Accepting that illness and death are part of our everyday lives

As you grow older you may have to face up to illness and, whether or not the complaint is life-threatening, your condition will obviously affect your loved ones. At this age, your grandchild, in particular, is likely to feel many different and confusing emotions in connection with what is happening to you.

Younger children find it difficult to comprehend illness or death and adolescents may have experienced it in their own or friends' families, but 8 to 12 year olds look to their family relationships for stability and like to consider them everlasting. Your attitude can help your grandchild to accept the nature of life and death. You may also find that concentrating on readying your grandchild for the inevitable gives you the strength to come to terms with your own mortality.

Find times when you are both relaxed and not overtired to introduce this topic in a low-key way. Ideally, discussions should take place while you are still fit, but if you are ill and not likely to recover fully you need to give your grandchild reassurance. By this stage in her education she will have looked at the life cycles of various small creatures and, if her school is church-based, discussed life and death in a religious context. But when it comes to someone dear to her, she will require guidance to accept what is going to happen.

Try to talk about your illness in a matter-of-fact manner; you don't have to go into too much detail but you can, at this stage, gently suggest that people don't usually make a recovery. If, despite the understated nature of your discussion, your grandchild becomes upset don't rush to change the subject, but acknowledge her feelings and try again on another occasion.

If you have a strong religious faith, you may not find it difficult to discuss death but you need to be absolutely sure what her parents believe before you talk to your grandchild about it. To receive conflicting explanations from the adults around her is confusing and distressing.

Make it clear to your grandchild that she can ask questions whenever she likes – you will probably find that she has already been thinking quite deeply. There are some good books for this age range that deal with illness and death within the family,

A child's first experience of death may well be the loss of a pet. Accepting that all creatures die – because of an accident, illness or old age – is the first step towards realising that you are not always going to be there. Burying the body in the garden introduces the idea of burial and that there is a special place where memories of a loved one are particularly resonant.

and if you find it hard to begin your discussions you could read one or two of these with her.

If you are ill, you may worry that your grandchild will be frightened by visiting you. But remember that it is the unknown – things that children are not allowed to see but can only imagine – that provokes the greatest fears. Keep an open mind about this: if your grandchild becomes distressed and her parents say she would rather not visit, accept her feelings and write to her instead (record a tape if you feel too tired to write).

Funerals

When your grandchild is talking to you about life and death she may want to know about funerals. Most children of this age will not have attended any and she may feel anxious about whether to attend yours when the time comes. Point out that many people will probably cry but that it is good to be able to express grief.

If you are both strong enough she may even want to play a part in choosing music and making sure that things will be as you want them to be. But whether or not her involvement is this detailed, make it clear to her that you are content with whatever she decides and that you do not expect her to attend if she would rather not.

Many children feel surprisingly strongly about attending funerals and sometimes parents try to stop them to spare their grief. There has been a growing tendency to try to minimise the trappings of death, especially where children are concerned, but it should be acknowledged that children have intense feelings of grief when someone dies and the funeral can often be as cathartic for them as it is for the mourning adults.

Loving memories

While you obviously do not want to dwell on your own death, especially if you are at present fit and well, you will undoubtedly gain comfort from knowing that you will

Funerals give children the chance to say goodbye. This can be particularly important if they feel they didn't do so – if you die in a hospital, for example. Funerals also give an opportunity for all family members to gather together to remember you.

be fondly remembered and talked about. Your grandchild's memories of you will be a means of keeping you 'alive' for her.

Make it easy for your grandchild to remember you happily. Arrange for some photographs to be taken of you together (without explaining your intentions) and give them to her to keep. If you feel able to, write a letter describing some of your best outings together and funny moments you treasure. Place the letter with your solicitor to be given out after your death.

Lastly, you may ease your grandchild's grief in advance if you can subtly convey to her some of the different emotions that people experience when a loved one dies. Children often feel total disbelief on their first experience of death. Disbelief can be followed by anger because you have left them and they miss you so much. These feelings may also be mixed with guilt because they didn't always behave as they know you wanted them to or they didn't come to see you as much as they could have. If you can tackle the difficult task of planting some understanding and acceptance in your grandchild's mind, you will have left her with the strength to remember you in the best possible way.

Then and now:
Personal freedom

As recently as a generation ago, on fine days parents suggested their children 'go out and play', and helped them to feel independent by asking them to run errands to the local shops. In today's world, such freedoms are no longer practical.

In recent years the freedom children enjoyed to come and go at will, play in the streets and roam through fields without supervision has been severely curtailed. Some psychologists place the blame firmly on the increased number of cars on the roads: children are driven everywhere so they do not develop the ability that previous generations had to judge situations and keep themselves safe. Furthermore, because everyone drives everywhere the streets are not full of benign adults, as they once were, to whom a child in trouble could turn.

Other professionals blame the media. Events such as road accidents and assaults, which would previously have gone largely unnoticed in the wider community, now make headline news, producing panic among parents. A combination of many factors is probably at the heart of the situation, but the result is that your grandchild will not experience the freedoms your own children had at a similar age, and her parents' attitude towards her safety will be different from your own when you were parenting.

It is important to keep your attitude towards children's safety and personal freedom at this age in perspective. Before your grandchild went to school, she was simply too young to be permitted to wander off alone; when she reaches adolescence it will be impossible and unfair to try to accompany her at all times. But 8 to 12 year olds are in the middle. If your grandchild is to grow into an independent person able to make sensible, safe decisions, she must be allowed some freedom, but striking the right balance can be difficult.

You must know the rules her parents impose and stick to them when she comes to stay or when you 'babysit'. If you feel that they are being obsessively protective, or turning a blind eye to potential dangers, speak out tactfully. But in the meantime, don't go against her parents' wishes.

For much of the time, 8 to 12 year olds enjoy being addressed as adults and want to achieve a sense of self-sufficiency, but they also want security. The favourite reading matter among this age group is stories in which children of the same age have incredible adventures without adult supervision. These tales always end with the children safe and sound. This says a lot about their growing need for independence

NOW

Few cars on the roads meant that streets were once safe for children to play in (above left); today, heavy traffic and fear of strangers make most parents unwilling to allow their children to make even short journeys alone (above).

and security in equal measure. You should support what your grandchild's parents are doing and saying, help to alert her in a non-alarmist way to the potential hazards of the outside world, and enable her to make positive and successful forays into that world.

Some children are sensitive to the fears of adults and react adversely to media coverage of accidents to and crimes against children. If your grandchild refuses to do anything independently, discuss the matter with her parents – in severe cases she may need professional help.

Noting the differences
• At the age of 8
You went to the cinema with a friend of the same age when you had the money to do so. Your grandchild asks to do the same.

Is there a safe way of making this happen which will be acceptable to all concerned? Is there a morning session which is properly supervised?

• At the age of 10
You slept in the garden in a tent in the summer and played at being in the wilds. Your grandchild asks to do the same.

Can you make your garden secure for her? If not, would she welcome you camping out with her? Will she accept the conservatory or attic as a temporary alternative?

• At the age of 12
You made short journeys alone to visit relatives and friends. Your grandchild asks to do the same.

Can you escort her to the start of the journey and make sure she is met at her destination? If she is travelling by bus, can you ask the driver to see that she gets off at the right place?

WHEN YOU ARE IN CHARGE

• Ask her parents how they would behave in certain situations; contact them if you are unsure about allowing a solo trip your grandchild proposes.

• You can negotiate with your grandchild, but don't be coerced into allowing her to go somewhere or do something you are uncomfortable with.

• Before you allow a solo trip, ask your grandchild what she would do if she was approached by a stranger/had an accident/was asked for help. Encouraging her to visualise possible problems and talking over solutions with her is a good way to prepare her to face them. Don't overdramatise.

• Make sure your grandchild knows how to use a public telephone to call you or the emergency services. Give her a phone card or enough coins to make the call.

• On joint outings discuss possible risks and ways to minimise them. Remember that there are many more road accidents involving young people than there are assaults and abductions.

• Do not leave your grandchild in your house alone even if her parents do so: she cannot be responsible for protecting your home.

Separation and divorce
Your special role when families are fractured

Apart from the death of a parent, the greatest upheaval a child has to face is her parents' separation and/or divorce. There is no way of making this a completely painless interlude for your grandchild. Your part in the proceedings has to be played with great delicacy and understanding if you want to achieve what is best for her and for you.

Remaining neutral
You may find your emotions are in turmoil as you try to understand what has gone wrong. It is possible to feel that your son or daughter has been badly treated or let down and that your in-law is behaving appallingly, but to act in an overtly partisan manner could ruin your chances of maintaining a close relationship with your grandchild in the future. This would be tragic for both of you. The child's interests must take precedence over what you would like to say to the adults involved.

At all costs, remain calm and appear impartial, stating from the outset that your main concern is for your grandchild's wellbeing. Do not be tempted to seek consolation through talking to other family members about the problem. When relationships turn sour, adults have to walk a tightrope to avoid being accused of taking sides and making matters worse. Keep telling yourself, even when you come under pressure to be partisan, that you must remain neutral for your grandchild's sake.

If you feel overwhelmed by what is happening – and it is common for grandparents to wonder if their own parenting skills are to blame for the failure of their children's marriages – talk to a professional counsellor or phone an appropriate helpline so that you can discuss your worries in confidence.

One of the damaging aspects of relationship breakdown for children is seeing the parents they love angry with each other. If you can shield your grandchild from some of the ugliness by offering temporary shelter while parents sort out their next move, you may help the situation.

Your grandchild's feelings
In the same way that you may hold yourself in some way culpable for your child's failure to sustain a happy marriage, your grandchild may think that the separation or divorce is her fault. She may have been the innocent pawn in a lot of arguments during the marriage and, as in so many cases, misunderstood the root of the trouble. It is usual for children in this situation to assume blame in an attempt to protect their parents from the burden: they would rather feel that they themselves are at fault than that their parents are imperfect, out of control, or willing to leave the family set-up.

Without forcing discussions, you should be ready to listen for as long as your grandchild wants to talk about what has happened to help her to make sense of it. If she is finding it hard to introduce the topic because she is so distressed you should recognise the signs and start by giving her a hug or a cuddle until she is ready to begin.

Your grandchild may well feel, as her parents start to make arrangements to live apart, that she, too, is being rejected. She may become insecure and revert to immature habits and behaviour. If her parents' divorce involves her changing schools, homes and possibly acquiring new step-siblings as well, she will have an immense amount to cope with and you may be the one stable element in her life. Try to stifle your own feelings about what is going on and concentrate in a positive way on hers.

You can help your grandchild to cope with and accept all the adjustments she will have to make. You may well be the difference between her facing the future with total panic or feeling positive about it.

She may choose to focus on aspects of the problem which to you seem rather less important – what will happen to the family dog, for example. This is her way of trying to chip away at a dilemma which will for some time seem all-encompassing. You could set about relieving her anxiety by suggesting temporary or, where possible, permanent solutions to such problems. Always check that her parents will agree to anything you suggest before telling your grandchild, but in the case of family pets you could help by agreeing to give them house room, at least until everyone is permanently settled.

When emotions are running high, as they are in this situation, you may receive unexpected snubs when trying to help. Brace yourself to bear them in silence because, however resolute the adults involved may seem – and even if you can accept that their decision may be the right one – they are most certainly suffering too.

CASE HISTORY

I always found my son's wife Trudy rather distant and cold, but made every effort to make her feel part of the family. And after my granddaughter Laura was born (she's eight now) we got on much better. Trudy was an only child and her mother was dead, so she seemed to turn to me for support and help with Laura. At the time my son seemed pleased and we all spent a lot of time together.

It came as a complete shock when they separated, but my first thoughts were for Laura. I panicked at the idea that Trudy would take her away and I would never see my granddaughter again. Imagine my surprise when my son told me that Trudy had agreed to his taking Laura abroad. He said it was the only way to become independent and get to know his daughter. He accused me of ganging up with Trudy against him and said I had turned his wife into a different person since Laura's birth. He needed to get away and start again.

That was six months ago and I have only just received a letter from my son, including a recent photograph of Laura. She looks well. They intend to come home soon and I am trying to prepare myself for seeing my son and Laura again. I feel bitter that he has blamed me for his marriage going wrong and deprived me of my granddaughter's company, but I do accept that, somehow, in making a great effort to include Trudy in the family and to get to know Laura, I must have excluded my son.

I intend to be very careful how I handle the situation, even though I'm desperate to see Laura.

Separation and divorce

If your time with your grandchild is more restricted after his parents' separation, you may feel reluctant to dilute it further by inviting a step-sibling to share in the activities and outings you enjoy. But your acceptance of change will help your grandchild come to terms with the upheaval in his life.

Practical arrangements

Once you have negotiated all the emotional challenges set by separation and divorce, you still have to face up to the practical arrangements that have been made.

You will, of course, have to respect the custody agreements that have been reached regarding your grandchild. If, for example, your son has access to your grandchild at weekends only, you will obviously be hoping that he will share some of this time with you, while appreciating that he will, at first anyway, be keen to have her to himself as much as possible. If you are lucky enough to have been able to maintain good relationships with both parents throughout their separation and divorce, you may be able to see your grandchild more frequently, as long as the parent with custody has not decided to move a long distance away.

There may be a problem regarding the venue for access to your grandchild. The parent with 'weekend only' access may not yet have found suitable accommodation, or

may have moved in with a new partner, making the new home unacceptable to the parent with custody. In these cases you could suggest that your home is used as neutral territory. The parents can meet there to hand over your grandchild and discuss her welfare when necessary. This could help ease some of the discomfort your grandchild will feel during these periods and give you some time with her.

If you are in the miserable position of having no access to your grandchild, make every effort to improve things. In the first instance, appeal to the parent with custody to allow you to spend time with your grandchild for the child's sake. If this has no effect you could try appealing to your grandchild's other grandparents if you know they have access and you think they might respond. If this is not appropriate, try to find someone who is known and liked by all parties concerned and who can be relied upon to act in a neutral, sensitive way. If there simply isn't anyone who can help you among family and friends, contact your social services department to see if they have a family mediation unit through which contact between you and your grandchild might be re-established.

If all informal mediation is to no avail, you have recourse to the law. Since the 1989 Children Act (UK) you are entitled to obtain permission through the courts to gain access to your grandchild. If this sounds impossibly expensive, it is worth contacting your nearest Citizens Advice Bureau or a solicitor specialising in children's law to find out if you are entitled to legal aid.

Seeking custody

If you believe that your grandchild would be better off living with you, either because the parent with custody is unable to care for her due to illness or has disappeared and left the child with you, or if you have been temporarily fostering your grandchild, you can apply through the courts for permission to seek a residence order. If your grandchild has already been living with you for three years or more, or there are other exceptional circumstances, you are automatically entitled to apply for a residence order.

A residence order legally settles the arrangements regarding whom the child will live with. It gives you parental responsibility for as long as the order continues, although you are not allowed to take the child abroad for more than a month or change her surname, unless everyone with parental responsibility agrees in writing or the court gives special permission.

In the United Kingdom some social services departments sever fostering payments when grandparents are given a residence order for their grandchild. And in order to obtain allowances you may have to declare your savings and pension provisions and be subject to detailed financial scrutiny. Contact your Citizens Advice Bureau or lawyer before you become involved in costly court procedures. Grandparents' pressure groups are also actively involved in campaigning against the severance of care payments when residence orders are granted. If financial considerations are not an issue for you, a residence order is obviously a more permanent arrangement than fostering.

Your overall aim should be to re-establish for your grandchild the solid foundations that may have been severely

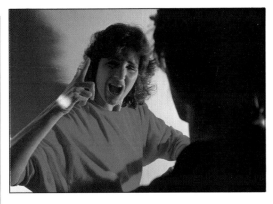

When emotions are running high, nobody behaves well. Apportioning blame when a relationship breaks down benefits no one. Your impartiality and fairness to all parties may help to relieve some of the tensions at this time, but be prepared to be caught in the crossfire.

shaken by her parents' divorce. In taking this on, bear in mind that the demands a child will make, in terms of your energy and time, will be considerably more than those of the normal grandparenting activities in which you have been involved. Because you are trying to repair the damage done by a family split, you should not try to aim for perfection or put yourself into the position of martyr. If there are other family members who can help, call upon them. This will help conserve your strength. You will need every ounce you possess to complete this most demanding but rewarding job.

Many children view packing their belongings to move to a new home as an adventure, despite their need for stability when relationships break down. Be sure that you can carry out any offers of help or support you make – the last thing children of separated parents need is more uncertainty and broken promises.

Separation and divorce

Extended families

The initial repercussions of your child's divorce centre around the care of your grandchild and any arrangements you are involved in making for her. But its impact does not stop there. Most couples who divorce remarry within a short time. One in five children will have divorced parents by the time they are 16, and about 80 per cent of divorcees marry again within five years.

A grandchild whose parents remarry may have to face step-siblings becoming a part of her life, or one or both of her parents choosing to have more children, or both. If the new partner comes to the relationship with children of his or her own, you may be needed to counsel your grandchild into accepting and coping with the shifts in the family set-up. In order to do this properly you must first come to terms with the changes yourself.

A child who is brought into your family by the new partner may be feeling every bit as bewildered and unsure of herself as your own grandchild. You need to have enough love to go round, without making your own grandchild feel she is losing her special place in your affections.

If you have not taken to the new partner or have not been given the chance to do so, you might find it difficult to accept the child. However, it is to the detriment of your own grandchild and all your family relationships if you cannot stretch yourself a little farther. If your step-grandchild has reached adolescence, be prepared for things to be a little more difficult than if she had met you earlier in her life; having patience and striving to be tolerant and understanding will pay dividends in the end.

Adolescents often take their parents' divorce and subsequent remarriage a lot harder than younger children. In addition to being forced to accept their parent's new relationship, they are simultaneously trying to cope with their own emerging adulthood. You could provide the steady influence that your grandchild needs; if you are able to do so, she will doubtless experience fewer problems in her own relationship with her step-sibling than might otherwise be the case.

Many children are thrilled when a baby comes along. But if your grandchild has not accepted his parent's new relationship, he may resent the new arrival. Although you will doubtless be delighted to have another grandchild, accept the older child's misgivings and reassure him that his place in your heart is unaffected.

A new baby

If your son or daughter and new partner produce a new baby, in theory your emotions will be less complicated than with step-grandchildren because the baby is, after all, a 'real' grandchild. In practice you may not have fully accepted the new marital arrangements and/or be overwhelmed with anxieties about how the grandchild you know and love will cope with yet another new development in the family situation.

If you let your fears show, your grandchild will pick up on them and judge that there must really be something to worry about. An addition to the family is surely a positive thing, something to be welcomed. With luck, your grandchild, like most other children, will be delighted with the novelty of the new arrival and you can allay any feelings of being left out by giving her lots of extra attention and time.

Parents who are still building their own relationship may seem to have time only for their new baby; if so, your task is to shield your grandchild from feelings of neglect. There are lots of good children's books on the subject of new arrivals and the mixed emotions they cause, so you could try reading some with your grandchild. You could also help to refocus the parents' attention on their older child by organising family get-togethers which include other children, or take the baby out so that the parents can spend some time with your other grandchild. Do not be afraid to tell them, politely, when you offer to look after the baby, that you think your grandchild is looking forward to spending some special time with them – they may simply not have noticed that they were leaving her out.

Fair shares

Once you have adjusted to the emotional changes that come with an extended family, you will need to make some practical readjustments. If you have put aside

The mixed emotions – fear, bewilderment, anger, betrayal, guilt, even relief – she feels towards her parents may spill over into your grandchild's relationship with you. At this time you need all your love and patience to accept that any behavioural problems are temporary and your easy rapport will return.

savings or a trust scheme, or have offered to pay for private education for your first grandchild, you should extend these benefits to the new arrivals in your family. By being scrupulously fair in this way you will show everyone that you have accepted what has happened and give your children and grandchildren the best possible chances of making a success of their new relationships.

In addition to any financial provisions you may have made, you will also have to rethink how you spend your time with your grandchildren. If you normally take your grandchild for an outing once a week, carry on with this exclusive arrangement for as long as she wants you to, but arrange a day for your step-grandchild to do something with you, too, or for you to spend time with the new baby. At first this may seem like a time-consuming and exhausting programme of events but eventually your first grandchild will probably suggest that her sibling comes along on your excursions. You will then have the satisfaction of knowing that you did the right thing – one of the reasons she is better able to accept and enjoy her new family is the help you have given her.

CHAPTER SEVEN

The Young Adolescent
12 to 15 years

There are likely to be times, even in the closest-knit families, when your adolescent grandchild's struggle for independence results in behaviour that will test the patience of the most even-tempered parents. The fact that he is treading a well-worn path towards adulthood does not make the going easier, especially if he seems to be attacking everything for which your family stands.

Your handling of situations can make all the difference to their outcome. If you can listen when everyone else is exhausted, you may help to protect your grandchild from harmful influences and keep his relationship with his parents on a more even keel. Through sharing activities and skills, you will broaden his experience and give him resources to fall back on when life gets difficult. And by letting

him know that you understand at least a part of his concerns, you will keep the lines of communication open between you and build on the friendship you have always enjoyed.

Areas of conflict

Dealing with the ups and downs of adolescence

Few families escape completely the tempers and tantrums of early adolescence, a particularly sensitive time in your grandchild's growing years. If you live far away and see your grandchild only infrequently, he may appear to be the polite sweet-natured person you have always known and you won't witness his more unattractive moments.

If, however, you spend a lot of time with his family, the strain of being on his best behaviour for you may be too much for him and you, too, may be on the receiving end of his moods and angst. This will be as hurtful for you as it is for his parents. At these times it is good to remember your own child's teens. Recall – silently – the moments when he was argumentative and moody, and tried your patience beyond endurance. Remember the rows about the length of his hair and what time he came home at night. And realise that you both survived!

The most challenging teenage behaviour usually occurs between the ages of 11 and 15 – the period of rapid growth and intense hormonal changes. Physically, your grandchild is almost an adult, capable of becoming a parent himself. Emotionally, he is still a child who is rather scared about what is happening to him and tries to hide the fact by being moody and self-centred. It helps if all family members understand that he is reacting to a real – and perhaps deep-seated – fear of leaving the security of childhood for a less certain adulthood.

Making friends

Some areas of dispute seem to be common to most families with an adolescent in their midst. High on the list come his friends. In this transitional period your grandchild begins to seek security in a group of people his own age and it is they who appear to exert the most influence over him. For the most part peer pressure is positive: members of the gang provide the

Snacks at all hours of the day and night – with fridge door left ajar, juice cartons not put away and debris much in evidence – are considered reasonable by most adolescents. But when your grandchild is at your house you can insist he and his friends tidy up after themselves.

Your granddaughter's parents may be horrified by dyed and gelled hair, eccentric clothes and body piercing. But your acceptance that such fashions are part of growing up – and your willingness to be seen having a good time in the company of your grandchild – may help her to come to terms with her emerging adulthood.

companionship and comfort of a family in this period. They can offer mutual support because each one is experiencing similar domestic conflicts.

Avoid criticising his friends unless they are truly objectionable. Of course, if you or his parents suspect that someone is leading your grandchild into criminal activities or drug abuse, the friendship should be discouraged as firmly as possible without actually driving a headstrong teenager into defiance. But if the only opposition is the way a friend dresses or the fact that he is not as bright at school as your grandchild, leave well alone.

Encourage his parents to get to know his friends and allow them into the house, however unattractive they seem. Be prepared to do this yourself if you live close by. They may be more willing to meet at your house and you may find that they are more pleasant than you imagined. Having a home where they are welcome also limits the amount of time young teenagers spend 'hanging around', usually on street corners.

You should probably worry more if your grandchild appears to have no friends at all. If he has a row with his parents, he has no one to call to get things off his chest, and no one with whom to share stories about

his diabolical family and their unreasonable ways. Step in and make it clear to your grandchild that you are always available when he is feeling particularly miserable. If you don't live close, encourage him to phone when he is lonely.

How he looks

The first signs of adolescent rebellion usually manifest themselves in a teenager's appearance. Your grandson may choose torn jeans and scruffy T-shirts and your granddaughter may wear too much make-up and skirts that you judge too short. And, at a time when you might expect them to be bold and extrovert, both sexes dress from head to foot in black.

People of this age also tend to experiment a lot with their hairstyles, since this is a quick and effective way of looking like a different person – which, of course, is what your grandchild now feels he is. Colouring the hair is popular, often in what you may consider outrageous shades. Try to conceal your dismay, or amusement; your grandchild is probably hoping to shock, so don't give him the satisfaction of reacting to his latest extravagance. Such crazes are usually short-lived and harmless.

Areas of conflict

More difficult to accept is a teenager's urge to have some part of his body pierced. You can probably accept pierced ears even in your grandson since it is now more common for boys to wear earrings, too. But you may find it incomprehensible that he wants to wear a ring through his nose or have a stud in his navel.

This is only a matter of fashion, but he should know that once a hole has been pierced, it will not close completely again. Reminding him of this (his parents may simply have forbidden it, which will make him even more determined) may persuade him to delay having it done, by which time he may go off the whole idea. If he goes ahead anyway, you don't have to like or admire it; but make sure he realises that it doesn't stop you loving him.

Annoying habits

Teenagers tend to slump lethargically in front of the television. The amount of channel-hopping that goes on indicates their lack of absorption in any particular programme. Your grandchild's parents may well decide to limit television viewing if it means he does nothing else or if it interferes with his schoolwork. Obviously, if you spend hours watching TV, you can't expect him not to do the same when he is with you. Suggest a a visit to see his local

If you are worried about your grandchild's safety when she stays with you, set limits. If you retire early and are unwilling to let her stay out as late as her parents do, explain why – she may accept from you what she would call thoroughly unreasonable from her parents.

team play, a game of tennis, a fishing trip, or whatever else might enthuse him.

Sloppy bedrooms – unmade bed, dirty laundry scattered over the floor, unwashed coffee cups – can infuriate parents. The usual teenage response is that it is not worth making a fuss. He has more important things to worry about, such as the meaning of life or whether his school rock band will achieve worldwide fame. If his parents complain to you about this,

One day there is a lovable child, the next a surly, uncooperative monster who argues about everything, makes unreasonable demands and sulks and slams doors when thwarted. Some parent–child conflict is inevitable in the teen years – try to support both sides.

console them with the fact that untidy teens often become highly house-proud adults.

It may be difficult to lure a teenager out of bed in the morning. While it is true that excessive fatigue can be a sign of depression or drug abuse, teenagers do need to sleep more than younger children because of all the hormonal and physical changes taking place. As long as he is active and fit when awake, there is nothing to worry about. When he stays with you, don't hang around waiting to make his breakfast when he does emerge – leave that to him.

The state of his room at home may drive his parents to distraction, but this is less likely to be a problem for you, even if your grandchild has his own room at your house, simply because you can go in and clear up once he has gone home. You won't find month-old coffee cups if he stays only a few days.

Reasonable hours

If you are a witness to arguments between your grandchild and his parents over the hour at which he should return after a night out, don't remind your child in your grandchild's hearing of your own rows on this subject. These disputes are best solved by compromise. If parents insist that he is home by a reasonable time when he has to get up for school but extend the curfew if he has a special party to go to, both sides should be happy.

Use your memories of parenting to advise his parents to get to know the parents of their teenager's friends. At least they may then learn where he is going, with whom and what time he may be back.

Education

One of the most serious concerns parents have at this time is that their child appears to be dropping out of school – mentally if not physically. He seems to be doing less and less work and endless rows result from the fact that he won't sit down and do his homework or study for an important exam. Often this behaviour is related to his fear of failing at school: he feels determined to reject school before it rejects him.

All parents like to believe that their child is intelligent and that any lack of academic achievement simply means he is not working hard enough. Encourage him to believe he can succeed by showing an interest in his schoolwork and making much of any academic success, however modest. Ask him about his plans for the future, and talk about the fun of university or college life rather than the effort of making it through exams. But if you suspect that your grandchild would be happier in a non-academic career, try not to be disappointed: support him in whatever he chooses to do and continue to value him for his numerous other qualities.

A safe haven

There will be times when your grandchild finds it easier to handle his anger and frustration away from his immediate family. Knowing that he can use your house as an escape route when things get tough can be reassuring. His parents may also use you as a refuge when the rows and angst get too much for them. Whether this means they just pop round for a chat or whether one of them packs their bags and comes to stay for a few nights, it enables all concerned to cool down.

Try not to take sides – you probably won't want to. In your special position you will have insight into both parent and child, which will help you to maintain a balanced viewpoint. It is this calm objectivity that is so valuable to all members of the family during these stressful times.

Gifts for 12 to 15 year olds

Choosing an appropriate present for a young teenager

It is easy, by the time children reach their early teens, to hand over cash every Christmas and birthday or whenever a gift is required. And 12 to 15 year olds do like to receive money. But it's important to strike a balance between encouraging your grandchild to choose some items for himself and letting him know that you still think about what he would like.

If you find you approach your grandchild's birthday every year without any good ideas of what to buy him, you need to pay more attention to his interests in the preceding months. When you see him, listen carefully for any information that may help you to find him an original present when the time arrives. If he is enthusiastic about music, for example, you could purchase concert tickets for around the time of his birthday; if he reveals an interest in car racing you could arrange a trip to a go-kart track or tickets for a Grand Prix event, and so on.

Consider alternating gifts of money and surprise items. You can vary the way you give cash by pledging a set amount for each month from this birthday until next or at the beginning and end of each school term. This may seem less exciting to him than receiving a larger sum, but it will be appreciated when he has spent all the rest of his cash.

If your grandchild has an interest in collecting CDs or tapes, you could buy vouchers to be sure that you don't duplicate what is already in his collection. Subscriptions to favourite magazines give a lot of pleasure because they are ongoing, and if your grandchild, like many of his peers, is concerned about endangered species you could pay for him to adopt a whale, gorilla or elephant, for example. He will then receive regular information on 'his' animal and how the protection programme is progressing.

Many young teens are adventurous about food. You could buy an appropriate cookery book, with wok or pan and some interesting spices and starter ingredients. Consider a course of cookery lessons, either at a cookery school or on video. He will appreciate that you share his new interests

FAIL-SAFE GIFT PLAN

• Season ticket to see his favourite sports team – this could be a combined Christmas and birthday present because of the cost.

• Toiletries: aftershave (it doesn't matter that he doesn't shave yet), deodorants, soaps, towels.

• High-interest savings account – for when he starts college or university, or wants to strike out on his own.

• Vouchers for favourite hairdresser, barber, shoe store, health club or games workshop.

• Fan club membership of his best-loved band.

• Block booking at squash club, ice rink, tennis court.

• Materials for redecorating his room (as long as his parents have given permission).

• Set of hand weights, gym kit, video workout.

• Bike, skates, skateboard – ask his parents if there are favoured brands to buy.

Ongoing gifts such as magazine subscriptions are often popular for this age group, although if you know which CD, computer game or video is on his list, it will be appreciated. If you prefer to give money, add a 'grown-up' purse or wallet. Sports equipment comes into its own for this age group, with many young teens taking an interest in physical fitness.

and treat him with a little sophistication. As well as catering for your grandchild's enthusiasms you could introduce him to some of yours. A teenager who scorns 'classic' movies may be surprised and won over by the stormy romanticism of *Wuthering Heights*, for example, and this may spark a lifelong interest and prepare him for outings you both enjoy.

If he has always liked looking at your collection of stamps or coins, start him off with his own set. This is a gift you can add to, as long as his interest is genuine rather than stemming from a desire to please you.

Although 12 to 15 year olds are fashion-conscious, buying clothes for them is a

minefield. Ideas about what is acceptable are so well defined by the peer group that it is virtually impossible for an adult to get it right. A way around this might be to plan a shopping trip together and stipulate an amount he can spend on clothes.

Gifts of an educational nature often seem unexciting, but if you can live with the initial lukewarm reception you may find your grandchild expressing his appreciation later when he realises the value of what you have given him. CD-ROMs, videos, books and tapes may make all the difference when he is studying.

With all gifts you may need to develop a thicker skin. Teens are hard to please and can be tactless about unwanted presents. Try not to be offended if a gift goes unused after a few weeks, and buy something longer-term like music or sports lessons that you know he will like if such fickleness upsets you.

Young teens use computers for schoolwork and pleasure. A game may bring him – and you – hours of fun while more educational CD-ROMs will help with his course work.

Outings with 12 to 15 year olds

Broadening your grandchild's outlook on your trips with him

Now that your grandchild is almost adult there are lots of grown-up places to go with him. You might have loved sharing his enjoyment of zoos and theme parks, but you may also find great pleasure in introducing him to your favourite pastimes – taking him to the theatre, to a classical concert, to art galleries or even to a good restaurant. These interests will enrich his whole life if he has an unpressured introduction to them in his youth and has the opportunity to learn to appreciate them at his own pace.

You may be hesitant about suggesting an outing in the belief that now he has an active social life of his own, the last thing he wants is to be seen with you. However, he is more likely to be prepared to fit in with any plans you make than he is to comply with his parents. He may even convince himself that he is doing you a favour by accompanying you to a concert or the theatre – which will make him feel grown up and good about himself.

Your grandchild may be antagonistic towards anything that smacks of 'culture', convinced that he is going to be bored, but you can overcome these prejudices in subtle, easy-going ways. A teenager who has shown no interest in the serious theatre may be keener to go if the first production he sees is related to texts he is studying at school, which might help him to get better grades. Most plays come to life with professional actors in a way they never can

Watching skilled performers act out a story in dance (above) may be an experience that your grandchild wants to repeat. For his first ballet, it will be easier for him if you explain the plot beforehand.

If you intend to take in an exhibition (left), try to get hold of a catalogue in advance so that you can both read up about particular artists and the work on display before you go.

in a school production or when they are intoned in the classroom. Plays by popular authors such as Arthur Miller or Arnold Wesker, which may appear on the school curriculum, are often performed in local or provincial theatres. Your grandchild will be pleasantly surprised at how absorbing he finds the play and be left wanting more. Build on this initial spark of interest by taking him to other plays or performances.

Music and art

If he listens to nothing but rock music he is likely to be reluctant to attend a classical concert. Do a deal with him – you will listen to a recording of his favourite band if he gives the classical composers a hearing. He may be surprised at how familiar some of the music is – a great deal is used as background music in films and television programmes. If he becomes 'hooked', imagine the hours of pleasure you can spend together, going to concerts and listening to music on CD and tape. Take advantage of birthdays and other special occasions to buy him recordings of pieces that you have enjoyed together – you may discover that he is listening to Mozart rather than heavy metal on his stereo!

If going to art exhibitions is one of your favourite pastimes, suggest that next time he might like to go with you. Like the theatre and classical music, art does not necessarily come into a young person's sphere of experience. A small exhibition by a single painter might be a good way to introduce him to the joys of viewing, rather than taking him to a gallery full of national treasures which can be rather overwhelming.

An outing with your grandchild might end with a meal in one of your favourite restaurants. It can be enormous fun giving a young person the chance to try new dishes, to learn to manipulate chopsticks or handle shellfish. Not only will he be proud of his new accomplishments, but he will also be acquiring social skills that will help him feel relaxed and confident in later life.

CASE HISTORY

*W*e *hardly ever ate out when I was a child, but once when I was about five we stayed with my grandparents and the whole family went to a restaurant. My Gran had a plate of what I was told were shellfish. While the rest of us ate chicken or steaks, she dismembered and peeled these fish of different sizes and ate them; some of them she just tipped into her mouth. I wanted to try them, so she slipped me a couple of things, which tasted delicious.*

When I was 12 my grandparents moved nearer to us and, for my 13th birthday, they offered to take me for a 'grown-up' meal. I remembered the plate of shellfish and said that was what I would like. They took me to a French restaurant, and ordered a similar dish for me. There were some things I didn't like much, but most of it tasted wonderful.

After that I went out regularly with them and ate all sorts of things I had never tasted before. They took me to an Italian restaurant with candles in wine bottles on the tables where I tasted pizza that bore no resemblance to those my friends and I had bought. On another occasion we had sushi at a Japanese restaurant; and we all laughed as we tried to master chopsticks the first time we went to a Chinese restaurant.

I'll never forget the fun we had over those years. Thanks to my grandparents, I went away to college with a social confidence I wouldn't have had otherwise and able to cook slightly unusual dishes that my friends loved. My Gran's been dead for five years now, but I still think of her every time I go to a restaurant and try to guess what she would have chosen from the menu.

Then and now:

Sex and sexuality

Hasty experimentation and fears of pregnancy characterised relationships between the sexes even two generations ago; today's teenagers are more relaxed about sex and sexuality.

THEN

Since the end of World War II there has been an enormous shift in attitudes towards sexual behaviour. Unless you moved in sophisticated society, sex was almost certainly an unmentionable when you were growing up. Now it is discussed freely and most children from the age of six or seven know something about the basic facts of life, not only about how a baby grows in mummy's tummy but also how the 'seed' gets there in the first place. You may find this openness embarrassing. But if you can remember the fear and ignorance that prevailed when you were young, perhaps you can understand the benefits of such frankness.

In the industrialised world, teenagers are physically ready for a sexual relationship and biologically capable of becoming parents long before society believes that they are emotionally prepared. Except in some religious communities, virginity is no longer seen as a precious commodity and many girls and boys consider it a burden to off-load as soon as possible. The result is that, although most countries set an age at which sexual intercourse is legal, some children experience it well before that age.

You may be able to take comfort from the fact that a majority of teenagers still say they believe lovemaking should take place in a stable, long-term relationship –

although not necessarily one that is leading to marriage. They also view decisions about sexual relationships as personal, rather than related to the moral values imposed on them by older generations or by religion.

Used properly, contraception – which is vastly improved and much more accessible than it was even a generation ago – has in the main relieved young girls of the fear of pregnancy. Research has shown that teenage pregnancies are less likely to occur when young people have the facts and are given access to family planning services. The old myth that knowledge will inevitably lead to experimentation is not borne out by the evidence – the rate of teenage pregnancies in the Netherlands, which has a liberal approach to teenage sexuality and excellent family planning services, is much lower than in other Western countries.

One factor that remains unchanged is that children still receive much of their information – or misinformation – from giggling groups in the school playground. Young people prefer this information to come primarily from their parents, with teachers as a back-up. But many parents continue to opt out of this responsibility, despite the widespread discussion of sexual matters on television and in

NOW

You may well have frequented coffee bars and bowling alleys to meet potential partners, then started dating them (far left). The relaxation of social attitudes has given young people greater freedom to get to know each other as friends (left) before they begin to consider having partners.

magazines and newspapers. The problem with sex as part of the curriculum is that school is an efficient forum for conveying the physical facts but less effective when it comes to discussing the emotional implications of sexuality. Children need to understand how strongly they can feel when aroused, and how much their emotions are tied in with physical drive.

Practical knowledge

Given that many young teens are sexually active, an important concern should be that they are sufficiently well informed to prevent conception. Many children of all ages find the concept of their parents' sexuality deeply embarrassing, so your grandchild may find it easier to talk to you than to them. If he feels he can discuss anything he likes with you and knows that it is in confidence, you may be able to give sensible advice that would be unacceptable coming from a parent. But do encourage him to talk to them too.

The earlier teenagers become sexually active the more important it is that they should always practise safer sex. They may only relate using a condom to avoiding pregnancy, but they need to know that condoms are also very important for the prevention of sexually transmitted diseases, including AIDS.

Advising a young person about contraception can pose a dilemma for parents and other adults. On the one hand, there is reluctance to appear to condone such behaviour. But on the other, teenagers must be made aware of the need to take responsibility for their actions.

• **The Pill:** There is concern that using the contraceptive pill before the menstrual cycle is well established can be harmful. However, both parents and doctors may think the advantages outweigh the risks if a young girl is regularly sexually active.

• **Diaphragm:** A young girl could be fitted for a diaphragm, but it's unlikely that this method will appeal to her or her partner. And because she is still growing, the diaphragm may not fit properly for long.

• **Condoms:** The most satisfactory way for young people to protect themselves against an unwanted pregnancy is to use a condom, as long as it is used properly. (The female condom is still not widely accepted.) This does not mean that the boy has to be responsible for carrying one. A girl who goes out on a date knowing that she is likely to make love may carry condoms in her bag. This may make her seem 'easy' in your eyes, but she should be commended for her sense of responsibility.

• **The morning-after pill:** This is an emergency form of contraception if a girl has had unprotected sex and risked becoming pregnant. It involves two special doses of a pill taken 12 hours apart, which prevent an egg from being released from her ovary, or a fertilised egg from implanting in the womb.

Drug awareness

Understanding teenagers' interest in legal and illegal substances

Lots of adults drink and smoke. You may be one of them – but you would be horrified if someone suggested that you were a drug addict. However, tobacco and alcohol are drugs and are more common causes of health and social problems than illegal substances such as cannabis or heroin. The difference is that they are socially acceptable. It is important to bear this in mind when you are discussing drugs with your grandchild.

Smoking

Despite expensive and extensive health education programmes and the damage caused by cigarettes (which young people might witness in their older relatives), more young adolescents are taking up smoking, with girls starting younger than boys. Teenagers know that over 80 per cent of lung cancer is related to smoking; that it also causes bronchitis and other serious breathing difficulties; and that thousands of smokers die prematurely and in pain each year. Smoking also makes the breath stale and discolours the teeth, and the smell of smoke lingers on clothes. Yet by the age of 15 nearly a third of adolescents have taken up the habit.

One reason children continue to find smoking so alluring is that they believe it makes them appear sophisticated. They are continually exposed to smoking (and drinking) if not at home, then in the street, on the screen and at social occasions. Family example is also influential. Children who have two parents who smoke are three times more likely to take it up than the children of nonsmokers; those with older siblings who smoke are even more likely to be attracted to the idea. The positive news is that teenagers become much more aware of the risks associated with smoking as they grow older. The problem then is the difficulty of giving it up.

If you and other family members smoke, it is difficult to argue that your grandchild should not. The idea that you are setting a bad example may spur you to kick a lifelong habit, but if this is impossible, the only thing you can do that is likely to have an impact is to emphasise to your grandchild the difficulties of giving up smoking once he starts. Telling him that nicotine is as addictive as heroin may catch his attention. If you have never smoked and disapprove, your grandchild may do it to defy you and his parents. That doesn't mean you have to allow him to smoke in your house.

The problem with alcohol is its ubiquity. If your grandchild often sees you enjoying a beer, cooking with wine and drinking with each meal, he will believe that he can do so too. Aim for moderate social drinking when he is around.

WARNING SIGNS

Your grandchild may mask a developing drink problem for several months, simply because many of the symptoms – such as irritability – are so common among adolescents. If he is suffering from several of the symptoms listed below, however, he could be in trouble. If you suspect that his drinking is getting out of hand, tell his parents.

- Mood changes
- Irritability
- Insomnia
- Poor appetite or a craving for sweet things or eating enormous amounts between drinking bouts
- Aggression
- Loss of interest in hobbies and other pastimes

Young teens are constantly exposed to street drugs – in the playground, at parties and in clubs and discos. Aim to teach the self-esteem to say no.

Alcohol

As serious for his parents as for your grandchild, alcohol abuse can cause a young person to harm himself and others. An easy-going, mild-mannered adolescent can become aggressive and violent under the influence of alcohol and may even end up on a criminal charge.

You and the rest of the family can play an important part in teaching your grandchild sensible drinking habits, which is more effective than locking the cocktail cabinet and warning him constantly about the dangers of the 'demon drink'. Forbidding a child to have any alcohol at all will only make him even more curious and determined to try it.

A child's first alcoholic drink tends to be given by parents or family and most 11 to 14 year olds drink only at home with family where they can experience the effects in a safe environment. A child who is gradually introduced to alcohol over a period of years, perhaps starting with a little wine mixed with water at special family meals, is likely to be able to handle it far better than someone without prior experience. A moderate attitude at home can encourage sensible drinking when the child is out with friends. Girls tend to receive less encouragement to drink than boys, for whom there is still something of a macho element attached.

From around the age of 14 teenagers tend to drink with friends and this is where problems can arise. Although laws govern the age at which young people can buy alcohol, many children openly flout them. This can be laziness or disregard on the part of the person selling the drink, but some teenagers look so mature that it does not occur to the vendor to ask for proof of their age.

When asked about the effects of alcohol, young people tend to emphasise the positive ones such as feeling happy and relaxed and having a good time, rather than remembering the headaches, nausea and hangovers. It's true that alcohol helps to relieve tension and aid relaxation, but it does not offer any lasting solutions, and young people need to be made aware – through calm discussion, not angry rebuke – that overindulgence will, in the long term, add to their problems.

If your grandchild develops his social skills under the influence of alcohol, he won't know how to behave without it. Those who drink heavily as teenagers are also more likely to use other drugs. A young person may develop a pattern of becoming inebriated with alcohol one evening and stoned on cannabis the next. You are likely to find this recklessness and disregard for health and wellbeing the most upsetting aspect of teenage drinking.

Drug awareness

Illegal drugs

Because it is something that might be out of your own experience, you may feel at a disadvantage when it comes to discussing drugs with your grandchild. Your own child might have smoked the odd joint but generally the use of illicit drugs was very low until the late 1960s. Today, a huge range of illicit drugs is on offer and your grandchild may be tempted to experiment with a variety of substances. Older people often do not know enough to tackle this issue confidently. Since you may have to confront it at some point in your grandchild's adolescence, it is important to read and absorb as much information as you can.

All young teenagers need to be aware of the dangers of drugs: it is an alarming fact that children of only 13 and 14, or younger, may be exposed to drugs in the school playground. The reasons they try them are many and varied, but background and performance at school do not seem to be relevant factors. Peer pressure plays an enormous part – a child may take drugs to avoid being the odd one out. He may be tempted in an effort to escape from problems at home, to dull the pain of failing an important exam or breaking up with a girlfriend. It may be simply curiosity,

Drug use first became common among young people in the 1960s as one aspect of the new emphasis on personal freedom. Then, as now, cannabis (marijuana) was the most common street drug.

TELLING ALL

If you suspect that your grandchild is smoking, drinking excessively or using illicit drugs you must tell his parents. The chances are that you will only be confirming their own suspicions but, at least, you can join forces at this particularly difficult time.

• Never offer your grandchild a cigarette.

• Encourage sensible drinking by allowing small amounts of alcohol at special meals.

• Be well informed about illicit drugs and their effects. A grandchild convinced of your ignorance may use drugs in your home.

• If you have charge of your grandchild and suspect alcohol or drug abuse, report the matter immediately to his school.

• Find out about counsellors and support groups for both him and his family.

or he may be intrigued by the notion that some drugs can offer him insight into the meaning of life or the existence of God.

Once he has tried them he may find it difficult to cope socially without the sense of euphoria or wellbeing these drugs initially induce. If he becomes physically addicted, he may be unable to function normally without a fix, and attempts to give up the drugs may result in withdrawal symptoms – from sweats and cramps to sickness, fever and a desperate craving for the substances he is trying to avoid. A calm, commonsense approach from adults he cares for may help him to refuse them.

If you find that your grandchild is in this position, condemn the behaviour but not him, and make it clear that you will do everything you can to help him kick the habit. Parents often find a child's drug problem difficult to deal with; you may be calmer and may also have more time to do some research and find your grandchild professional help. The people who go on to become lifelong alcoholics or drug addicts are most likely to be those who do not have a loving and supportive family.

| NAME | USAGE | EFFECTS AND HAZARDS |

Cocaine/Crack

Cocaine, also known as coke or snow, is a powerful stimulant. Crack is cocaine that has been treated with chemicals to be absorbed faster. Both come as white powder.

Powder is sniffed (snorted) through a tube or dissolved in water and injected with a syringe.

Creates a feeling of wellbeing, makes the user indifferent to pain and tiredness and increases confidence. Users become dependent and tempted to increase dose and frequency; they often become nervous, excitable and paranoid. Repeated sniffing damages the membranes lining the nose and the structure separating the nostrils. Smoking crack can cause various breathing problems and pains in the chest.

Ecstasy

White, brown, pink or yellow tablets and capsules, also known as disco burgers, diamonds, New Yorkers and rhubarb and custard.

Tablets or capsules taken by mouth.

The user experiences a 'rush' followed by a feeling of calm and wellbeing; often gives a heightened perception of colours and sounds. Dangers include dehydration and heat stroke from prolonged non-stop dancing; water is necessary to combat their effects but excessive water consumption can lead to medical complications and be fatal.

Heroin

An opiate, also known as smack, junk and skag. White powder often adulterated with other substances such as talcum powder so dose is unclear.

Injected, sniffed or smoked.

Makes the user feel drowsy and content, although the first time he can feel nauseous and may vomit. Dependence develops quickly. There is also a danger of contracting HIV if needles are shared with other users.

LSD

A colourless, odourless, tasteless powder or solution; other names include acid, tabs and trips.

Comes as tablets or capsules but usually supplied on small squares of blotting paper – tabs or trips – taken orally.

Causes hallucinations for up to 12 hours. The brain is affected by the tiniest amount of the drug. A user can lose all sense of time and place, and sounds and colours can become confused.

Marijuana

Also known as cannabis, dope, hash, weed and ganga, this can be bought as leaves, stalks or seeds.

Usually smoked in a pipe or mixed with tobacco and rolled in a cigarette; can also be brewed into a drink or eaten.

Makes user talkative, cheerful and relaxed; increases the appetite. May cause feelings of paranoia if taken when depressed. Like smoking nicotine, marijuana can cause lung cancer and breathing problems.

Solvents

Most common drug used by children aged 12 to 16. Involves sniffing chemical fumes in glues, aerosol sprays, nail polish remover, butane gas and other household substances.

Sniffed, sometimes with a plastic bag over the head, until user feels 'high'.

A user feels light-headed and giddy and may have hallucinations; death can occur from choking, vomiting or suffocation. Long-term heavy use can damage the brain, liver and kidneys. Damaged brain function can trigger long-term mental illness. Nightmare-like flashbacks can happen years later without warning. Although solvents are not usually addictive, a regular user can feel out of touch with the real world.

Understanding the jargon
Keeping up with current trends in music, film, clothes and speech

Once he reaches adolescence, it is important to be aware of what is happening in your grandchild's life, without being intrusive. If you know the kind of films he enjoys, the music he listens to and the TV programmes that appeal, you will have an opening on to his world.

There is a very fine line between being sufficiently well informed to make communication easy and becoming an embarrassment. Never let your grandchild know that you watched his favourite film in order to understand him better. This is

patronising. But recognising the references he makes to a film – even if it is one you would normally shun – shows your grandchild that you are broad-minded enough to talk to, and that it is age which separates you, nothing more.

It is likely that, for a variety of reasons, his parents will react in traditional fashion to their child's taste in clothes, music and film and the way he speaks. But you can be more objective. You may remember your parents' disapproval of your generation's choices. Perhaps you took the stern parental role with your own children.

Popular culture and styles of dress and speech give adolescents a chance to express their separateness from the previous generation and to identify with and be accepted by their peers; these are safe ways of rebelling. Put your opinions forward, but listen to what your grandchild has to say, too. Resist the urge to ridicule current styles and popular heroes, even if they seem sadly lacking to you – and don't make comparisons with bygone trends. Your grandchild needs to feel that he is discovering something new that 'belongs' to him. Pointing out that a current favourite owes everything to John Lennon or that it's all been done a hundred times before is the most cynical kind of put-down.

Sharing his interests
Don't become obsessive about keeping up with your grandchild's chosen interests, but do a little 'homework'. Teen magazines are

You don't have to share all your grandchildren's interests – nor they yours – but if you look regularly in the 'what's on' section of the newspaper or a local listings magazine, you are sure to discover films, plays, concerts or exhibitions that appeal to you all.

You don't have to buy computer games or CDs to understand popular culture, but it is important to realise how central that culture is to your grandchild's life.

a good source of information on current fads, trends and heroes and you will absorb a lot of new language as well. Many magazines are criticised for their explicit nature and the fact that they are read by people younger than their professed target audience. Nevertheless, you can be sure that your grandchild will be familiar with everything discussed on their pages. You may feel shocked, but remember that the writers are pandering to the young people's sophisticated ideas about themselves rather than truly reflecting their everyday lives.

Your grandchild is sure to watch a lot of videos, since these are a less expensive option than the cinema. If his parents object because they often want to use the VCR themselves, consider inviting him to use yours if you live close by. Stipulate the maximum number of friends he may bring with him and reserve the right to know exactly what they plan to watch. Most parents are flexible about older children watching videos which are classified for older or more mature audiences, but you should tread carefully. If in doubt, seek his parents' advice and/or ask to view the movie before he watches it.

As long as everyone acts consistently with regard to this kind of supervision, your grandchild will respect you for it, regardless of his protestations about what all his friends watch. Most young people see some unsuitable material but that does not mean that they crave it or that it should be encouraged. Help your grandchild to resist unsuitable peer pressure by maintaining a level-headed, broad-minded attitude.

Think, too, about watching some films together. Perhaps you could take him to the cinema (there is bound to be at least one film you might both enjoy), and gradually extend the range of films he watches so that it includes some of your favourites you think he might appreciate.

Television is a more accessible medium and it is not difficult, when you have the time, to tune into programmes aimed at his age group in order to discover what is popular and important now. You may be surprised at how central the issues of ecology and conservation are to young people today and in what depth they are examined and discussed.

Computer games are an integral part of being a young teen and it is hard to understand their appeal until you have played them yourself. You do not need to be pre-informed here; your grandchild will be only too willing to have a convert. If you find you play for long periods every time you are together, try to compromise. Suggest a board or card game for a change and entice him outdoors occasionally, but don't denigrate his interest.

Perhaps the hardest part of understanding your grandchild at this stage is making sense of the jargon and his manner of expressing himself. There is a vocabulary attached to computers and games, terms used in connection with music and dance, and language that bonds peers together. Remember that language constantly shifts and develops and people use words and phrases in order to feel part of a chosen group. It's important to be able to understand what he is saying to you, but you will embarrass everyone if you start peppering your conversation with his terms. Don't encroach on his desire to be different.

Shared skills: crafts

Introducing your grandchild to practical skills and handicrafts

This is the age at which your grandchild may give the impression that he thinks you have nothing to teach him. Don't respond too harshly to this attitude – everything about the adult world is new to him and it takes some time to realise how much there is to learn. If you have skills you think are worth passing on, go ahead and try to do so; sharing practical knowledge may make up for some of the closeness you feel you are losing due to his growing independence.

All children, but especially those at this stage, respond well to the 'hands-on' approach, rather than being lectured on the subject. Useful skills, such as woodwork, home decorating and DIY, all lend themselves to this way of working. To begin with, your grandchild may need the enticement of seeing you tackling a project of your own. Without placing pressure on him or letting him see it as a chore, enlist his assistance in a small way at first. If this type of working together goes well, you could then discuss a future project.

If you have redecorated your house recently, he may be keen to paint and paper his own room at home. There are three considerations to bear in mind if home decorating is the skill you are sharing. First, your grandchild's parents must be privy to your intentions and happy to let you and your grandchild get on with the project in their home. Second, you have to keep your advice and guidance low-key – as if you were helping an adult, not instructing a child – and this means accepting results which may not be up to your own high standards. Last, be certain before agreeing to any project that you have the time to be present at each stage and see it through to the end. Half-finished enterprises and unfulfilled promises are no way to promote good workmanship or maturity in your grandchild.

With an expensive project – such as redecorating a room – decide how much you are willing to contribute and budget accordingly before you begin. Going to

Your grandchild may still be living with her parents' choice of decoration – which may be more appropriate for the child she was than the young adult she is becoming. Your help in redecorating her haven is sure to be appreciated.

All of a sudden the child who wanted to hand you screws or hold your screwdriver or hammer is eager to learn some of the finer points of working with wood. Passing on traditional skills is a wonderful way to bring the two of you closer and a marvellous antidote to the frenzied pace of your grandchild's everyday life.

a few stores and planning and costing everything together will give your grandchild a firm grip on these basic aspects and prevent him from becoming too ambitious. Encourage him to buy good-quality materials and tools that will last and can be used again and again so that he views the skill he is acquiring as something he can develop rather than a one-off lesson.

Start small

If you are sharing your love of carpentry or joinery with him, be patient. Discuss the idea that this must be a long-term commitment, since these are skills it takes time to learn. Start in a small way to avoid early frustration and disappointment. These skills may be part of his school curriculum, but students often have little choice as to what they make and frequently lose interest because the object they have produced is of little relevance to them. You may start off, as with decorating, by encouraging your grandchild to assist you with one of your own projects, then progress to working on one of his own ideas.

It may help to consult a library for ideas about what can be made simply and also appeal to someone of this age. Forget old standbys such as pencil boxes, bookends and small stools unless they are of an unusual design and your grandchild is genuinely keen to make them. Suggest that he produce Christmas or birthday gifts for his family – a spice rack for the keen cook, or a stand to hold the music lover's CDs. Young people often have little or no money to spend on others, so this could be a satisfying solution for all concerned.

Other skills

You may have other skills which you had not realised would interest someone of your grandchild's age. Knitting has an old-fashioned image, but bright, bold knitwear is always in vogue and your grandchild may jump at the idea of making something eyecatching for himself. The quality of yarns and availability of different textures and colours has improved dramatically over the years and is sure to interest a style-conscious adolescent. You could also point out that knitting can be therapeutic and an antidote to pre-exam stress. If you are competent in this area, encourage your grandchild to design his own patterns: with your knowledge and his eye for fashion you will make a winning team.

If you are skilled at sewing your own clothes try to pass this on to your grandchild. Both boys and girls will benefit later from being able to make a pair of curtains, cover some old cushions, shorten trousers and sew on buttons.

Shared skills: cooking

Fostering your grandchild's interest in choosing and preparing food

Cooking food for and with others is one of the most fulfilling things we do, enjoyable in itself and with a satisfying end result. Preparing a favourite dish for a friend; making a special dinner for the family; and baking a cake or some biscuits for someone who is feeling unwell or upset all show we care. They cement the undeniable connection between giving generously of our time and resources and loving people.

The negative side of the busy lives we all lead is the lack of time and energy to cook on a regular basis for families and friends. Your grandchild will probably have a greater experience and knowledge of convenience foods and takeaways than he will of home cooking and the pleasures of concocting special meals and treats. His parents may be pressed for time or simply lack the inclination to show him how important and rewarding this particular skill can be, so if you decide to play the role

Inviting his friends to sample a dish you have created together is probably the highest accolade your grandchild can give the skill you have shared with him.

of 'master chef' you will find it a satisfying way of maintaining closeness, as well as having fun with your grandchild.

Children have enough formal teaching at school – make the time your grandchild spends with you easy and calm. If you have never done much home baking or special cooking yourself but are keen to learn, now is a wonderful time to begin. Your grandchild will enjoy the experience of your learning step by step together just as much as he would enjoy your being the expert sharing your skills.

Whether you are a competent cook or not, begin your sessions with something that is sure to achieve results worth eating. Don't opt for a dish so simple that your grandchild will have done it when he was younger – this is an affront to his adolescent dignity. But if despite your more exotic suggestions he wants to cook burgers, you can still make them special. Use the freshest mince or mince your own meat. Add herbs and spices to improve on the bland taste he knows from burger chains and, for a real home-cooked touch, bake your own buns. If you are planning more than one session around this staple, consider making your own sauces and relishes.

If, like some of his peers, your grandchild is vegetarian and you are not, choose recipes you know he will eat and that you can make successfully. You may need to consult some books on the subject to ensure that your meal is nutritionally balanced. Don't comment on his decision over this issue or try to pressure him into eating meat or anything else he declines.

Cooking is not always about transforming ingredients: the approach to presentation is equally important in some national cusines.

Adolescents often develop a desire to try foreign cuisines, which could be a worthwhile area to pursue since you can adapt and tailor curries, stir fries, chillies and so on to suit your individual palates. This is a particularly rich area if you have a strong ethnic cuisine which, perhaps, his parents have not shared with him. Spend time leafing through recipe books and make up a list of things you both want to try. Once you are used to working together and become a competent team you may want to invite the rest of the family to sample your efforts.

Baking bread can be highly satisfying if your grandchild has never tasted homemade loaves. Alternate these time-consuming recipes with making cakes and biscuits which give quick results. If your grandchild is unsure of what to buy for family members or friends – or financially unable to afford a present – introduce him to the delights of homemade chocolates, toffee and fudge. Attractively packaged, these make great gifts.

SHARING COOKERY SKILLS

• If a recipe is not familiar to you try it out before you involve your grandchild in the process.

• Have all the ingredients and utensils you will need ready before you begin working. Your grandchild will be disappointed if you find that a vital element is missing.

• Alternate recipes he wants to try with surprises you think he will enjoy eating.

• Always leave enough time at the end of a session to sample what you have cooked.

• Do not comment during your cooking sessions (or at any other time) on his parents' cooking abilities, or lack of them.

• Suggest he starts a notebook of the recipes you try together, adding comments and tips of your own which may help him. He may well use it for years to come.

Don't worry if things go wrong. Even the best chefs produce sponge cakes that sink and soups that are unappetising. But these efforts will be outnumbered by your successes. If you are not upset when the worst happens, your grandchild will learn to try again.

Shopping for new and unusual ingredients is half the fun of learning to cook international dishes. If you, too, are unused to such an array and unsure of what to buy or overwhelmed with too many choices, ask for advice – most deli staff are pleased to reward your interest with helpful tips of their own.

Pocket money and allowances

Deciding when to offer financial help to your grandchild

Heated discussions over pocket money seem to reach a peak at this stage in your grandchild's life. You may remember from your parenting days the problems this contentious issue caused; and you may also be able to empathise with your grandchild because you know he is under peer pressure, as well as being lured by advertising, to buy expensive items and not to be different from everyone else. Because you can see both sides of the argument over the precise amount of money – whether or not it should be given in return for chores done or withheld as a punishment – you are in a position to help both your grandchild and his parents.

If you are aware that his parents have financial difficulties that are genuinely exacerbated by your grandchild's demands, you could, tactfully, offer to supplement the amount he receives. If his parents are set in their attitudes and concerned that their child is being greedy, you could offer a regular amount for chores to be done for you. If you settle the matter in this way you must ensure that your grandchild really

does complete the chores you agree upon. You must be sure that they are not beyond his abilities or too time-consuming.

Find something that is a real help to you so that he does not feel you are patronising him. Window cleaning, car washing and gardening all fall into this category. But remember, if you do contribute to your grandchild's allowance on a regular basis, you must operate with impeccable fairness: if you have other grandchildren be prepared to give the same amount to them.

Young teens' allowances vary enormously. If you think your grandchild's parents are unrealistic in how little they give their child you could casually mention the fact the next time you read of a survey on the subject; these items appear regularly in the press.

If, on the other hand, you can clearly see that your grandchild's ability to spend is limitless and that he shows no signs of saving anything or wanting to do anything with his money than spend it all on himself, you may prefer to save a small weekly amount for him without telling him you are doing so. Then, when he has no

Gardens can be hard work, particularly if you are not as fit as when you acquired the house of your dreams. Asking your grandchild to rake leaves, mow grass, dig and plant vegetable beds and carry out numerous other seasonal tasks – with your advice and participation – helps you and gives him the chance to supplement his allowance.

Young teenagers are under intense pressure to conform, and many of the latest 'must haves' are expensive. If you want to help, consider offering half the cost of a pair of trainers or new jeans as a birthday gift; your grandchild should pay the rest with her own money.

money to buy gifts, you can introduce him painlessly to the pleasure of spending money on others. Make it clear that you saved the money for him so that he would not be embarrassed by his inability to buy a present for anyone – though obviously you can only do this once he has admitted that he is penniless.

You must accept his parents' decision if they have made it clear that they do not want you to become involved in the pocket money issue. Lavish time and attention on your grandchild instead of money, and help him make his allowance go further by showing him how to shop wisely, encouraging saving, and teaching him games and recreations that do not depend on expensive equipment. You can also, if you feel strongly on this matter, open a savings account in his name for when he becomes an adult. If you do, keep silent about it, and do the same for all your grandchildren, or you may run the risk of family discord.

CASE HISTORY

Every time we visit our grandchildren we notice that seven-year-old Andrew has more new toys. His mother says they are educational or they were bought because Andrew doesn't get pocket money yet. We are sure that his parents spend more on Andrew than they give 14-year-old Paul for pocket money, yet it is always Paul they argue with, usually over something he has asked for or that he can't afford. We have tended in the past to give Paul rather expensive birthday and Christmas gifts, when we have been sure that they were what he wanted, but his parents have asked us not to – they think we are spoiling him, and are concerned that he is growing up ignorant of the value of things. So, on recent visits although we have bought Paul the T-shirt he wanted and a new pair of trainers, we have also been careful to buy something for Andrew, even though he has so much already.

Now we have decided to give Paul a small monthly amount to ease everybody's burden and we've made it clear that we are putting exactly the same amount in savings for Andrew. We were surprised that there were no arguments over this, but we talked about how to word it before we made the offer. In the past we have tried to supplement Paul's pocket money on occasion and been accused of undermining parental authority, but I think this time it was different because we took care to include Andrew and made it clear that Paul's allowance would stop if his parents said so.

The arrangement has been in effect for three months now and there have definitely been fewer arguments in that household. Paul is making a real effort because he knows we have, and the extra amount we give him has brought him on a par with most of his friends.

Understanding the world

Helping your grandchild to make sense of his life and experiences

If your grandchild allows you into her room, you may be overwhelmed by the visual material that attests to her support for a number of environmental and other causes. These may vary from large, international organisations trying to act on a global scale to local groups working on small specific projects.

There are sure to be times when you may wonder what happened to the obedient little child who looked to you for advice and information. And you may ask yourself how he turned into the young person with highly charged emotions and passionate views. At such times, you are witnessing the development of your grandchild into an adult.

But the next time you feel overwhelmed by his opinions, remind yourself that this is what growing up is all about and congratulate yourself that he feels sufficiently confident of your support to be using you as his sounding board. You should be far more concerned if he has nothing to say for himself and no ideas about the world in which he is about to enter. Be prepared for him to accuse your generation of making nothing but mistakes – this is simply a part of his trying to make sense of the larger issues that confront him.

Try to remember how angry or desperate you felt about causes before you gained enough maturity to cope with the often harsh realities of our world.

Politics

Whether they study politics as a subject in its own right or as part of a 'general studies' course, adolescents are frequently encouraged to discuss current global and local problems. As a result, politics is often the key issue for young teens.

There will, inevitably, be times when your grandchild reveals naiveté or impracticality in what he says. He will probably come across some adults (both in his own family and among the parents of his friends) who put him down because he is young and who use age and experience as weapons in discussions. Make sure that you are never among them. This is a crucial stage for your grandchild in terms of self-confidence. Even if you disagree most strongly with everything he is saying, he deserves respect for his opinions and – obviously – has the right to express them.

Your grandchild is far more likely to take notice of your different ideas if you have first listened to him without interruption. Treat him as an adult. If you fear that his politics are dangerous or verging on the illegal, or that he is being influenced by an unsavoury group, keep a close but unobtrusive eye on things – he may share what he is involved in with you rather than his parents – but take into account this age group's delight in exaggeration.

If you live at a distance, it's important to maintain telephone or written contact. If your grandchild has been used to discussing issues with you, he is likely to talk about his enthusiasms and you will have a picture of the depth of his interests and involvements. If anything he says gives you cause for concern, ask him about it calmly, and explain why an aggressive political stance, say, concerns you.

Religion
One aspect of life that usually comes in for close scrutiny at this age is religion. If your family is devout, you may find that your grandchild chooses to rebel in some way. However offended you feel about this, it helps to recognise that questioning of assumptions shows intelligence and doesn't mean that he will be a permanent non-believer.

A lively discussion centred around the issues of the day, using newspapers and magazines to support your views, helps your grandchild to understand the complexities of the adult world.

If his parents find this difficult to deal with, take some of the burden off them by listening to what your grandchild has to say. If you can't counter his arguments objectively – and if he is genuinely interested in discussion – you could enlist the help of your minister. But applying pressure to bring him back to the family's way of thinking is a sure way to strengthen his resolve to be different.

By contrast, if your family is not committed to any faith you may find that your grandchild suddenly becomes attached to one. This is often a way in which young people try to make sense of a difficult world and as long as the group he has chosen does not seek to take him away from his family or alter the way in which he lives there is little to fear. If, however, your grandchild becomes involved with a sect that you feel is an unwholesome influence, it is worth investigating – or at least discussing the matter with his parents – sooner rather than later.

Understanding the world

Prejudices

It is common to find that your grandchild's views on such matters as race and prejudice are entirely different from yours. If he has experienced hostility from a particular racial group he may have developed a less than liberal attitude, but gentle reasoning on your part – emphasising that the characteristics of the individuals who have mistreated him cannot be attributed to an entire race – should help him to develop more tolerance. If, as is more likely, he has grown up among ethnic groups of which you have less experience and the prejudice is on your side, listen to him carefully.

Sex

A major interest for all adolescents is sex, and if you have always had a close relationship, your grandchild is more likely to talk to you than to his parents on this subject. Any personal information he shares with you should be treated in total confidence, even if you feel he is placing you in a difficult position with regard to his parents. If you are concerned that you are betraying his parents' trust, tell your

In a religious group or sect your grandchild may find the sense of belonging that he lacks in his school or social life. Listen sympathetically to his views, even if they are not ones you feel you can share.

grandchild so in a way that does not make him turn from you completely.

He is more likely to talk about sex in a general way and his attitudes are almost certain to differ from your own. Silently recall how many of us say we will never get married or have children and how many of us recant; and how our attitudes towards sex, monogamy and relationships in general evolve and mature. Allow for his youth without being patronising or revealing too much of your worldly wisdom. Be careful what you let slip about yourself. A risqué tale told to convince your grandchild that things aren't that much different now from how they were in your youth could prove embarrassing when it spreads around your family. (See also pages 156–57.)

Supporting a cause today is not simply a matter of sending a donation. For many young teens, support also means a fashion statement.

A multitude of causes

Your grandchild may espouse different causes with a fervour bordering on the obsessive. Don't make light of his concerns. While you do not have to accompany him on protest marches or write letters of support to various organisations (unless you want to), you should be pleased that he cares deeply about something other than himself. It is easier as we get older to turn our backs on global problems with feelings of helplessness – we have, after all, witnessed so many. But your grandchild's energy and enthusiasm should remain untainted by cynicism for as long as possible.

Even if you think his zeal could be better directed elsewhere, it is important to realise that he is learning to care in the broadest sense – which is good practice for when he has a family of his own. You might be bewildered by how often his concerns change, but this is simply a sign of how quickly his feelings and ideas are developing. He is experiencing a tumult of emotions and ideas which will calm down as he nears adulthood.

ARE YOU LISTENING?

It is vital to listen to children. But it is when the skill of listening is perhaps most valuable that it can be difficult to maintain. Adolescents can be so strident and overbearing that it is frequently easier to switch off for a time or to try to silence them. But you will miss out on an exciting part of your grandchild's development if you cannot listen effectively.

• After a visit, make a list of what your grandchild said to you and recall any times when a conversation was begun but not finished. Write down what you told him of your concerns and life. If you discover that he has tried to tell you things that you didn't hear properly, or that you have interrupted and finished the conversation, you need to approach things differently.

• Improve your listening skills. If you spend a lot of time on your own you may have got out of the habit of listening, so make an effort to concentrate – it will be worth it.

• Develop the skill of 'reflective listening'. Rather than interject with helpful remarks or sympathetic words, simply feed back what your grandchild is saying in order to encourage him to say more:

Grandchild: 'I feel really angry with mum.'
Grandparent: 'You're angry with your mum?'
Grandchild: 'She picks on me all the time.'
Grandparent: 'She's picking on you?'
Grandchild: 'She's annoyed about work and takes it out on me.'

This may seem like a self-conscious mode of speaking but in fact the grandparent's lack of reaction and interference encourage the grandchild to think about why his mother is annoyed and acknowledge that it is not his fault. In reflecting back enough of what is being said to let the speaker know you are listening, you can also give him the chance to think things through.

Comments designed to 'help' like 'Well, your mother has problems of her own' or 'You know what her temper is like' would not have encouraged the grandchild to pursue his line of thought and understand the problem, but would have turned the attention away from the child, back towards the grandparent.

CHAPTER EIGHT

Becoming an Adult
16 and up

As your grandchild moves into adulthood your relationship is likely to change. You may find that the decades between you lead to misunderstanding, or feel that the way she lives conflicts with your own values. She may believe she can no longer be as open with you as before. On the other hand, with the worst upheavals of adolescence behind her, she may be more relaxed about herself and more responsive to you. With a little tolerance on both sides, your relationship can be as richly rewarding as ever.

Leaving school, finding work and forming serious relationships are exciting, but daunting, prospects. Your grandchild still needs your love and support, especially when things do not work out as planned. You can sympathise if she fails an examination or breaks up with a boyfriend. You can offer financial or practical help when she is establishing a home of her own. And, most important, you can take pride in the capable, independent individual she has become – and take some of the credit.

School-leaving rituals and gifts

Marking the transition from school to the adult world

Teenagers leave school with a variety of feelings. Childhood is now truly behind them and they will shortly have to learn to be self-reliant and responsible adults. Some can't wait for the day that they walk out of the school gates for the last time. These are most likely to be children who have already assumed the outward appearance and habits of adulthood, and who have felt for some time that school was irrelevant to them. Others may feel nervous about leaving the comparative safety of school for the unknown world of higher education or the workplace. How teenagers view this rite of passage also depends on how they have performed at school; whether they were academically successful and appear to have a glittering future ahead or whether they feel they have not made the most of their opportunities and are entering a new world ill-equipped and with few qualifications.

However she feels about the future, your grandchild is likely to want to mark the end of her schooldays in some way. Some teenagers – even in the most exclusive schools – rip up their uniforms or burn their books. A more civilised way to mark the occasion, however, is to have a dance or disco or to share a formal dinner with the teachers who have supported them throughout their school years.

The school-leaving celebration may be the first grand occasion your grandchild has attended and her first opportunity to dress up. If a fancy dress or evening gown is required and you are a competent dressmaker, you may be called upon to help out. You will both have fun poring over pattern books and fashion magazines and may be able to create something special and original for her big night. It's important that she looks her best and she

Regardless of your grandchild's overall opinion of his schooldays, leaving school is a milestone in his life. In addition to the formal recognition of the occasion by his peers and teachers, his graduation from school to the world of work or college is an excellent opportunity to get the family together to wish him well in whatever he chooses to do next.

and her friends will no doubt spend days, if not weeks, preparing for this occasion.

It would not be surprising if your idea of a formal outfit differed from your grandchild's. Formal, for your grandchild, may mean anything that isn't jeans and heavy boots – and that applies to both sexes – so don't be disappointed if she opts for smart trousers and a tunic instead. Your grandson may decide to hire a dinner jacket for the occasion but this could be an opportunity for him to buy a suit, which will also be useful for job interviews. Consider giving him the money to go shopping for suitable clothes. Don't offer to accompany him unless he asks you to and don't insist on him having the most expensive suit in the store. If he is still growing, a suit will not last long. If he already has a suitable jacket and trousers, suggest he smarten it up for the evening with a colourful waistcoat or a silk tie.

Because fashion is cyclical it is possible that the clothes you wore in your youth will be acceptable to your grandchild. If you have stored a few of your favourites away in a trunk it might be fun to let her rifle through to see if there is anything she could wear. What could be more special than going off for an important evening in one of Grandma's evening dresses or Granddad's dinner jacket?

You may want to mark your grandchild's school-leaving with a gift. If she is going on to college or university a cheque will be appreciated. But if she is not particularly good at budgeting and likely to blow the money in one go, you might decide to pay a certain amount into her bank account each month. A grandchild who is starting work immediately may also be glad of financial help to buy appropriate clothes for her new life or to tide her over until her first pay cheque.

Grandparents often like to help out with the cost of driving lessons or with the purchase of a car. A licence is always a useful qualification and may be an advantage in securing your grandchild's first job. If you are considering buying her a car, check with her parents to make sure they agree that she is ready for the responsibility. Boys, in particular, need to be aware that a car is not something in which to prove to their friends how many risks they are prepared to take. Young people often forget, too, that the cost of owning a car goes far beyond the purchase price and that they need to put money aside for tax, insurance and upkeep as well as petrol. A knowledge of maintenance is handy, too (see also pp. 182–83).

There is no need to buy a new car. The chances are that your grandchild will prefer an older one which she can individualise. This may mean respraying it shocking pink or decorating it with stickers. Secondhand cars do not need to be smart but they must be safe. Unless you are an expert, get any car you are considering checked by one of the motoring organisations.

Perhaps your grandchild is celebrating leaving school by taking her first independent holiday with friends rather than family. Once again money is a welcome gift. Alternatively, she might be planning to travel more seriously, perhaps by taking a year off between school and college in order to see the world. You could offer to pay for an air ticket or a month's rail ticket or consider buying a backpack or something similar as a way of wishing her bon voyage.

Your grandchild's first thought as she leaves the inflexible routine of her schooldays behind her may be to see something of the world. She may want to travel before she becomes too involved in a career and forming lasting relationships.

Activities to share
Making the most of your adult grandchild's time with you

There is no reason why you and your grandchild should not continue to do things together now that she is a young adult. But the fact that you may not see her as much as you would like makes it even more important that your times together should be fulfilling.

If you still have hobbies and interests in common, you will almost certainly continue to share them whenever possible. What could be better than striding across the golf course with your grandchild, putting on your walking boots in preparation for a trek in the country with her or going off to a ball game together? Especially if you introduced her to an activity in the first place, there is great satisfaction in knowing that it continues to enrich her life. You may, however, have to resign yourself to the fact that your grandchild is now better at these activities than you are and to accept this graciously. But you can, at the same time, take some credit for her achievements.

There are quite a few grandparents who sparked the first interest in an activity or spotted a particular talent.

With their steady encouragement a child may have developed and perfected skills that now mean she is winning medals for athletics or has turned artistic leanings into a profession. The little granddaughter you taught to sew may now be taking a course in fashion design and the small boy you introduced to the *Asterix* books in French may be an accomplished linguist. Even if your grandchildren have not reached these pinnacles of achievement, the dressmaker who makes all her own clothes may need your advice from time to time, and a weekend athlete may like you to come and watch him run.

Such developments can be even more satisfying if your own child showed no interest in your particular hobbies. Artistic skills and other

Your grandchild may still value your help and advice – even if you think that by now you have taught her everything you know about dressmaking. There may be times when you are the only one who can get an outfit for a special occasion to look exactly right.

Teaching your grandchild to play golf – and continuing to play with him even when his handicap betters yours – is an ideal way to keep the channels of communication open. It also gives you both some undemanding exercise in pleasant surroundings.

both be filming family occasions.

It may be that all the interests you once shared have lapsed as your grandchild has grown. Or perhaps ill health or reduced mobility have made your common passion for outdoor activities difficult for you to pursue. If so, invite her out for a meal every couple of months or so – try different restaurants and experiment with new foods. This will give you a regular opportunity to find out what is going on in her life and for her to learn that grandparents are among the most interesting dinner companions.

talents often seem to skip a generation. There is a great deal of enjoyment to be had in the role of onlooker, too – particularly if you have previously always been too active yourself to study the finer points of another's skill. Following your grandchild's progress may bring back happy memories of the fun you had at that age.

Now that your grandchild is a grown-up and your relationship is a more balanced, two-way affair it may be her turn to introduce you to some new interests. It is sometimes difficult to admit that the younger generation may know more than you do, but in the area of new technology this is almost always the case. If you would like to know more, ask your grandchild for information and try to keep up with developments together. Before you know it you may be the owner of a computer and discovering a fascination with computer games or with surfing the Internet.

Similarly, if photography is a shared interest you might extend this to video taping. Once again your grandchild may be the best person to introduce you to the intricacies of the camcorder. Soon you may

KEEPING IN TOUCH

Now that your grandchild has left school, and is away at college or working full-time, you are inevitably going to see less of her than you once did. You will miss her, but her absence doesn't mean that she has stopped caring about you; rather her life is now so full of new experiences and new friends that she probably finds it difficult to keep open the lines of communication. If she is a long way away, and you can afford it, you might suggest that you pay the bus, train or air fare, but make the offer graciously, so that it doesn't seem like a bribe. Regular letter-writing is a good way to stay in touch, especially if – like many other older people – you are unused to long, personal conversations on the phone. You will probably write much longer and more frequent letters than she does, and may have to be content with a quick postcard from her, but keep writing – she will be delighted to hear from you even if she doesn't often have time to reciprocate.

Then and now:
Flying the nest

Today's young adults often have the freedom to decide when to leave the parental home, but, as before, it is a matter of financial expediency versus the yearning for independence.

It is perfectly normal and healthy for your young adult grandchild to want to leave home. You may be part of the generation that left home only when they married, took a live-in job or joined the armed forces. And, if you did go from your parents' home to your own, you probably saved during your engagement in order to buy what you needed before you married to make that home comfortable. Or perhaps you married and lived with your parents while you saved long and hard for a place of your own.

In either case, you may find it strange that your grandchild prefers to share a grubby flat with a group of friends rather than remain in her comfortable family home. She may even decide to live alone: single-person households are an increasing feature of modern life. Respect her need for independence and self-reliance; if she has a number of siblings at home she may be longing for time and space to herself

If your grandchild is setting up home, expect her to beg and borrow from you. Now is the time to clear out some of the things you have been saving. Your granddaughter is unlikely to have been putting things away in preparation for the day she leaves home. Such forward planning is not characteristic of today's younger generation. Your grandchild will

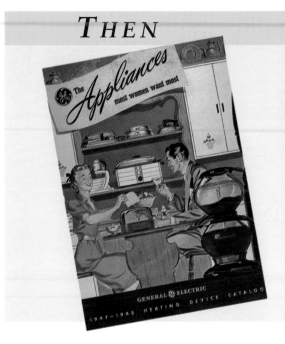

THEN

probably need everything – china, cutlery, cooking utensils and even furniture. (What is provided in 'furnished accommodation' tends to be very basic.) Make sure that you really can live without the things you give away, even if you only give them on an 'extended-loan' basis. And think about your other grandchildren. If you help one grandchild, are others going to ask for a similar gesture from you?

Stay-at-homes
Although you may have resented living at home when you reached your 20s or even 30s, the fact that many of your peers were doing the same probably made it less onerous than it might otherwise have been. Today, however much they are longing to lead independent lives, many young people are forced – for economic reasons – to remain in their parents' home for far longer than was expected. According to recent research, many young men, in particular, are still living at home with Mum and Dad and having everything done for them well into their 20s and 30s.

This can be a difficult situation for both your grandchild and her parents. Parents can gain a great deal of satisfaction from

NOW

Some years ago advertising certainly supported the view that it was impossible to set up home satisfactorily without every modern appliance (far left). Today, your grandchild is likely to be happy with a starter pack of the basic essentials (left), or even with odd bits and pieces from garage sales until she can afford something better.

watching their child establish herself as a separate entity. If she remains at home it can be more difficult for them to accept that she is truly grown up and she may consider that her parents are unnecessarily interfering in her life. If this sounds familiar from your young adulthood, you may feel nothing but sympathy for her, and you may be able to use your own experience to lessen the tension between her and her parents.

Perhaps even more worrying than an unwilling stay-at-home is the adult child who seems quite happy to remain with her parents, having her meals cooked, laundry done and bedroom cleaned long after she might be expected to be living independently. With no experience of living alone, such children find life difficult when their parents are no longer around and they have belatedly to fend for themselves.

Young people who have lived away from home may find themselves forced back after a long-term relationship has ended. Your grandchild's parents have probably become accustomed to having their home and lives to themselves again. Do you remember the sense of relief you felt as you waved your last child off and got on

with doing the things you had always wanted to do? A mother, in particular, may have embarked on a new career or resumed old interests and may feel restricted by the return of her child. The same tensions that occur with a stay-at-home child may surface here.

In this situation the ideal solution is to adapt the house to provide separate living quarters for the adult child so that she can entertain friends and have overnight guests to stay. Making these arrangements, even if only for a few months while she sorts herself out, may, in fact, be the only means of maintaining good family relations.

If the tension between your grandchild and her parents is becoming unbearable you may be able to intervene. Can you offer accommodation in your home? Some families find this an excellent compromise: if you are not in the best of health and do not leave the house much it is good to have someone around on a daily basis, although it is important not to get too dependent on what will inevitably be a temporary arrangement. But it may allow you to stay in your own home for longer than might otherwise be possible, especially if your grandchild is helping out with the household bills (if you expect her to do this, or to perform her share of the household chores, discuss it with her in advance). It is also a way of preserving the extended family network which is so lacking today compared with even a generation ago. But take care not to pry into her life and resist the temptation to ask her where she is going and with whom, every time she leaves the house. Respecting each other's privacy is essential if you are to live in harmony under the same roof.

Shared skills: practical competence

Helping your grandchild make the most of what she owns

It is a mistake to think that once your grandchild is grown up you have nothing further to offer her. Perhaps the most valuable skill she can continue to acquire from you is the ability to live life to the full, surmounting problems, getting along with the people around her and being as contented and fulfilled as possible. Neither of you may be aware of it, but if you have had a long and close relationship there will often be times when she draws on your experiences in order to deal with her own circumstances.

In particular, she may be lacking the very abilities that she needs now that she is branching out on her own. The modern school curriculum often omits to teach children practical skills and your grandchild may only become aware of her limitations when she is trying to fix her car, maintain her home or balance a budget. Unless she wants to pay someone every time she needs to change a plug or do a routine service on her car, she needs to learn to do these things fast.

This is where your help and advice can be of tremendous value. If the first car she owns is rather old it is likely to need a lot of maintenance. With your help she can learn how to do basic servicing. Understanding the rudiments of the combustion engine may help her to resolve problems that occur. You – and her parents – may also feel happier about the prospect of her breaking down on a lonely road if you know that she might be able to do something about it.

This is also the time to initiate her into the art of reading maps, if she has not had experience of them before. Even teenagers who have studied geography extensively are often unable to make sense of a road map. Take her for drives in the country and ask her to navigate. Make sure neither of you is on a tight schedule, and don't be angry or make fun of her if you get a bit lost.

Girls need to know as much about home maintenance as their brothers, if not more, since girls tend to lead independent lives earlier than their male peers. Your granddaughter may buy her own home, perhaps one in a state of disrepair, and feel obliged to pay people to knock down walls, replaster and repaint. The grandchild with family members ready to take on those jobs for her is lucky indeed. But there is no reason why she should not do some of the work herself – with

Sharing your passion for repairing precision instruments, a skill requiring both understanding and dexterity, can reap rewards in many areas of home maintenance.

Professional help is not necessary for many routine tasks. If you pass on your knowledge of motor maintenance, your grandchild will gain an invaluable skill. It's important that she feels safe and confident in her car.

your help, perhaps. You may find that you both develop such enormous enthusiasm for converting her rather unprepossessing basement flat into something cheerful and special that in no time you are showing her how to plaster walls or lay a wooden floor.

Being able to spot the potential in the most unlikely pieces of furniture is also a talent worth passing on. It's amazing what can be done with second-hand furniture: pieces that might have looked decrepit at auction can often be transformed by simple repairing, stripping, painting or reupholstering. A little skill and imagination will work wonders.

If you are a keen carpenter, your abilities will again be valuable at this point in your grandchild's life. You may be enlisted to help build a set of kitchen cupboards or to put up bookshelves. Don't take on all the work yourself. The only way to pass on practical skills like these is to allow your pupil some 'hands-on' experience.

This is also the time when she may begin to develop a genuine love of gardening. If you are already an enthusiastic gardener, you have probably been encouraging her to grow plants and flowers all her life. But now she may have her own garden to take in hand and who better to consult than you? You can show her how to sow or turf a lawn, lay a simple paved path or – if she is ambitious – how to build and stock a small garden pond. Once again, you will be able to share the pleasure and satisfaction of transforming a bleak, neglected area into a thing of beauty.

Your grandchild will be delighted with all the tasks she has been able to accomplish with your help. Working together in this way will leave you both with some very happy memories.

CASE HISTORY

Everything I know about home repair my granddad taught me in the year I moved into my first home. The kitchen, in particular, was awful – small and dark with old cupboards on the wall, a tiny walk-in pantry and cracked lino on the floor. I had used all my savings to buy the place, so had to do everything as cheaply as possible. Granddad offered to help me.

He showed me everything, starting with how to draw a scale plan. He moved his workbench in, then suggested we open the kitchen out into the larder. I carried rubble away as he knocked down the wall, then he demonstrated how to make good the edges of the hole he had made and plaster its surface. He showed me how to fit a large new window which made an enormous difference to the light levels, and made me one wall cupboard. Then he lent me his tools and told me to copy his cabinet – and with his help, I did! Under his guidance I fixed wall tiles and hired a sander to strip the lovely old floorboards he found buried by the floor covering. After all that, the decorating was the easy bit. My parents, who had been quite shocked at how much work needed to be done, couldn't believe the transformation.

When he died, my granddad left me his workbench and tools in his will – they are my most prized possessions.

Further education

Knowing the choices facing your grandchild when she leaves school

When you – and, indeed, your own children – left school, there were probably two directions for young people to take. Those who had performed well academically moved on to college or university, while others looked for work, probably in the local area.

The situation facing your grandchild today is more complex. It is no longer only the high achievers who go on to do tertiary courses; even those who find employment immediately probably spend some time in formal training. There has been an enormous increase in the number of people staying in education long after they are legally required to do so. It is argued that this is the result of the prolonged and worldwide recession which has thrown people out of work and reduced job opportunities. Many claim that young people continue their education simply as a means of delaying the need to search for work. It is certainly true that finding a first job, whether straight from school or after further education, is more difficult for the current generation than it ever was for you and perhaps for your children.

You may remember the days when entire communities were employed by just one or two local industries. All your friends and neighbours worked in the same place, whether on the shop floor or in a clerical or managerial position. Young people frequently followed in their parents' footsteps and in some industries having a parent already employed in a certain area almost guaranteed the school-leaver a job. This gave young people a great sense of security even if in some cases it may have limited their full potential.

Acquiring additional skills

The basic unskilled jobs that offered young people their first experience of employment and demanded whole armies of male and female workers have almost disappeared. Computer-driven machinery invariably copes with such tasks today. Now,

Going to college is still an enormous and exciting step for young people. But today it is less likely to be a once-in-a-lifetime experience. College courses and retraining are becoming increasingly necessary in order for workers' skills to keep pace with technological innovation and the demands of the marketplace.

employers are looking for skilled workers, and acquiring skills almost invariably requires some form of post-school vocational education or training. Much of this training used to occur through apprenticeship schemes whereby a young person learned a trade step-by-step from experienced colleagues in the workplace, with perhaps one day each week spent at a college. Apprenticeship schemes still exist in some areas of employment – in catering or in the printing trade, for example – but they are much less common than they once were.

As a result, there has been a huge increase in the range of courses available and almost everyone can gain a certificate, diploma or other paper qualification of some kind. Although academic qualifications reflect the ability of the student and prove that she has successfully progressed through a course of higher education, they do not necessarily tell a prospective employer what that person is capable of in the workplace.

The main growth area in further education has been in vocational courses, which are intended to train a young person for a particular job and are, therefore, more closely geared towards the needs of industry and commerce than are traditional academic programmes. Many courses include a 'sandwich' element, in which the student is required to spend a specified period in relevant employment before completing the course.

Partly because technology is advancing so rapidly and partly because throughout the Western world in general jobs are insecure, it is necessary for people to become competent at more than one task. Many employers demand that each member of the workforce be multiskilled. There are very few jobs now that do not demand some knowledge of information technology – even doctors and nurses need to have basic computing skills. A single course is unlikely to train your grandchild for all the demands that will be made on her during her career.

Today's young adults may well opt for manual work, but that is likely to involve periods of theory-based learning, interspersed with more 'hands-on' experience.

Consider secretaries, for example. In the past they were trained in shorthand and typing at a commercial school. These skills meant that they could move easily from job to job – one typewriter was much like another – without further training. Now, if your grandchild wishes to pursue such a career, she needs keyboard skills in addition to familiarity with a range of computer software programs. And every time she wishes to change her job she may first have to acquaint herself with several different computer programs.

Many mature people begin a course in their late 20s or 30s, or even later, in order to extend or acquire the skills they need for the constantly changing world of work – an increasing proportion of college and university students are over the age of 25. Further education is no longer simply for school-leavers. Throughout her life your grandchild may find herself dipping in and out of education and vocational training in order to learn the varied work techniques that the modern world continues to demand of her.

The gay grandchild

Accepting your grandchild's sexual preferences

The revelation that your grandchild is gay may come as a complete shock to you, but if you have always been close to her, the chances are you have suspected for some time that this is the case. However you learn the truth, you may find that you have to battle with some turbulent emotions.

It isn't surprising that people in their middle and later years often find it difficult to accept the fact that a relative or friend is gay, since until recently this would have been considered shameful at best and certainly would not have been discussed openly. In your youth sexual relationships between men were actually illegal. Enlightened thinking and support and pressure groups have helped to remove much of the stigma from homosexuality. Nevertheless, discrimination on the grounds of sexual proclivities is still rife and many people remain repelled by the idea of someone making love to another person of the same sex, believing it to be perverted and evil.

If this is how you feel, you need to be aware, first of all, that your grandchild cannot help being what she is. No one knows exactly why someone is gay and although theories abound – particularly about the effects of sexual abuse and traumatic parent/child relationships – it seems more likely that homosexuality is the result of random genetic make-up. Just as no one can control whether she has blue or brown eyes, so no one can stop being gay. Homosexuals comprise a large minority group all

The fear of AIDS may haunt you when you learn that your grandchild is gay. But heightened awareness and health education programmes on the importance of safer sex are having an impact.

Adolescent crushes on people of the same sex are common. But by mid to late teens, the feelings of being 'different', which most gays say they experienced from an early age, have usually coalesced into the certainty of their homosexuality. Your grandchild needs your support as he comes to terms with his feelings at this time.

over the world and are to be found in all walks of life. Despite the stereotypes, most have no obvious identifying features but look just like everyone else.

You also need to realise that once she is in her late teens or early 20s, homosexuality is not a phase that your grandchild may grow out of. It is a physical and emotional preference, and it is disrespectful and inappropriate to think in terms of 'curing' her of her sexuality.

If your religion or culture condemns homosexuality, you may find it difficult not to reject your grandchild. But remember that she is never more in need of your love and support than when she is coming to terms with her own sexuality. The world can seem a harsh place, particularly if family and friends are unsupportive. Her sexuality is only one part of her: she is still the same person with the same lovable characteristics that you have always known. If you feel the need to discuss honestly how you feel, there are support groups for the families of young homosexuals. It may help you to contact such a group and talk to other people in the same situation.

Of course, accepting your grandchild's sexual inclination may be easier than welcoming her partner when she establishes a steady relationship. Some people are embarrassed by open displays of affection between gays. If you would prefer that your grandchild does not bring her partner with her when she visits, say so, but remember that you risk alienating her. If your relationship is strong she will be sensitive to your feelings and will adjust her behaviour accordingly.

World AIDS Day

THE FACTS ABOUT AIDS

Media paranoia has been of little help to those keen to establish the truth about HIV and AIDS and many misconceptions prevail. If you are unsure of the facts, these notes may help.

• The World Health Organisation (WHO) estimates that 18 million adults and about 1.5 million children have been infected with HIV since the beginning of the world epidemic in the 1970s. Of these, 4.5 million have already developed AIDS.

• HIV is a virus which attacks the body's defence system against disease. At first, a person with HIV may feel completely well and have no symptoms. In time, he or she may develop rare illnesses and cancers because of this weakened immune system. When that happens the person is said to have AIDS.

• To become infected with HIV a sufficient amount of it must enter the bloodstream. The body fluids capable of containing enough HIV to infect someone else are blood, semen, vaginal fluids and breast milk. Other body fluids, including saliva, sweat and urine, cannot contain enough virus to infect another person.

• In Australia, New Zealand, the United States, the United Kingdom and northern Europe, the most serious impact of AIDS has been felt by the homosexual community. However, in the non-industrialised world, HIV is most often transmitted by heterosexual intercourse. In parts of the United States, Scotland and southern Europe, sharing needles for injecting drugs is the most common way to contract the infection.

• It is possible to be infected with HIV through transfusions of blood which contained the virus. In most Western countries blood and donor organs are screened for the virus, but in some countries infection rates through blood transfusion are still significant.

• A mother infected with HIV can pass the virus to her baby during breast-feeding.

• Although there is no cure for AIDS, contracting it is not an immediate death sentence: many people with AIDS have lived in relatively good health for several years. New drugs to combat AIDS are constantly being developed and there are grounds for hoping that a cure may be found.

Changed relationships

Treating your grandchild as your peer rather than your junior

As your grandchild moves into adulthood your relationship will be no less valuable but you must expect it to change. For one thing, she is now a person in her own right, a separate entity, and will not necessarily accompany her parents each time they come to see you. When you visit you might catch a glimpse of her as she rushes out of the front door, but don't expect her to cancel a date with friends simply because you have arrived.

Accepting that your grandchild is grown up can be even more difficult than accepting your own child as an independent adult. The decades between you make her still seem very young and you probably can't help feeling protective. Unless you come from a culture in which older people are treated with respect and deference, don't expect her to continue to view you as the fount of all wisdom. Her opinions and beliefs are now being formed by her own experiences and other social contacts.

If you have had a strong relationship over the years, however, there is no reason why you should not continue to be friends. She knows that you are there for her and may well seek your advice when she has problems. She may, indeed, feel freer to talk to you than she does to her parents because she wants them to be confident that she can stand on her own feet. Perhaps she will find it easier to admit mistakes to you than to her immediate family and, when she does so, avoid saying, 'I told you so' – however much you may long to.

When she asks for your advice don't shrug and say that your values and opinions are out of date and have no connection with the world she lives in.

CASE HISTORY

My wife Anna and I were always very close to our granddaughter Sarah. She lived with us for several years when she was a child while her parents were working abroad and she made a point of involving us in her life. Even after her parents returned and settled here, Sarah and her friends were as likely to meet at our house as at her own.

This changed when Sarah went to college. Shortly afterwards, Anna died. I was totally bereft and very lonely. I looked forward to hearing from Sarah and to seeing her in the holidays. At first she rang me often but then her calls became less frequent. I wrote to her every week but had only the briefest and occasional note in return. I couldn't help feeling hurt.

Then one day I was sorting through some old papers and came across some letters that my mother had sent to me when I first left home to join the army. In them she berated me for not writing, called me ungrateful and accused me of forgetting my father and her. Re-reading them helped me to recall my feelings when I left home. In the excitement of establishing a new life, my family became less significant and there was never time to write letters. I realised in retrospect that this detachment from home was part of growing up – and that this was exactly what Sarah was going through. I also knew that she hadn't really forgotten me and that when the novelty of her new life had worn off, she would be in touch again.

Shopping trips with your grandchild take on a new excitement now that you no longer have to worry about 'losing' her in the shopping centre and she can settle you and your purchases in her own car to take you home.

attitudes. Who better to explain the complexities of the modern world to you than your grandchildren?

And if you can treat your grandchild as the adult she is, rather than the child you remember, you may find that she gives you more than emotional support. It is very difficult as we age to admit physical frailty, particularly to our children for whom we have always had to be strong. But if you are finding some aspects of your daily life increasingly onerous, your grandchild may be the one person in the family to whom you can turn. Tell her your concerns honestly. Young adults today rarely take no for an answer and if, for example, you are having trouble getting a health screening or help in the home, ask your grandchild for advice. Unintimidated by 'the system', she may be able to pick up the phone and sort out in minutes a problem that has been bothering you for weeks. Even something as straightforward as choosing some new spectacles can be easier if you have a friendly person on hand to offer an opinion – and drive you to the appointment and back. Don't feel guilty about this – your grandchild will accept your confidences as the final proof that you have come to terms with her adulthood.

While it is probably true that her lifestyle is very different from your own young adulthood, you have a wealth of experience upon which she can draw. She will fall in and out of love, experience rejection and failure just as generations of people before her have done, and will sometimes feel that no one else has ever been so unhappy. Do your best to be reassuring. Life has shown you that, however painful the situation seems at the time, the hurt does pass and the most appalling dilemmas can be solved.

Your relationship can be mutually supportive. Sometimes it will be her turn to offer you advice, particularly if you are baffled by technical innovations or changing social

You may feel some pangs that your grandchild's early years seemed to pass so quickly and that their charms are lost for ever, but when an assured young woman arrives for a visit, you can take pride in the part you played in fitting her for a fulfilling role in the adult world.

Coming-of-age celebrations

Marking your grandchild's entry into adulthood

If your son's or daughter's childhood seemed to pass in a flash, you probably feel that your grandchild has grown up even more quickly. She is now planning to celebrate her coming of age and you are probably wondering where all the years have gone.

The age at which someone is considered a full adult – most commonly this means being able to vote and, therefore, participate actively in the running of her country – is usually marked in some way, especially in Western culture. However, in cultures in which religious rites of passage are considered more important than a civil acknowledgement, the legal coming of age can be quite a low-key affair.

How your grandchild celebrates her coming of age is her decision. Some young people want to mark the occasion with a big party. Others prefer to have a few drinks with friends or go to a favourite restaurant. If she is being supported by her parents she may not have enough money for anything more. Or she may simply not be a 'party animal'. But most young people will want to have a special celebration of some kind.

If her parents' finances are overstretched, there's no reason why you shouldn't offer to help if you are able to. But, whoever foots the bill, the party must be the one your grandchild wants to have, with her choice of guests. Most teenagers do not want their parents, let alone their grandparents, around when they are planning to have a good time with their friends. Don't be offended if you are not invited. A sensitive grandchild will probably agree to some kind of compromise which can involve everyone in the celebration in some way.

One option is to have a family gathering at home or in a restaurant and for your grandchild to have a less sedate affair with friends at another time. If you come from a culture that has retained traditional forms of entertainment in which everyone can become involved, whatever their age, a large family party may be a particularly appealing idea. Anyone from 2 to 80 can enjoy an Irish set dance, for example,

A meal in a favourite restaurant may be a good way for the family to celebrate your grandchild's coming of age, leaving her free to enjoy a less formal occasion with friends. But if this is too difficult to arrange, invite her to your home for a glass of champagne to wish her well.

ALTERNATIVE CELEBRATIONS

In some families religious rites of passage such as confirmation or bar and bat mitzvahs are more important than coming-of-age celebrations. The legal majority may be considered less important than the 15th (significant in Hispanic culture) or 16th (as in 'Sweet 16') birthdays. It is then that families and friends gather at a large party to wish the young person well. Depending on the family, this may also be the birthday at which 'extra special' gifts are offered.

Most 18 and 21 year olds appreciate a high-quality watch or other piece of jewellery, but if you want to offer something more unusual consider a beautiful photograph album with pictures of family members. Practical gifts, such as a sewing machine or electric drill, are also popular gifts.

but for the most part, the generations do not share the same tastes in either music or dancing. A more satisfactory alternative might be to arrange a buffet supper or cocktail party for everyone, followed by a disco for the young people only. If you are holding this party in your own home don't forget to warn your neighbours.

If you have been asked to provide the food for a coming-of-age party find out how many of the guests are vegetarian and whether there are special cultural requirements or specific food allergies. If you serve traditional ethnic food that is spicy, offer a few other options, too. If you love making cakes, now is the time to put your skills to the test. A coming-of-age cake can be as original and witty as you can make it. Restrict drinks to soft drinks, beer and wine – plus champagne for the toast. Although many young people boast of their drinking prowess, most are not used to drinking spirits and overindulgence by one guest – young or old – could spoil the entire evening for everyone.

The most traditional gift for this important occasion is jewellery, for both girls and boys – watches, rings, earrings, lockets, cufflinks – but you might want to choose something a little more original. Students may appreciate a beautiful fountain pen, for example, or a first edition by a favourite author. If your grandchild is living away from home she might like to have some luggage, a travel clock, a leather writing case or a silver frame with a photograph of her immediate family.

While coming-of-age gifts are usually those things which can be treasured for life, some young people prefer to have money spent on things they currently need. A young person involved in sport, for example, might appreciate a good tennis racquet or some golf clubs. If it is appropriate to your grandchild's interests, you might also consider a computer, a CD player, a camera or even a car. Check with her or her parents to ensure that you are buying an appropriate brand or model. Particularly on this special occasion, you don't want to spend a lot of money on something that will not be appreciated.

Another way in which to mark the occasion is to have your grandchild professionally photographed or, if you can afford it, to have her portrait painted. This is something which will give her – and her parents – enormous pleasure now and can also be passed on to future generations.

Weddings

Accepting your grandchild's wishes on her most special day

Your grandchild is getting married and you may be longing to help out with some of the arrangements. But this is a time to wait to be asked. Although weddings are, for the most part, joyful occasions, the run-up to the event can be fraught with problems and cause many a family row. As the day draws nearer, the bride and groom often get tense and the bride's parents, who usually fund and arrange the wedding, can become overstressed and weary of the whole business. They may also be worried about escalating costs. It might be appropriate to offer financial help if you are able, but don't let any member of the family pressure you into doing so.

A traditional ceremony, with friends and relatives throwing rice or confetti, is still the dream of many women and quite a few men. Contributions do not have to be financial – if you are able to, consider offering to make the cake or the bridesmaids' dresses.

A RELIGIOUS CEREMONY?

Your grandchild may have a strong faith and prefer to have a traditional religious wedding. If she is marrying outside the faith, however, and her partner does not wish to convert, she may face problems.

In general, Protestant ministers may marry couples at their discretion, so that if she has her heart set on a church service she may get one. Similarly, some rabbis are more liberal than others and will marry 'outsiders'. The Roman Catholic church often insists on regular attendance at mass and, in common with other faiths, a period of premarital counselling. The Eastern Orthodox churches generally do not favour mixed marriages.

Some faiths are pragmatic about the marriage of divorcés, allowing second marriages as long as the joy is tempered with a measure of 'contrition' that the first marriage ended. Others are less accepting. If a religious wedding is difficult, a blessing after a civil ceremony may be an option, but many couples choose just a civil ceremony.

One important part you can play at this time is to offer your grandchild and her parents – on separate occasions – an escape from the wedding-obsessed household when it all seems too much to cope with. You can act as a sounding board for all the minor irritations they may feel about each other, none of which you will ever divulge, of course.

The problem with weddings is that the needs and wishes of the couple can become lost in all the concerns and interference of their relatives. It is too easy to offer advice, to try to impose your ideas of how a wedding should be conducted and to show disapproval if the bride and groom do not plan things in a way you would like. Don't look aghast, for instance, if the bride announces she is wearing an emerald green dress, and don't try to convince her that she should have all your other grandchildren as her attendants.

Many reasons prompt the decision to marry overseas. Remember that the bride and groom are the most important people on this day – and their wishes should come first.

Some brides want to do things the traditional way even if their lives so far have seemed to you highly unconventional. Your granddaughter may choose to wear a white dress and veil although she and the groom have been living together for years. Other couples choose to have only a civil ceremony. Registry office weddings are usually brief and space is limited. On the other hand, ceremonies conducted by marriage celebrants can be held in almost any venue, indoors or out, and space is rarely an issue. Even so, some couples want only parents and siblings – with perhaps a couple of close friends to act as witnesses – to be present. If you are not invited, accept their decision with good grace and make a point of asking the couple round for a prenuptial or postnuptial meal; this is your opportunity to give them a gift and your best wishes.

Whatever kind of ceremony she chooses to have, the day can be difficult for your grandchild if her parents are divorced or separated and there are step-parents involved, too. Many families believe that the estranged parents and any respective new partners should come together and

smile happily for the photographer for the sake of their child. But too often the wedding becomes an occasion to re-enact previous quarrels. If this is likely to happen, use all your tact and sensitivity to defuse some of the tension.

To avoid the possibility of family confrontation, some couples choose to travel abroad to marry without the benefit of any guests at all. Regardless of your disappointment, try to accept the positive aspects of such a decision – marrying without family members in attendance ensures that your grandchild's special day does not degenerate into family wrangling. In such circumstances, most couples have a party for all their important relatives and friends on their return.

Wedding presents can be a source of great anxiety. If you are living on limited funds and there really is nothing on the wedding list that you can afford, a gift made at home with lots of love will be just as precious to the couple. Perhaps you could make a tapestry cushion or some other item which could easily become a family heirloom in years to come. If you are not good with the crochet hook or the needle, is there an ornament or a piece of china you know your grandchild has always loved? Now may be the time to pass it on to her. Don't feel that you have to compete with the other set of grandparents. They may be able to afford the washing machine but a sensitive grandchild will be aware of your financial circumstances and cherish your gift just as much.

Many grandparents do not play a major role in the weddings of their grandchildren, but the day is still a special one. You are able to share fully in the bride's and groom's happiness without having to worry about arrangements going wrong – as you probably did when your own child got married.

When there isn't a wedding

Accepting your grandchild's decision to cohabit rather than marry

Once upon a time people fell in love, married, set up home together and had children. Most still do these things; the difference is that today many rearrange the order in which they do them.

It has become common for the man the bride meets at the altar to be her partner of several years; and for the flower girl or page boy to be the couple's own child. Many older people, especially those who have had long and happy marriages, find it incomprehensible that so many young people appear to treat this important relationship so casually. It's true that some couples move in together after knowing each other for what may seem like a very short time, and some young men and women live with several different partners before they settle down with one. However, the majority see the decision to cohabit as a commitment and a possible prelude to a future marriage.

In the light of the number of marital breakdowns that happen today – particularly if your grandchild has experienced divorce in her own family – it is not surprising that she wants to be sure that this is the person she can live with before she ties the knot.

There are two ways to handle the situation if your grandchild sets up home with a boyfriend. One is to remember that she has grown up in a different moral climate. Perhaps the major reason that many older people find it difficult to accept cohabitation is that it is an open acknowledgement that a young couple has a sexual relationship. Her parents, probably young adults in the 1960s or 1970s, are likely to be more relaxed than you about premarital sex. Also, today great emphasis is placed on people finding out for themselves what is right for them and seeking their own personal happiness, rather than behaving as their grandparents, parents, the church and society think they should. You, of course, are entitled to stick to your

CASE HISTORY

My mum, in particular, gave me a really hard time when Bill and I moved in together – at one point we were barely on speaking terms. I'd introduced Bill to Grandma soon after I met him as I knew they'd get on, and it was Bill who suggested I talk to her to see if she could bring Mum round.

Rather to my surprise, Grandma seemed to understand why I felt Mum was being so unreasonable. She told me that, although she was engaged to Granddad at the time, while he was overseas during the war she had gone to live with another man. She had thought maybe Granddad wouldn't come back, and this man offered her a chance of happiness. She was with him for a couple of years, then the relationship fizzled out. She told Granddad all about the affair before they married and he understood what had prompted her decision. She thought Bill and I were sensible to get to know each other 'properly' – that was the word she used – before we made a more serious commitment.

I don't know what she said to Mum, but after that she was okay about things. I never realised Grandma had a past – perhaps Mum didn't either!

beliefs and maintain your own standards. But don't expect your adult grandchild to conform to those standards.

The other way to retain a sense of proportion in this situation is to remember the attitudes that prevailed when you were growing up. Despite the perception that no one then had sexual intercourse outside marriage, the number of illegitimate babies born proves that they did.

Can you look more positively on the younger generation's straightforward approach? They may have a different set of values but they do not condemn those who contravene a social code. Remember, too, that double standards often existed as far as sexual morality was concerned – there was an assumption that most men were experienced on their wedding night, while their brides remained virgins.

If you cannot accept the fact that your grandchild is cohabiting, you run the risk of not seeing her often, if at all. The situation is more difficult if the couple live together in the parental home since you may resent your child's collaboration in the whole thing. But you will not make things better by refusing to visit when you know the couple are going to be present.

No one claims that it is easy to come to terms with change in sexual and social mores. However, your disapproval is unlikely to make any difference to the way your grandchild leads her life. You obviously do not want to lose contact with her, so perhaps both of you would be happier if she visited you on her own. But in asking this, you risk alienating her by rejecting her chosen partner.

Invite them to call on you. If the

visit has to involve an overnight stay and you really cannot bring yourself to give them a room together, suggest that they would be more comfortable at a hotel and offer to pay part or all of the cost. This is preferable to insisting on separate sleeping arrangements, which only leads to embarrassment and play-acting all round. The grandchild with whom you have always had a close relationship will behave sensitively and probably make those arrangements herself.

It is a truism that people can become used to anything. However much you may dislike her lifestyle, your grandchild is showing the independence of mind and capacity for love that you have helped foster in her, and remains the person you have always loved. And, if it really matters to you, remember that the majority of people who live together do eventually marry and that one day you may receive an invitation to her wedding.

Your grandchild may choose not to marry her partner, but their commitment to each other may be just as strong and binding. Their life together, like many marriages, is probably based on shared incomes, both names on a mortgage and a happiness in each other's company that is obvious to all.

Then and now:

Careers and relationships

Among the many rapid changes in our society in the last half century, the role of women has evolved at breakneck speed. Now, as well as being partners and mothers, they may also have full-time jobs outside the home.

THEN

The way in which your grandchild conducts herself as both a partner and a parent probably bears little resemblance to the way you fulfilled those roles two generations ago. There has been a huge revolution in how families run their lives and this has taken place so recently that even members of your children's generation can find it difficult to come to terms with.

Historically, the principal ambitions of generations of women were to be wives and mothers. Single women often had jobs but were expected to give them up when they were married; many professions were barred to married women. As a result, most became financially dependent upon their husbands immediately after plighting their troth. Certainly, as soon as children came along, most women opted to stay at home and bring them up while fathers became the sole breadwinners. Now both parents are likely to work, perhaps full-time, and their children are cared for in day nurseries or by childminders.

There are several reasons why so many young mothers work outside the home. One is often economic necessity – two salaries are necessary to pay a large mortgage or rent on a house. They may

also have become used to a certain lifestyle and do not want to give that up because they have had a baby. But the main reason is that women no longer want to be 'only' housewives and mothers. They have the opportunity to become as well educated and as highly skilled as men; they seek fulfilment in the workplace, take pride in earning money for themselves and enjoy making a contribution to society as well as to the home.

A man's place
This development has inevitably brought about changes in the way men see themselves. Not so long ago fathers played little part in the day-to-day running of the home and the care of their children. It was rare to find a man who could change a nappy or make up a bottle of formula, or who did not feel deep embarrassment at being seen pushing a pram.

In fact, fathers often worked such long hours that they rarely saw their children. When he did come home from work, the man of the house probably expected his meal to be on the table, the house tidy and the children tucked up in bed asleep. With the exception of the war years – when women were encouraged to work outside

NOW

Traditionally, women were housewives and – with their children – welcomed the breadwinner home at the end of the day (far left). Today, many fathers are happy to take on this role, either through genuine longing or economic expediency (left).

the home – this was the pattern of domestic life for generations. And there were doubtless many men and women who were happy with this arrangement, just as there were some who were resentful of the fact that their roles were so strictly defined on the basis of gender.

The gradual emergence of the 'new man' has heralded a more flexible approach. Today's young father is likely to be present at the birth of his children, having attended antenatal classes with his partner. He will know as much about changing, bathing and feeding the new baby as his partner and chart each stage of development as avidly as mothers and grandmothers have always done.

But even if he has been allowed to take paternity leave, he is soon obliged to go back to work, while his partner's employer may be obliged to give her several months' leave to spend at home with the baby. According to most surveys, women – including those who have demanding careers – still take on the primary responsibility for childcare and running the home.

High unemployment and redundancy force some men to remain at home as 'househusbands' and main child carers,

dependent on their wife's salary. Some men are lucky enough to find this immensely satisfying; others are happy to make this contribution to their family life. Nevertheless, the old assumptions and values persist and a man may feel emasculated when he is put into this position. He is also likely to be in a minority when he takes his children to 'parent and toddler' groups. His self-esteem may be further diminished if his father, grandfather and other family members cannot empathise with his situation and hold him up to ridicule.

Can you help?

If a couple is fortunate enough to have both partners in work, the double income may allow them to pay for domestic help, as well as full-time care for their child. So while you may be appalled at the idea of your granddaughter or your grandson's partner handing over a new baby to a daycare centre or nanny and returning to work, remember that some new mothers are back behind their desks weeks, even days, after the birth.

You may be enlisted to help out with some baby-sitting but your grandchild is more likely to use professional childcare. This can be a tricky area for you and your adult child – the new baby's grandparent. You may think a nanny is far too young and inexperienced to be in charge of your precious great-grandchild but remember that the last thing she wants is a grandmother and great-grandmother coming round to check up on how she is getting on. It is essential for everyone to stand back and allow the young couple to lead their life in the way they wish – even if you find that lifestyle incomprehensible.

Inheritance

Leaving your treasured possessions in loving hands

There are doubtless many things you would like to pass on to your grandchild, some of which you may have mentioned in your will (see p. 209), but it can be difficult to be sure that you are giving what she would like to receive. Of course, you can ask her outright if she would like to be left the antique dresser you have treasured for years or the pearl necklace that you inherited from your own mother. But questions of this nature can be upsetting for your grandchild because they remind her that one day you will no longer be here as her friend and supporter. She may dismiss such queries with remarks like 'You're going to be around for years yet, Gran,' and refuse to discuss the subject.

Throughout your grandchild's growing years, you have undoubtedly picked up leads to objects she has admired in your home, pieces of jewellery she has exclaimed over, or the patchwork quilt which has always seemed to fascinate her. Make a mental or written note when you observe her enthusiasm for some item or other. Be realistic about what you leave each grandchild. While one with a more sentimental streak will obviously appreciate possessing your collection of photographs or other bits and pieces of family memorabilia, others may attach no importance to such things. Don't give them to one who you suspect is going to put all those cherished family photographs in the bin once you are no longer around.

Sometimes bequests are obvious. Keen musicians will love an instrument you used, for example, and the grandchild who shares your passion for fishing will enjoy having your rods and tackle. Rather than waiting until you die and are denied seeing how much pleasure your gifts bring, you may, like many other grandparents, decide to give away some of your possessions while you are still around to watch the recipient enjoying them. This is particularly appropriate with gifts of money. If you were planning to leave a sizeable sum to your grandchild, consider giving some of it to her now, perhaps to help her further her education, buy her first home or set up her own business.

You may believe that the money you leave should be equally divided between your children and their children. This

Some of your more valuable possessions have obvious 'homes' among your children and their children, but there are many curios and mementos that one of your grandchildren will love as being part of you – irrespective of financial value.

is entirely up to you. However, it may often seem illogical to treat all your grandchildren equally, since they have different needs at different times. One may be a single parent struggling to bring up a family on a minuscule income to whom any sum of money could make a huge difference. Another may already be running a successful business and have no need of your cash help. She may prefer to be given a piece of furniture or a painting.

In any case, you may choose to have an open, friendly discussion with family members about what you have decided to leave everyone and why. Otherwise, if you opt for equal shares, the less well-off members of the family may resent it; in the other scenario, your wealthier grandchild may be hurt at your apparent neglect. Better to explain your motives now, to avoid misplaced anticipation or an uncomfortable atmosphere.

Helping your grandchild out financially when she could do with some assistance makes more sense than forcing her to wait until you die. By that time she may be well established and no longer in need of your investment. But resist the temptation to be overgenerous; leave yourself enough funds

to live as comfortably as you would wish. Neither should you bow to pressure from relatives to give them money if that is not what you want to do. If you ever have the uncomfortable feeling that your grandchild is already planning how she will spend her inheritance, try to ignore it. It may be all in your mind, and if it isn't, raising the issue will only cause unpleasantness: she is bound to deny it and may be genuinely hurt. Don't reciprocate by threatening to cut her out of your will whenever she does something that meets with your disapproval. It is unwise to allow the promise of a future inheritance to become a form of manipulation. Love and attention should not be bought in this way.

If you decide to sell the family home and move to a smaller property or into a retirement home, you will almost inevitably have to reduce drastically the number of your possessions. You may, in fact, need to sell much of your furniture and other valuables in order to make money to subsidise your income, but this also offers you a good opportunity to invite your grandchildren around and ask them to choose things they would like to have. You could even hold the opposite of a house-warming party for the entire family, when, instead of your guests bringing presents, each one takes some favourite item away with them.

Of course, it can be a sad occasion when you relinquish those things that have been part of your life for so many years. But at least you know they will be in good hands and you will continue to gain enormous satisfaction from seeing your favourite pieces loved and cherished by the younger generation.

CHAPTER NINE

Becoming a Great-grandparent

In the same way that your life changed irrevocably when you became a parent, and again on becoming a grandparent, so it will change as another generation enters the world.

To help you focus positively on this new stage in your life, look back to when you became a grandparent. Perhaps you feared that you were no longer important in your child's world and that you might be excluded from his or her family life. But as your new role evolved and you achieved a blend of involvement and detachment which allowed you to take part in your grandchild's development, these misgivings were soon dispelled.

As a great-grandparent, your role will change again, but this does not make you superfluous to the rest of the family. You have the wisdom and experience that only come from witnessing generations of children growing up. You have probably slowed down a little, shed a few commitments and can devote more time to family matters. Until one of your children takes up the mantle, you are the keeper of your family's history, the one who lived the stories that the others enjoy. Relax and savour the continuity of family life in which you are still playing a key part.

Your new role

Taking pride and pleasure in your expanding family

Attitude is an all-important part of becoming a great-grandparent. You can feel justifiably proud of your place at the top of the family tree; or you can take change in a negative way, choosing to think that your own role is slipping away and you are being pushed to one side as the generations move on.

Focus on the positive. You are in the enviable position of having three generations come after you. Your family is a great, lasting, growing clan, which has been and will continue to be influenced by you. If your family members see that you have a positive attitude and commonsense approach to life, they will continue to make sure that you are a part of their social gatherings and day-to-day business.

You may have moved into sheltered accommodation, a retirement village or a nursing home where it is easier for you to live comfortably. If this means you are not as geographically close as you once were to the rest of your family, take steps to ensure that you do not feel left out of things. If you find writing long letters tiring, ask a sympathetic member of staff to help you or use a tape recorder to send taped messages to your grandchildren and great-grandchildren.

Make the most of the visits members of your family pay to you. Do not use these sessions as a forum for complaints about what is happening where you live; instead, let your family know that you are totally interested in their lives and in how everyone is getting along. It may be, with all the new arrivals over the years, that you sometimes find it difficult to remember names, ages and other details such as jobs or study courses. This happens to all of us, but to clarify things, take time when you are on your own and not feeling too tired to draw up a family tree so that when visitors come you are able to talk confidently about what stage the children are at and ask relevant questions.

If your family tree is of particular interest to you, make it something special, using photographs and additional information from the past which may otherwise be forgotten. This is sure to grab the attention of younger members of your family and they may feel inspired to join in with your efforts, hunting out unusual photographs or even tracing people with whom you might have lost touch. It is certainly something that will be treasured in the years to come.

Your grandchildren and great-grandchildren will continue to enjoy your company as long as you enjoy theirs and take an interest in their concerns. Find subjects of mutual interest for conversation, and activities within your capabilities that you both enjoy – such as going for a walk, or to the theatre or a restaurant.

Enjoy your position as matriarch. It is a great achievement to have three generations of descendants. And if your grandchildren's babyhood seems a long time ago, you now have the chance to relish the pleasures of grandparenting all over again.

Western society has such a horror of old age that it sometimes tries to deny its existence. Never view yourself as an inconvenience or allow yourself to be patronised. Younger people will learn from your attitude and respect your age and experience as something to be valued rather than hidden away.

Of course, if you are ill and simply feel too weak to receive visitors, you are entitled to rest alone. But don't feel that you have to be isolated. Continue sending your letters and tapes and telephone when you can; let your family know that you love hearing from them and that you think about them even though you can't see them at the moment. If your great-grandchildren are very young, they will appreciate a funny drawing just as much, if not more than, a letter from you, and the older ones will enjoy hearing your voice.

If you choose not to see the youngest members of the family, make it clear that you still want and need to see the adults. They will be sure to understand your reasons for not having the children to visit and will be able to keep you up-to-date with photographs and snippets of information on how everyone is doing.

Although some loss of health and strength is almost inevitable at this stage in your life, it can be a marvellous consolation to be able to witness the continuity of your family. So many people, throughout the world, are denied this satisfaction, but you have succeeded in rearing your own children and supporting your grandchildren and, in turn, their children. You and your family have succeeded at the most central function in life, and you have much to be proud of.

Coping with infirmity

If you have health problems you may not wish the younger members of your family to visit you. This is an issue which only you can decide, but it helps to remember that children see illness and infirmity differently from adults.

Your great-grandchildren will love you for who you are. To them, you have always been old (children consider their parents, never mind their grandparents, as old) and even, perhaps, frail. As a result, what you see as greatly increased infirmity or lack of health may hardly be noticed by much younger members of your family and will certainly not be feared for any reason, unless you are frightened yourself and let them see it.

Continue to see all your family and make your voice heard for as long as you feel well enough and strong enough to do so. Unlike cultures in which the oldest family members are considered the wisest and are cared for within the extended family unit,

Accepting your mortality
Coming to terms with the fact that life has an end

Whether you are fighting fit or struggling with ill health, whether you hold sustaining religious beliefs or have none, becoming a great-grandparent will inevitably cause you to consider your own mortality. Another generation has arrived, introducing new life and vitality at a time when you are bound to be slowing down a little and having the chance to take stock of all that has happened in your own lifetime.

Many people say that they have an intuitive feeling that they should start to tie up loose ends and prepare for what is to come. For many a full, if exhausting, life leaves them unperturbed and ready to accept death. But for others the end is unthinkable. This book has been an exploration of life, of the different stages of childhood and adulthood and the logical progression from one to the next. When we have passed through all the stages, the natural conclusion is life's end.

Whatever your spiritual beliefs, there are three generations of your flesh and blood who live as they do because of you. Do not underestimate how much you have influenced them. People really do live on in the memories of others. Think of your own parents and grandparents; inevitably you have carried some of their beliefs, wisdom, funny sayings and even looks through your life. These links carry on and on.

If, despite this knowledge, you find it difficult to accept your own mortality, don't be ashamed of the fact. All counsellors and spiritual leaders agree that this is the hardest thing to accept because it is so difficult to comprehend. It is probably best for you to speak with a trained professional or member of your church, rather than your immediate family.

If there are matters you wish to clear up or things that need saying, don't wait until you are influenced by illness or infirmity. Talk to your family now. And don't be surprised if people change the subject when you speak of your mortality, because it is painful for them to think of your death, and they cannot conceive of your acceptance of it as inevitable.

Funeral arrangements

One, often very calming, way of accepting your own mortality in a positive manner is to begin by managing practical matters.

Ensure that your will still represents your wishes, or if you haven't made one, do so. You may find it a surprisingly affirmative thing to plan, as far as is possible, your own funeral. If you are a music lover, for example, choosing one or more of your favourite pieces to be played at the service is

Putting papers in order, updating a will to include the newest arrivals, and sorting family photographs are not morbid actions but positive affirmations of how much you value life and your family. By leaving your affairs in good order, you can be sure that members of your family will abide by your wishes once you are gone and you will save them unnecessary hard work at a time when they want simply to remember you.

CASE HISTORY

I was only 38 when my grandson David was born. His parents' marriage was always rocky and David spent a lot of time with me as they tried to sort out their differences. But they split up when David was six.

David had a good relationship with both his parents, who always seemed to put him first, regardless of their problems. Then two years ago, when he was just 18, David was killed in a car crash. In the midst of all our grief his parents started to argue about the funeral arrangements. His father wanted a religious service; his mother was adamant that David had had no faith and would have thought it inappropriate. I tried to keep out of the wrangling, but found myself dragged in to arbitrate. It was ghastly. Eventually we reached a compromise that satisfied no one, but at least allowed us to bury David with some dignity.

Obviously no one had expected David to die and part of the problem was that we were taken unawares. But then I started to consider what would happen if I died suddenly. I'm still relatively young and in excellent health, but you never know what's in store. I realised that no one knew what my wishes would be if anything happened to me.

My daughter thinks I'm unnecessarily morbid, but I've written a letter to her detailing my wishes for my funeral. I hope it will sit in my lawyer's safe for the next 20 years or more, but at least I know none of my family will have to go through again what happened when David died.

fitting. There may be poetry or Bible readings that hold special significance for you and these, too, could be included. In writing all this down and placing it in the hands of your lawyer or a member of the family you are ensuring that your final goodbye bears your personal stamp. You will also be saving your family from some of the distress that surrounds funeral preparations for those who are grieving.

If you do not hold any religious beliefs and feel strongly about how your funeral will be conducted, make your wishes known. Contact a humanist society for advice and information on non-religious funeral ceremonies that your family may be too upset to organise otherwise.

Positive affirmations

If you feel you should start to do something to acknowledge your own mortality to yourself, consider writing a letter or letters to your family. Perhaps you have not always found the right words to praise them for their achievements and the way they have related to you. If you think these things would otherwise go unsaid, try to commit your thoughts to paper. Make everything positive – you will not have the chance to undo what you are going to say.

You will find you gain satisfaction and some peace of mind from writing a letter, whether you send it now or leave it with your other papers to be read after your death. Your family will take comfort from knowing you were thinking about them.

Death is the strongest taboo subject in our society. Even among people with strong religious faith it is often skirted around as if it were not the one certain fact of life. If you feel secure and composed enough, try to break this mould by letting your family know that because of them you are accepting and, hopefully, largely unafraid. Face this last step positively and frankly and imagine how you will be remembered by those you love and are loved by in the years to come.

Remaking the heritage chest

Presenting the whole story to your family

Most people rethink their position within the family when they become a great-grandparent. Now you can start to see your descendants stretching out in a long line before you; this is the time to savour the sense of continuity.

On becoming parents and grandparents many people start a heritage chest (see p. 15) containing significant family items, which can be added to as the years go by and may include a lock of a child's hair, a first swimming certificate, wedding invitations and birth announcements. This is the ideal time to update your family's memento box and check that the contents are properly stored so that they will last. You are in the unique position within your family of having lived through all the experiences that are represented in the box, and it will be helpful for future generations if you write some notes giving a date and brief explanation where necessary.

Never underestimate the delight that this type of tangible family history can bring. If you are able to make a thorough job of your family's heritage casket you will be providing them with a sense of background and roots. The younger children will be fascinated by some of the items they view as part of a bygone age and you will make their ancestors real for them.

Practical considerations

Wrap locks of hair individually in tissue paper, and place them in labelled envelopes. Remember, also, to continue the tradition by taking a snip of your new great-grandchild's hair and adding it to the collection. The adults will be fascinated by how their hair colour and texture has changed.

Certificates and other documents fade with age and start to disintegrate when handled. Fingerprints can also be a problem, so use clear plastic wallets to hold these items.

Many families keep children's first shoes or bootees. If you have some of these, remind your great-grandchild's parents not to throw their baby's away but to let you have them in due course. These keep better if they are stuffed with tissue or a sachet of cut, dried lavender.

If you have saved petals from wedding bouquets or ornaments from wedding or christening cakes, store them in small cardboard boxes, label them and, if possible, keep the flower petals pressed; otherwise they will break.

Another popular keepsake is a piece of the fabric from a wedding dress or christening gown. Store these between sheets of acid-free tissue, and expect them to fade with age (black paper slows down the rate of fading). Finding time to sew the names and dates of the wedding or christening party on the back or edge of the fabric pieces will add to the enjoyment of those who want to examine the contents of the box in years to come.

Younger family members will be fascinated by the bits and pieces you have saved from previous generations. A stylish box adds to the charm and if it has a number of compartments it will help you file things away neatly. Don't rely on your memory – make sure everything is labelled and dated.

Invitations, birth announcements or cards for special occasions deserve a folder of their own. All the family will be amazed at how design styles have changed over the years. Again it is important that these are properly dated.

Degree diplomas and other certificates keep better if they are rolled and fixed with ribbon rather than a rubber band (these perish over time). The nonchalant graduate who casually passed you his diploma years ago will appreciate the care you have taken of it when the time comes for him to show it to his own grandchildren.

Photographs generally keep better if they are stored in albums out of direct sunlight. If you have a collection of school or college photographs showing each member of your family at the same stage in their development and want to group them together, choose a small box or folder.

Plastic name and weight tags from the hospital or disposable paper baby gowns (unworn) can also form part of the collection, even if they may look less appealing than other items. In years to come the children will be fascinated by how tiny their wrists must have been to wear the tag and will have difficulty imagining how they fitted into the gown.

If, like most families, you have had your share of tragedy, don't omit the evidence from your heritage chest. If family members have died before their time, you should include a photograph, funeral card or special poem they liked, or even a toy or game which was special to them. Everyone in your family deserves a place here and should be remembered in some way.

As new babies come into your family you might like to purchase a newspaper for the day they were born, or put away a coin with their birth year on it or even some postage stamps. In the future those babies will be fascinated by how different things were when they were born.

Perhaps you have also been drawing up a family tree and if so you could place this, or a copy of it, in the chest. If you let your family know that you are maintaining a chest, they will be more likely to save appropriate things to go in it. Doubtless they will be keen to look at what you have collected and this will provide you with pleasure as well, but watch what the younger ones are doing to ensure that everything remains in the chest and is kept as it should be.

Survey of grandparents' legal rights

If talks fail, you have rights in law regarding your grandchildren

As recently as ten years ago, grandparents' rights to protect the welfare of their grandchildren were exremely limited. Since the Children Act of 1989, however, that situation has changed. Although your rights are neither extensive nor – in most circumstances – automatic, there are situations in which you can act. It is important to remember, however, that discussion and compromise are usually the best way to resolve family conflicts.

Court hearings that relate to a child are usually referred to as 'family proceedings'. In such proceedings the court has the power to grant an order relating to a child in response to an application made to it (for access, for example) or to grant an order on its own authority. The court is bound only by two principles: first, that the welfare of the child is the most important consideration; second, that an order must only be made if it results in a better situation for the child than if no order is made at all.

In circumstances in which applications are contested (for example, if you applied for a contact order and the child's parents opposed your wishes), the court has a checklist of factors it is bound to take into acount in reaching a decision. One of these is the child's wishes.

Keeping in touch

You have to apply to the court for permisson to seek a contact order if you have lost (or fear you are about to lose) touch with your grandchild. You have no automatic right to apply direct but, in the words of the Act, 'close relatives such as grandparents' should usually be granted leave. A contact order, if granted, requires the person with whom your grandchild lives to allow you to visit, or have your grandchild to stay, or to make sure that you maintain contact in some other way.

If your grandchild is in care

Parents who are unable to take care of their child can place her voluntarily in local authority care. The local authority also has the right to seek a care order for a child considered at risk at home.

If your grandchild is in care voluntarily, her parents retain responsibility for her. The child, her parents and anyone else the authority considers relevant – such

Grandparents' special role in the life of their grandchildren is acknowledged in law. As long as the court is satisfied that your visits are in your grandchild's best interests, you are likely to be able to maintain contact in most circumstances.

as grandparents – must be consulted before any decisions are made about her. If your grandchild has been taken into care, you can apply for a contact order in the normal way and the normal criteria apply. If your grandchild is placed with foster parents, the authority should help you to maintain contact with her.

Every day in Britain the partners of 550 women and 120 men die. Contrary to popular belief, the bereaved partner automatically inherits their spouse's estate only when there are no living children, parents or siblings. Making a will is a simple matter, and prevents any discord over your intentions after your death. You can buy a simple form at a stationer's, but it is much better to get advice from your solicitor to be sure that your intentions are clear. Alternatively, the charity Age Concern (see pp. 210–11) produces an information pack on the subject.

Applying for a residence order

A residence order (see p. 143) gives you some parental responsibility for your grandchild (although not the right to consent to adoption). You may find it easier to get a residence order than a non-relative would, but in the case of conflict with the parents you are less likely to succeed. Obviously you stand more chance of success if neither parent contests your application.

A grandparent with parental responsibility for a child can remove that child from the voluntary care of the local authority. If the child has been taken into care, and you successfully apply for a residence order, the care order comes to an end.

If your grandchild lives with you under a residence order and you decide you want to adopt, there may be financial considerations (see p.143). In addition, an adoption panel may turn you down if it deems that you are not suitable, although it would have to be sure that it was in your grandchild's best interests for you not to adopt. The normal age criteria applied to adoptive parents do not apply to grandparents and there has been at least one case of an adoption panel turning grandparents down, only to have its decision reversed when the grandparents appealed.

If your grandchild is adopted

Adoption is no longer automatically a matter of secrecy and loss of contact with natural relatives, so the granting of an adoption order to someone else need not mean the end of your contact with your grandchild. The court can impose any conditions on such an order that it thinks 'fit', which can include granting contact for any relative, including grandparents, if it deems such contact to be in the best interests of the child.

Taking a child abroad

If your grandchild's parent wants to take the child abroad, you can apply for a prohibited steps order to prevent it. But the court would have to be satisfied that such a move was not in the child's best interests. You can also apply for a contact order, which places some onus on the parent to allow you to visit the child.

It is an offence to attempt to take a child out of the country without permission so that if you or your grandchild's parent has reason to suppose that an estranged partner is planning to do so, go to the police immediately. The 'attempt' alone is an arrestable offence. Police can also warn immigration officers at ports and airports to be on the look-out.

Useful addresses and resources

BABIES AND TODDLERS

Association for Post-Natal Illness
25 Jerdan Place
London SW6 1BE
0171 386 0868

Association for Spina Bifida
Asbah House
42 Park Road
Peterborough PE1 2UQ
01733 555988

British Agencies for Adoption and
Fostering (BAAF)
Skyline House, Union Street
London SE1 0LX
0171 593 2000

British Diabetic Association
10 Queen Anne Street
London W1M 0BD
0171 323 1531

British Dyslexia Association
98 London Road
Reading RG1 5AU
01734 668271

Children's Aids Trust
12 Flitcroft Street
London WC2H 8DJ
0171 209 4066

Cot Death Research and Support
14 Halkin Street
London SW1X 7DP
24-hour Helpline
0171 235 1721

Downs Syndrome Association
153 Mitcham Road
London SW17 9PG
0181 682 4001

La Leche League of Great Britain
27 Old Gloucester Street
London WC1N 3XX
0171 242 1278

National Asthma Campaign
Providence House
Providence Place
London N1 0NT
0345 010203

National Childbirth Trust (NCT)
Alexandra House
Oldham Terrace
London W3 6NH
0181 828 4448

National Society for the
Prevention of Cruelty to Children
42 Curtain Road
London EC2A 3NH
0171 825 2500

Nursery Schools and Montessori
Information Line
P.O. Box 5
Brecon LD3 8YX
Helpline: 0800 181561

Play Matters
(National Toy Libraries
Association)
68 Churchway
London NW1 1LT
0171 387 9592

SCOPE (Spastics Society)
Helpline: 0800 626216

Toy Aids
Lodbourne Farm House
Lodbourne Green
Gillingham
Dorset SP8 9EA

SCHOOLCHILDREN

Child Abduction Unit
Official Solicitor's Dept
Chancery Lane
London WC2A 1DD
0171 911 7094

Centre for Young Musicians
Morley College
61 Westminster Bridge Road
London SE1 7HT
0171 224 0743

ChildLine
50 Studd Street
London N1 0QJ
Helpline for children: 0800 1111

Kidscape Campaign for Children's
Safety
152 Buckingham Palace Road
London SW1W 9TR
0171 730 3300

Museums Association
42 Clerkenwell Close
London EC1 0AU
0171 608 2933

National Association of
Bereavement Services
20 Norton Folgate
London E1 6DB
0171 247 0617

Royal Society for the Prevention
of Accidents
Canon House, The Priory
Queensway
Birmingham B4 6BS
0121 200 3461

Sports Council
16 Upper Woburn Place
London WC1 0QP
0171 388 1277

Stepfamily
72 Willesden Lane
London NW6 7TA
0171 372 0844/46

ADOLESCENTS

AIDS LINE
17 Chase Side Crescent
Enfield EN2 0JA
0181 363 6660

Alcohol Concern
49 Copperfield Street
London SE1 0EJ
0171 928 7377

ASH (Action on Smoking and
Health)
109 Gloucester Place
London W1H 3PH
0171 224 0743

British Pregnancy Advisory Service
Austy Manor
Wootton Wawen
West Midlands B95 6BX
01564 793225

Brook Advisory Centre
165 Grays Inn Road
London WC1X 8UD
Helpline: 0171 617 8000

Career and Educational Counselling
Tavistock Centre, Belsize Lane
London NW3 5BA
0171 794 1309

Drinkline
Weddell House
13–14 West Smithfield
London EC1A 9DL
Helpline: 0171 332 0202

Drug and Alcohol Service
Colindale Hospital
Colindale Avenue
London NW9 5HG
0181 200 9525/75

Drugline
9a Brockley Cross
London SE4 2AB
0181 692 4975

Family Planning Association
27 Mortimer Street
London W1N 7RJ
0171 636 7866

Gay & Lesbian Switchboard
Helpline: 0171 837 7324

National AIDS Helpline
0800 567123

Samaritans
LinkLine 0345 909090

Terence Higgins Trust
52-54 Gray's Inn Road
London WC1X 8JU
Helpline: 0171 242 1010

FOR PARENTS AND GRANDPARENTS

Child Benefit Centre
PO Box 1
Newcastle upon Tyne NE88 1AA
0191 417 9999

Child Poverty Action Group
1–5 Bath Street
London EC1V 9PY
0171 253 3406

Child Support Agency
PO Box 55
Brierly Hill
West Midlands DY5 1YL
0345 133133

Families Need Fathers
134 Curtain Road
London EC2A 3AR
0171 613 5060

Gingerbread Association for
One-Parent Families
16 Clerkenwell Close
London EC1R OAA
0171 336 8183/84

Grandparents' Federation
78 Cook's Spinney
Harlow
Essex CM20 3BL
01279 37145

Independent Financial Advisers
Association
12 Henrietta Street
LondonWC2E 8LH
0171 240 7878

Legal Aid Head Office
29–37 Red Lion Street
London WC1R 4PP
0171 831 4209

LOGIC (Love of Grandparents
in Conflict)
9 Gainsborough Road
Warrington
Cheshire

National Council for One-Parent
Families
255 Kentish Town Road
London NW5 2LX
0171 267 1361

RELATE
Little Church Street
Rugby CV21 3AP
01788 573241

BOOKS

Ahlberg, Janet and Allan *Starting School* Penguin, London, 1988

Anholt, Catherine and Laurence *Sophie and the New Baby* Orchard, London, 1995

Brown, L.K. and M. *Dinosaurs Divorce* Little, Brown, London, 1996

Briggs, Raymond *Grandpa* Red Fox, London, 1992

Cole, Babette *Drop Dead* Jonathan Cape, London, 1996

Fine, Anne *Goggle Eyes* Penguin, London, 1990
——*Madam Doubtfire* Penguin, London, 1995
——*The Angel of Nitshill Road* Methuen, London, 1992

Gray, Nigel and Rogers, Gregory *Running Away from Home* Red Fox, London, 1997

Mole, K. B. *What's Happening? Splitting Up* Wayland, 1994

Nystrom, C. *Mike's Lonely Summer – A Child's Guide Through Divorce* Lion, London, 1986

Ross, Tony *I Want My Potty* Anderson Press, London, 1988

Simmons, Posy *Fred* Jonathan Cape, London, 1987

Varley, Susan *Badger's Parting Gift* Collins, London, 1984

Waddell, Martin and Dale, Penny *When the Teddy Bears Came* Walker, London, 1994

Index

Acknowledgments

l = left; *r* = right; *b* = bottom;
t = top; *c* = centre

2/3 Jay Silverman/The Image Bank;
4 Zefa; 5*l* Zefa; 5*c* Anthony A.
Boccaccio/The Image Bank, 5*r* The
Image Bank; 6/7 The Image Bank;
8 P Barton/Zefa; 9*t* & *b* Zefa, 9*c*
David Young Wolff/Tony Stone
Images; 10/11 Zefa; 12 L D Gordon/
The Image Bank; 13 Zefa; 14 Robert
Harding Picture Library; 15 Andrew
Sydenham; 16 Frans Rombout/
Bubbles; 17 David W Hamilton/The
Image Bank; 18/19 Zefa; 20*t* Robert
Harding Picture Library, 20*b* Silver
Cross; 21*t* Sue Ann Miller/Tony
Stone Images, 21*c* Zefa, 21*b*/25
Andrew Sydenham; 26*l* Robert
Goldman/Zefa; 26*r*/27 Andrew
Sydenham; 28 Robert Harding
Picture Library; 29 P Joseph/Bubbles;
30 J Nettis/Zefa; 31*l* Butch Martin/
The Image Bank, 31*r* Zefa; 32/33
Robert Harding Picture Library;
34 John P Kelly/The Image Bank;
35 Andrew Sydenham; 36 Zefa;
37*t* Andrew Sydenham; 37*br* Andrew
Lazell; 38/39 Zefa; 40 Andrew
Sydenham; 41*t* Robert Harding
Picture Library, 41*c* & *b* Andrew
Sydenham; 42*t* Early Learning Centre
42*b* Andrew Sydenham; 43*t/tc/b*
Andrew Sydenham, 43*bc* Early
Learning Centre; 44/45 Robert
Harding Picture Library; 46/47
Andrew Sydenham; 48 John Birdsall;
49*t* Zefa, 49*b* Andrew Lazell; 50*l*
The Hutchison Library, 50*r* Terje
Rakke/The Image Bank; 51 Andrew
Sydenham; 52/53 Zefa; 54 Mugshots/
Ace Photo Agency; 55 P Barton/Zefa;
56*t* Andrew Sydenham, 56*b* Zefa;
57*t* Jo Browne/Mick Smee/Tony
Stone Images, 57*b* Andrew Sydenham;
58*t* The Image Bank, 58*b* Richard
Walker/Ace Photo Agency; 59*tl/tr*
Zefa, 59*trc/cr/b* Andrew Sydenham,
59*cl* Early Learning Centre; 60 Derek
Dryland/Bubbles; 61 Richard
Pharaoh/Robert Harding Picture
Library; 62*t* Andrew Sydenham, 62*b*
Colin Thomas/Ace Photo Agency;
63*t* Dale Durjee/Tony Stone Images,
63*b* Andrew Sydenham; 64 Ian Cook/
Topham Picture Point; 65 Jennie
Woodcock/Reflections; 70/71
Andrew Sydenham; 72 Zefa; 73
Andrew Sydenham; 74/75 Zefa;
76/77 Andrew Sydenham; 78 Zefa;
79/81*t* Andrew Sydenham, 81*b*
Zefa; 82*t* Popperfoto, 82*b* Andrew
Sydenham; 83 Jeff Smith/The Image
Bank; 84 Andrew Sydenham;
85 Robert Harding Picture Library;
86 The Image Bank; 87/88 Andrew
Sydenham; 89/90 Zefa; 91/96
Andrew Sydenham; 97/99 Zefa; 100*t*
Werner Bokelberg/The Image Bank,
100*b*/101 Andrew Sydenham; 102*t*
Zefa, 102*b* Walter Hodges/Robert
Harding Picture Library; 103*tl/tr*
Early Learning Centre, 103*bl/br*
Andrew Sydenham; 104/105 Zefa;
106 Robert Harding Picture Library;
107 Zefa; 108 Steve Chenn/Robert
Harding Picture Library; 109/111
Andrew Sydenham; 112/113
Mugshots/Ace Photo Agency; 114*t*
Andrew Sydenham, 114*b* Zefa; 115*t*
Zefa, 115*b*/117 Andrew Sydenham;
118 T & D McCarthy/Zefa; 119
Zefa; 120/122*l* Andrew Sydenham;
122*r* Anne Yelland; 123 Andrew
Sydenham; 124/125 Zefa; 126 The
Image Bank; 127 David Madison/
Tony Stone Images; 128 Andrew
Sydenham, 128/129 Image Finders/
Ace Photo Agency; 129 Andrew
Sydenham; 130 Zefa; 131/132
Robert Harding Picture Library;
133*t* Chip Henderson/Tony Stone
Images, 133*b* Andrew Sydenham;
134 Alan Hicks/Tony Stone Images;
135*t* Zefa, 135*b* J Feingersh/Zefa;
136 Andrew Sydenham; 137 Zefa;
138 Robert Harding Picture Library;
139 Michael Bluestone/Ace Photo
Agency; 140 Robert Harding Picture
Library; 141 Andrew Sydenham;
142 David Young Wolff/Tony Stone
Images; 143*t* Roy Morsch/Zefa,
143*b*/144 Andrew Sydenham;
145 Jennie Woodcock/Reflections;
146*t* R Kanjman/Zefa, 146*b* Robert
Harding Picture Library; 147 Zefa;
148 Andrew Sydenham; 149 Zefa;
150*l* Nikki Gibbs/Bubbles, 150*r*
Zefa; 151 Jennie Woodcock/
Reflections; 152/153*t* Andrew
Sydenham, 153*b* Bill Bachmann/
Ace Photo Agency; 154*t* Robbie
Jack, 154*b* Laura Wickenden; 155
Andrew Sydenham; 156 Redferns;
157 Zefa; 158 Andrew Sydenham;
159 Anthony Medley/S.I.N.1;
160 Cortis; 161*t* Zefa, 161*c* David
Hoffman, 161*b* Andrew Sydenham;
162 Laura Wickenden; 163/164
Andrew Sydenham; 165 Dennis
O'Clair/Tony Stone Images; 166
Andrew Sydenham; 167 Zefa; 168
Bill Bachmann/Ace Photo Agency;
169*t* Robert Cundy/Robert Harding
Picture Library, 169*b*/172 Andrew
Sydenham; 172/173 Tim Morris
Cerullo/Rex Features; 174 Zefa; 175
The Image Bank; 176/179*b* Andrew
Sydenham, 179*t* Anthony Boccaccio/
The Image Bank; 180 Retrograph
Archive; 181/183 Andrew Sydenham;
184 Jon Henley/Zefa; 185 Zefa;
186 Chris Craymer/Tony Stone
Images; 187 National Aids Trust;
190/191 Andrew Sydenham; 192
Zefa; 192/193 Sylvain Grandadam/
Tony Stone Images; 193 Andrew
Sydenham;194 Corbis-Bettmann/UPI;
195 Laura Wickenden; 196 R
Willinger/FPG/Robert Harding
Picture Library; 197 Andrew
Sydenham; 198*t* Clive Corless,
198*b* Andrew Sydenham; 199 Clive
Corless; 200*t* Zefa, 200*b* Andy Sacks/
Tony Stone Images; 201 Zefa;
202 Mary Kate Denny/Tony Stone
Images; 203 Ron Sutherland/Tony
Stone Images; 204/210 Andrew
Sydenham; 211/212 Zefa; 213
Robert Harding Picture Library;
214/216 Andrew Sydenham.

The publishers wish to thank the
following:

Greenpeace (for poster)
Canonbury Villas, London, N1 2PN

Friends of the Earth (for T-shirt)
26–28 Underwood Street,
London N1 7JQ

Amnesty International (for T-shirt)
99–119 Rosebery Avenue,
London EC1R 4RE